Jazz
Poetry

JAZZ
POETRY

From the 1920s to the Present

Sascha Feinstein

Westport, Connecticut
London

Library of Congress Cataloging-in-Publication Data

Feinstein, Sascha, 1963–
    Jazz poetry : from the 1920s to the present / Sascha Feinstein.
        p.   cm.—(Contributions to the study of music and dance,
    ISSN 0193–9041 ; no. 44)
    Includes bibliographical references and index.
    ISBN 0–313–29515–8 (alk. paper)
    1. American poetry—20th century—History and criticism.   2. Jazz
in literature.   3. American poetry—Afro-American authors—History
and criticism.   4. Music and literature—History—20th century.
5. Afro-American musicians in literature.   6. Jazz musicians in
literature.   7. English language—Rhythm.   8. Poetics.   I. Title.
II. Series.
PS310.J39F45   1997
811'.509357—DC20   96–25006

British Library Cataloguing in Publication Data is available.

A hardcover edition of *Jazz Poetry: From the 1920s to the Present* is available from Greenwood Press, an imprint of Greenwood Publishing Group, Inc. (Contributions to the Study
of Music and Dance, Number 44; ISBN: 0–313–29515–8).

Library of Congress Catalog Card Number: 96–25006
ISBN: 0–275–95915–5 (pbk.)

First published in 1997

Praeger Publishers, 88 Post Road West, Westport, CT 06881
An imprint of Greenwood Publishing Group, Inc.

Printed in the United States of America

The paper used in this book complies with the
Permanent Paper Standard issued by the National
Information Standards Organization (Z39.48–1984).

10 9 8 7 6 5 4 3 2 1

For my wife, Marleni, and our son, Kiran

Contents

Acknowledgments

I am enormously grateful to Donald J. Gray, James H. Justus, Yusef Komunyakaa, Terence Martin, David Wojahn, and, especially, Robert Eugene Gross for their editorial assistance and personal support in the early stages of this project. Thorpe Feidt and Bob Reid helped shape parts of this book at a critical point in the writing; in the final stages I received invaluable advice and criticism from David J. Rife. I also want to thank Lycoming College for a Professional Development Grant that made the publication of this book possible.

Chapter 6, "The John Coltrane Poem," originally appeared in a shorter form in *The Southern Review*.

Every effort has been made to trace copyrights for the poems included in this book.

The epigraphs were reprinted from various excerpted materials:

Chapter 1: Etheridge Knight's poem "Haiku" from *The Essential Etheridge Knight* by Etheridge Knight (Pittsburgh: University of Pittsburgh, 1986).

Chapter 2: Vachel Lindsay's poem "A Curse for the Saxophone" from *The Poetry of Vachel Lindsay: Volume I* edited by Dennis Camp (Peoria, Il: Spoon River, 1984) and Carl Sandburg's poem "Jazz Fantasia" from *Complete Poems* by Carl Sandburg (Harcourt, Brace and Company, 1950).

Chapter 3: Langston Hughes's essay "The Negro Artist and the Racial Mountain" from *The Nation* (Vol. 122, no. 3181, 1926) and Sterling Brown's poem "Odyssey of Big Boy" from *The Collected Poems of Sterling A. Brown* by Sterling A. Brown (New York: Harper & Row, 1980).

Chapter 4: Kenneth Rexroth's essay "Jazz and Poetry" from *Esquire* (Vol. 49,

May 1958) and Kenneth Rexroth's "Introduction" to *Seasons of Sacred Lust* by Kazuko Shiraishi (New York: New Directions, 1978).

Chapter 5: Charlie Parker's statement in *Hear Me Talkin' to Ya* edited by Nat Shapiro and Nat Hentoff (New York: Rinehard and Company, 1955) and Bob Kaufman's poem "A Remembered Beat" from *Solitudes Crowded with Loneliness* (New York: New Directions, 1965).

Chapter 6: Amiri Baraka's poem AM/TRAK from *The LeRoi Jones/Amiri Baraka Reader* (New York: Thunder's Mouth, 1991) and Michael S. Harper's poem "Dear John, Dear Coltrane" from *Images of Kin* (Urbana: University of Illinois, 1977).

Chapter 7: Whitney Balliett's letter to the author dated 13 February 1988 (also printed, in a slightly different form, in his essay "Majesty" from *American Singers* by Whitney Balliett [New York: Oxford University Press, 1988]) and Lynda Hull's poem "Lost Fugue for Chet" from *Star Ledger* by Lynda Hull (Iowa City: University of Iowa, 1991).

Chapter 8: Yusef Komunyakaa's discussion with William Matthews titled "Jazz and Poetry: A Conversation" moderated by Robert Kelly and published in *The Georgia Review* (Vol. XLVI, no. 4) and Al Young's poem "Jungle Spout" from *Heaven: Collected Poems 1956–1990* by Al Young (Berkeley: Creative Arts Books, 1992).

In addition, I gratefully acknowledge the following permissions:

Every reasonable effort has been made to trace the owners of copyright materials in this book, but in some instances this has proven impossible. The author and publisher will be glad to receive information leading to more complete acknowledgments in subsequent printings of the book and in the meantime extend their apologies for any omissions.

COPYRIGHT ACKNOWLEDGMENTS

The author and publisher gratefully acknowledge permission for use of the following material:

Excerpts from "Archangel" in *Greed* (NY: Norton) by Ai. Copyright © 1993 by Ai. Reprinted with permission.

Excerpts from "Bessie" and "Bessie Smith's Funeral" in *If Winter Come: Collected Poems, 1967–1992* (Pittsburgh: Carnegie Mellon University Press, 1994) by Alvin Aubert. Reprinted with permission.

Excerpts from "AM/TRAK" and "Black Art" in *The LeRoi Jones/Amiri Baraka Reader* by Amiri Baraka. Copyright © 1991 by Amiri Baraka. Used by permission of the Publisher, Thunder's Mouth Press.

Excerpts from "Glass" and "Trane" in *Black & Blues* (Cuba: Ediciones Casas de las Americas, 1976) by Kamau Brathwaite. Reprinted with permission.

Excerpts from "Cabaret," "Ma Rainey," "New St. Louis Blues," "Odyssey of Big Boy," "Old King Cotton," "Southern Road," "Strong Men," and "When De Saints Go Ma'ching In" in *Southern Road* by Sterling A. Brown. Copyright 1932 by Harcourt, Brace, & Co. Copyright renewed 1960 by Sterling Brown. Included in *The Collected Poems of Sterling A. Brown*, selected by Michael S. Harper. Copyright © 1980 by Sterling A. Brown. Reprinted by permission of Harper-Collins Publishers, Inc.

Excerpts from "An Expatiation on the Combining of Weathers . . . ," "Billie Holiday," "Freedom and Discipline," "Letter to Maxine Sullivan," " 'Sure,' Said Benny Goodman," and "What a Wonder Among the Instruments Is the Walloping Tramboone!" in *Collected Shorter Poems* by Hayden Carruth. Copyright 1992 by Hayden Carruth. Reprinted with permission.

Excerpts from "Paragraphs" in *Brothers, I Loved You All* by Hayden Carruth. Copyright 1978 by Hayden Carruth. Reprinted with permission.

Excerpts from "Strange Fruit" by Cyrus Cassells in *The Jazz Poetry Anthology* (Bloomington: Indiana University Press, 1991). Edited by Sascha Feinstein and Yusef Komunyakaa. Reprinted with permission.

Excerpts from "Coltrane" by J.G. Cobo-Borda, in *Poems for John Coltrane* (Syracuse: Syracuse University Press, 1969). Ed. John Taggart. Trans. Evelyn Pagán and John Taggart. Reprinted with permission.

Excerpts from "How Long Has Trane Been Gone?" in *Pissstained Stairs and Monkey Man's Wares* (NY: Phrase Text, 1969) and "Rose Solitude" in *Mouth on Paper* (NY: Bola, 1977) by Jayne Cortez. Copyright 1996 by Jayne Cortez. Reprinted with permission.

Excerpts from "For the Marriage of Faustus and Helen" by Hart Crane, reprinted from *Complete Poems of Hart Crane*, edited by Marc Simon, with the permission of Liveright Publishing Corporation. Copyright 1933, © 1958, 1966 by Liveright Publishing Corporation.

Excerpts from "The Bird, The Bird, The Bird" "Chasing the Bird," and "Le Fou" in *Collected Poems of Robert Creeley, 1945–1975* by Robert Creeley. Copyright © 1983 The Regents of the University of California. Reprinted with permission.

Excerpts from Creeley's letter dated June 24, 1950. Copyright © 1980 by Robert Creeley. Reprinted from *Charles Olson & Robert Creeley: The Complete Correspondence, Volume 1* with the permission of Black Sparrow Press.

Excerpts from "ta," "god pity me whom(god distinctly has)," and the lines from "even a pencil has fear to" are reprinted from *Complete Poems, 1904–1962*, by e. e. cummings, edited by George J. Firmage, by permission of Liveright Publishing Corporation. Copyright © 1923, 1925, 1951, 1953, 1991 by the Trustees for E. E. Cummings Trust. Copyright © 1976 by George James Firmage. "ta" is also reprinted by permission of W.W. Norton & Company Ltd. Copyright © 1976, 1991 by the Trustees for the E.E. Cummings Trust and George James Firmage. "god pity me whom(god distinctly has)" and "even a pencil has fear to" are also reprinted by permission of W.W. Norton & Company Ltd. Copyright © 1925, 1976, 1991 by the Trustees for the E.E. Cummings Trust and George James Firmage.

Excerpts from "Coltrane's Alabama" in *Blue Lights and River Songs* (Detroit: Lotus, 1982) by Tom Dent. Reprinted with permission.

Excerpts from "Almost Blue" in *My Alexandria* (Urbana: University of Illinois Press, 1993) by Mark Doty. Reprinted with permission.

Excerpts from "The Bison Keyboard." Copyright © 1989 by Clayton Eshleman. Reprinted from *Hotel Cro-Magnon* with the permission of Black Sparrow Press.

Excerpts from "Bud Powell." Copyright © 1975 by Clayton Eshleman. Reprinted from *The Gull Wall* with the permission of Black Sparrow Press.

Excerpts from "Un Poco Loco." Copyright © 1986 by Clayton Eshleman. Reprinted from *The Name Encanyoned River: Selected Poems 1960–1985* with the permission of Black Sparrow Press.

Excerpts from "Jackie-ing" in *Well You Needn't: The Thelonious Monk Poems* (Independence, Missouri: Raindust, 1975) by Dave Etter. Reprinted with permission.

Excerpts from "Autobiography" and "[sometime during eternity]" in *A Coney Island of the Mind* by Lawrence Ferlinghetti. Copyright © 1958 by Lawrence Ferlinghetti. Reprinted by permission of New Directions Publishing Corp.

Excerpts from "Coltrane Blues" by Jaime Ferran in *Poems for John Coltrane* (Syracuse: Syracuse University Press, 1969). Ed. John Taggart. Trans. Evelyn Pagan and John Taggart. Reprinted with permission.

Excerpts from "Howl" in *Collected Poems, 1947–1980* by Allen Ginsberg. Copyright © 1991 HarperCollins Publishers. Reprinted with permission.

Excerpts from "Memorial for Trane" in *Blues for an African Princess* (Detroit: Third World, 1971) by Sam Greenlee. Reprinted with permission.

Excerpts from "Jazz" in *The Light Guitar* (New York and London: Harper and Brothers, 1923) by Arthur Guiterman. Reprinted with permission of HarperCollins Publishers.

Excerpts from "Healing Animal" from *In Mad Love and War*, © 1990 Joy Harjo, Wesleyan University Press by permission of the University Press of New England.

Excerpts from "Brother John," "Dear John, Dear Coltrane," "Effendi," "Elvin's Blues," and "Here Where Coltrane Is" in *Images of Kin* (Urbana: University of Illinois Press, 1977) by Michael S. Harper. Reprinted with permission.

Excerpts from "Ben Webster and a Lady," "Bird," "Birding with Charlie Parker," "For Christianne," and "Moonlight on the Ganges" in *Selected Poems: Six Sets, 1951–1983* (Berkeley, CA: City Miner Books, 1984) by Howard Hart. Reprinted with permission.

Excerpts from "Elvin Jones Gretsch Freak" in *Felix of the Silent Forest* (New York: Poets, 1967) by David Henderson. Reprinted with permission.

Excerpts from *Jasbo Brown and Selected Poems* by DuBose Heyward. Copyright 1924, 1931 by DuBose Heyward. Copyright © 1959 by Dorothy Heyward. Reprinted by permission of Henry Holt & Co., Inc.

Excerpts from "Blind Saxophonist Dies" by David Hilton in *Bright Moments* (Madison: Abraxas, 1980). Ed. Jim Stephens. This poem first appeared in *Waves* magazine, Ed. Eric Torgersen, 1978. Reprinted with permission.

Excerpts from "Roots" from Yellow Light, © 1982 by Garrett Kaoru Hongo, Wesleyan University Press by permission of the University Press of New England.

Excerpts from "Homesick Blues" in *The Dream Keeper and Other Poems* by Langston Hughes. Copyright 1927 by Alfred A. Knopf Inc. and renewed 1955 by Langston Hughes. Reprinted by permission of Alfred A. Knopf Inc. and Harold Ober Associates Inc.

Excerpts from "Trumpet Player" in *Selected Poems* by Langston Hughes. Copyright 1947 by Langston Hughes. Reprinted by permission of Alfred A. Knopf, Inc. and Harold Ober Associates Inc.

Excerpts from "Hey" in *Collected Poems* by Langston Hughes. Copyright © 1994 by the Estate of Langston Hughes. Reprinted by permission of Alfred A. Knopf, Inc. and Harold Ober Associates Inc.

Excerpts from "Song for Billie Holiday" in *Selected Poems* by Langston Hughes. Copyright 1948 by Alfred A. Knopf, Inc. Reprinted by permission of Alfred A. Knopf Inc. and Harold Ober Associates Inc.

Excerpts from "Morning After" in *Selected Poems* by Langston Hughes. Copyright 1942 by Alfred A. Knopf, Inc. and renewed 1970 by Arna Bontemps and George Houston Bass. Reprinted by permission of Alfred A. Knopf Inc. and Harold Ober Associates Inc.

"Jazzonia" in *The Weary Blues* by Langston Hughes. Copyright 1926 by Alfred A. Knopf, Inc. and renewed 1954 by Langston Hughes. Reprinted by permission of Alfred A. Knopf Inc. and Harold Ober Associates Inc.

Excerpts from "Negro Dancers" in *The Dream Keeper and Other Poems* by Langston Hughes. Copyright 1932 by Alfred A. Knopf, Inc. and renewed 1960 by Langston Hughes. Reprinted by permission of Alfred A. Knopf Inc. and Harold Ober Associates Inc.

Excerpts from "The Negro Speaks of Rivers" and "The Weary Blues" in *Selected Poems* by Langston Hughes. Copyright 1926 by Alfred A. Knopf, Inc. and renewed 1954 by Langston Hughes. Reprinted by permission of Alfred A. Knopf Inc. and Harold Ober Associates Inc.

Excerpts from "Lost Fugue for Chet" in *Star Ledger* (Iowa City: University of Iowa and University of Iowa Press, 1991) by Lynda Hull. Reprinted with permission of the Estate of Lynda Hull.

Excerpts from "Hollywood Jazz" in *Ghost Money* (Amherst: University of Massachusetts, 1986) by Lynda Hull. Reprinted with permission of the Estate of Lynda Hull.

Excerpts from "A Remembered Beat," "Bagel Shop Jazz," "Battle Report," "Mingus," "Walking Parker Home," "War Memoir," and "War Memoir: Jazz, Don't Listen . . ." in *Solitudes Crowded with Loneliness* by Bob Kaufman. Copyright © 1965 by Bob Kaufman. Reprinted by permission of New Directions Publishing Corp.

Excerpts from "Newark" by Robert Kelly in *Poems for John Coltrane* (Syracuse: Syracuse University Press, 1969). Edited by John Taggart. Reprinted with permission.

Excerpts from Choruses "221," "239," "240," and "241" in *Mexico City Blues* by Jack Kerouac. Copyright © 1959 by Jack Kerouac; copyright renewed © 1987 by Jan Kerouac. Used by permission of Grove/Atlantic, Inc. Reprinted by permission of Sterling Lord Literistic, Inc.

Excerpts from "Con/Tin/U/Way/Shun Blues," "Haiku," "Ilu, the Talking Drum," and "Indiana Haiku" are reprinted from *The Essential Etheridge Knight*, by Etheridge Knight, by permission of the University of Pittsburgh Press. © 1986 by Etheridge Knight.

"For Eric Dolphy" and "Max Roach" in *Belly Song* (Detroit: Broadside, 1973) by Etheridge Knight. Reprinted with permission of Estate for Etheridge Knight.

Yusef Komunyakaa, "Speed Ball" first appeared in *New England Review*. Used by permission of Yusef Komunyakaa.

Excerpts from Yusef Komunyakaa, "The Plea," "Blue Light Lounge Sutra . . . ," and "February in Sydney" from *Neon Vernacular*, © 1993 by Yusef Komunyakaa, Wesleyan University Press by permission of the University Press of New England.

Excerpts from Yusef Komunyakaa, "Copacetic Mingus" and "Elegy for Thelonious" from *Neon Vernacular*, © 1993 by Yusef Komunyakaa, Wesleyan University Press by permission of the University Press of New England.

Excerpts from "Jackie-ing" in *The Monk Poems* (NY: Frontward, 1977) by Art Lange. Reprinted with permission.

Excerpts from "I Remember Clifford" in *One For the Rose* (New York: Atheneum, 1981) by Philip Levine. Reprinted with permission.

Excerpts from "Crab-Angel," "Lady Laura in Bohemia," "Mexican Desert," and "The Widow's Jazz" in *The Last Lunar Baedeker* (Highlands: The Jargon Society, 1982) by Mina Loy. Edited by Roger L. Conover. Reprinted with permission of The Jargon Society.

Excerpts from "Don't Cry, Scream" in *Don't Cry, Scream* (Detroit: Broadside, 1969) by Don L. Lee (Haki Madhubuti). Reprinted with permission.

Excerpts from "Averted Eyes," "Bmp Bmp," and "Unrelenting Flood" in *Flood* (Atlantic, Little Brown) by William Matthews. Reprinted with permission.

Excerpts from "Alcide 'Slow Drag' Pavageau," "Bud Powell, Paris, 1959," and "Listening to Lester Young" in *Rising and Falling* (Atlantic, Little Brown) by William Matthews. Used with permission.

Excerpts from "Alice Zeno Talking" in *A Happy Childhood* (Atlantic, Little Brown) by William Matthews. Used with permission.

Excerpts from "Blues for John Coltrane, Dead at 41" and "Coleman Hawkins (d. 1969), RIP" in *Ruining the New Road* (New York: Random, 1970) by William Matthews. Used with permission.

Excerpts from "Don't Say Goodbye to the Pork-Pie Hat," "The Life: Hoodoo Hollerin' Bebop Ghosts," "Malcolm X—An Autobiography," and "Lady's Days" in the book *Vision of a Liberated Future* by Larry Neal. Copyright © 1989 by Evelyn Neal. Used by permission of the publisher, Thunder's Mouth Press.

Excerpts from "The Day Lady Died" in *Lunch Poems* by Frank O'Hara. Copyright © 1964 by Frank O'Hara. Reprinted by permission of City Lights Books.

Excerpts from "[and in another place]" in *Collected Poems of Kenneth Patchen* by Kenneth Patchen. Copyright 1939 by New Directions Publishing Corp. Reprinted by permission of New Directions Publishing Corp.

Excerpts from "Boss Guitar" and "Death of Jazz" in *Silhouette* (Chicago: Free Black, 1970) by Eugene Perkins. Used with permission.

Excerpts from "Thou Shall Not Kill" in *Shorter Poems* by Kenneth Rexroth. Copyright 1956 by New Directions Publishing Corp. Reprinted by permission of New Directions Publishing Corp.

Excerpts from "5 Winos" and "Me, In Kulu Se & Karma" in *Songs of a Black Bird* (Chicago: Third World Press, 1969) by Carolyn M. Rodgers. Used with permission.

Excerpts from "Tuskegee Experiment" by Sadiq in liner notes to Don Byron's CD, *Tuskegee Experiments* (Elektra Nonesuch (9 79280–2), 1992). Used with permission.

Excerpts from "a/coltrane/poem" in *We a BaddDDD People* (Detroit: Broadside, 1970) by Sonia Sanchez. Used with permission.

Excerpts from "The Windy City" in *Slabs of the Sunburnt West* by Carl Sandburg, copyright 1922 by Harcourt Brace & Company and renewed 1950 by Carl Sandburg, reprinted by permission of the publisher.

Excerpts from "Honky Tonk in Cleveland, OH" and "Jazz Fantasia" in *Smoke and Steel* by Carl Sandburg, copyright 1920 by Harcourt Brace & Company and renewed 1948 by Carl Sandburg, reprinted by permission of the publisher.

Excerpts from "Singing Nigger" in *Cornhuskers* by Carl Sandburg, copyright 1918 by Holt, Rinehart and Winston, Inc. and renewed 1946 by Carl Sandburg, reprinted by permission of Harcourt Brace & Company.

Excerpts from "Dancing to Ellington" by Jan Selving in *The Jazz Poetry Anthology* (Bloomington: Indiana University Press, 1991). Edited by Sascha Feinstein and Yusef Komunyakaa.

Excerpts from "Dedication to the Late John Coltrane" in *Seasons of Sacred Lust* by Kazuko Shiraishi. Copyright © 1975 by Kazuko Shiraishi and Sanrio Ruo Co. Reprinted by permission of New Directions Publishing Corp.

Excerpts from "Ellington Indigos" by Aleda Shirley in *The Jazz Poetry Anthology* (Bloomington: Indiana University Press, 1991). Edited by Sascha Feinstein and Yusef Komunyakaa.

Excerpts from "Homage to John Coltrane" in *This Is Our Music* (Detroit: Artist's Workshop, 1965) by John Sinclair. Printed by permission of the author. All rights reserved.

Excerpts from "John Coltrane" in *The Beautiful Days* (NY: Poets, 1965) by A. B. Spellman. Used with permission.

Excerpts from "Did John's Music Kill Him?" in *Understanding the New Black Poetry* (NY: Morrow, 1973) by A. B. Spellman. Edited by Stephen Henderson. Copyright by A. B. Spellman. Used with permission.

Excerpts from "Song for Bird and Myself" by Jack Spicer. Copyright © 1975 by the Estate of Jack Spicer. Reprinted from *The Collected Books of Jack Spicer* with the permission of Black Sparrow Press.

"In Memorian John Coltrane" from *Memories of Grace Street* (unpublished manuscript) by Michael Stillman. Copyright © 1972 by Michael Stillman. Reprinted by permission of the author.

Excerpts from "Giant Steps" in *Peace On Earth* (Berkeley: Turtle Island Foundation, 1981) by John Taggart. Used with permission.

Excerpts from "Peg Leg Snelson" reprinted from *A Gallery of Harlem Portraits* by Melvin B. Tolson; edited, with an afterword, by Robert M. Farnsworth, by permission of the University of Missouri Press. Copyright © 1979 by the Curators of the University of Missouri.

Excerpts from "Lambda" and "Mu" in *The Harlem Gallery Book 1: The Curator* (New York: Twayne, 1965) by Melvin B. Tolson. Used with permission.

Excerpts from "Extension" and "JuJu" in *JuJu* (Chicago: Third World, 1970) by Askia Muhammad Toure. Used with permission.

Excerpts from "Elegy for Wes" in *Embryo* (NY: Barlenmir, 1972) by Quincy Troupe. Used with permission.

Excerpts from "The Day Duke Raised: May 24, 1974" in *Weather Reports: New and Selected Poems* (NY: Harlem River, 1991) by Quincy Troupe. Used with permission.

Excerpts from "Ben Webster: 'Did You Call Her Today?' " in *Heartland* (Detroit: Lotus, 1981) by Ron Welburn. Copyright by Ron Welburn. Used with permission.

"Gonsalves" from *The Look in the Night Sky* (Kansas City, Missouri: BkMk, 1977) by Ron Welburn. Copyright by Ron Welburn. Used with permission.

Excerpts from "Ol' Bunk's Band" in *Collected Poems 1939–1962 Vol II* by William Carlos Williams. Copyright 1946 by William Carlos Williams. Reprinted by permission of New Directions Publishing Corp. Also reprinted by permission of Carcanet Press Limited.

"Jazz", a postcard written by William Carlos Williams. Published with the permission of the Poetry / Rare Books Collection, University Libraries, State University of New York at Buffalo. Also, with permission of New Directions Publishing Corporation.

Excerpts from "Satin Doll" by David Wojahn in *Glassworks* (Pittsburgh: University of Pittsburgh Press, 1987). Reprinted by permission of the author.

Excerpts from "Billie," "Dance of the Infidels," "A Dance for Ma Rainey," "Jug," "Jungle Strut," "Lester Leaps In," and other poems in *Heaven: Collected Poems*

1956–1990 (Berkeley: Creative Arts Book, 1992) by Al Young. Used with permission.

Excerpts from "The Duke Ellington Dream" is reprinted from *Family Reunion*, by Paul Zimmer, by permission of the University of Pittsburgh Press. Copyright © 1983 by Paul Zimmer.

Excerpts from "To the Pianist Bill Evans" in *Theories of Rain* (NY: Sun, 1975) by Bill Zavatsky. Used with permission.

Excerpts from "Elegy (for Bill Evans, 1929–1980)" in *You Must Believe in Spring* (Warner Bros. CD 3504-2; tape WB W5 3504 by Bill Evans) by Bill Zavatsky. Used with permission.

1

Jazz Poetry: An Introduction

Making jazz swing in
Seventeen syllables AIN'T
No square poet's job.
          —Etheridge Knight

When I think about the poet Etheridge Knight, I often reflect on the times I heard him read his work, or evenings when we listened to jazz at various clubs in downtown Indianapolis. I also remember, bittersweetly, a symposium on poetry and jazz that featured him as well as other writers from the region, including myself.[1] The symposium preceded a performance of jazz-related poetry, and when Etheridge arrived, he elevated our enthusiasm just by smiling. We joked a bit, got him settled in. I think he was genuinely pleased to be there, although his awkward walk and stilted gestures reflected the physical pain he was trying so hard to hide. Everyone knew at least two things about this poet: He was the most celebrated writer on the panel, and he was dying of inoperable cancer.

I invoke this afternoon with Etheridge Knight partly because the union of grief and joy was also central to his poetry. "I died in Korea from a shrapnel wound," he once wrote, "and narcotics resurrected me. I died in 1960 from a prison sentence and poetry brought me back to life." For Knight, and for many other poets including Langston Hughes, a major relationship between poetry and jazz concerned the integration of exuberance and despair. Jazz for him was not merely an intellectual pursuit but rather a function of his life and work.

So it may be surprising to hear that, despite his presence, the symposium became tedious and pedantic. It failed to illuminate anything substantial about the topic, and that failure gave me some perspective on several crucial and controversial issues concerning the nature of jazz poetry. We never fully discussed the inspiring, creative forces behind jazz-related poems. We never addressed the various kinds of jazz poems that have been written, nor did we talk about the complex history of jazz poetry. Instead, the panel argued over unanswerable questions: What is jazz? How can we define jazz poetry if we can't define jazz or poetry individually? Knight began to fidget and participate less frequently.

After awhile, the panel agreed that there was music in the world commonly referred to as "jazz" and that jazz has inspired poets for about three-quarters of a century. But then the conversation took a new argumentative turn: Does a jazz poem, someone asked, have to be about jazz, or can it simply suggest jazz in its rhythmic structure? This question (an important one, I think) evoked some energetic responses, as it has with many poets and critics for years now, and the afternoon concluded with several people steadfastly defending either the first or second premise.

That the panel remained unresolved over the issue should not surprise anyone. Some writers feel passionately that a jazz poem must in some way emulate the rhythmic pulse of the music; others claim that "jazziness" is an arbitrary term at best and that allusions to jazz musicians might be the only sure way to know whether the poem has been influenced by jazz. Proponents of the first approach criticize the other, particularly the work by West Coast writers and performance artists, for not substantiating the poetry as strong verse. Those in the other camp, however, strongly criticize narrative presentation for avoiding the essence of jazz—or, to use a more colloquial phrase, for being square.

This book does not attempt to solve that debate because I reject the binary premise—and so, I might add, did Etheridge. "I think," he said in a somewhat frustrated tone, "we should perhaps pay closer attention to the distinction made on this flyer [for *The Jazz Poetry Anthology*] which refers to the poems as being jazz-*related*."[2] And in that spirit I offer this brief definition: A jazz poem is any poem that has been informed by jazz music. The influence can be in the subject of the poem or in the rhythms, but one should not necessarily exclude the other. By emphasizing that a jazz poem should be informed by the music itself, I have tried to bring together the opposing views, not simply in an effort to avoid controversy but because I feel that it is both rational and necessary. In doing so, I hope to present a broad overview of the cultural and aesthetic developments of jazz-related verse.

The nature of jazz poetry, with its synesthesia of musical and literary innovations, has highlighted for me the nature of modern and contemporary American poetry. "If we want to understand the poetry of our time fully," explains David Jauss, "then we must try to understand why it so often turned to jazz for inspiration" (126). Like the ebullient spirit in Whitman's verse and that by other modern poets from the first half of this century, the emergence and evolution of jazz might be seen as a musical parallel to the innovations in American poetry, which explains why both Hart Crane and William Carlos Williams wrote about the American idiom and its relationship to jazz—how poets should somehow integrate the rhythmic drive of jazz into verse.

Similarly, Etheridge Knight felt that the strongest connection between the two arts concerned the oral tradition of poetry, and when he read that evening, the audience could sense tangible rhythmic connections between the two art forms. But this issue of orality does not and should not negate other poems that seem informed by jazz primarily in subject matter (or, to put it another way, that pay homage to jazz and jazz musicians). In fact, direct references to the blues and jazz permeated Etheridge's work, even his haikus, such as "Indiana Haiku" ("Mirror of keen blades / Slender as guitar strings; Wes / Montgomery jazz" [*Born of a Woman*, 98]) and "Haiku" ("To write a blues song / is to regiment riots/and pluck gems from graves" [*Poems from Prison*, 18]). In the poem "For Eric Dolphy," the poet unites Dolphy's sound with associative imagery of violence, racial and family conflict, as well as expressions of love, and, to speak more generally, the poem acts as an excellent introduction to jazz poetry:

```
on flute
spinning spinning spinning
love
thru/ out
the universe

I
know
exactly
whut chew mean
man

you like
titi
my sister
who never expressed LOVE
in words (like the white folks always  d
she would sit in the corner            o
and cry                                i
everytime                              n
ah                                     g
got a whuppin
```

(*Belly Song*, 54)

Is this a jazz poem? Yes, certainly—but why? Is it a matter of form, where the vertical spelling of "doing" and the parenthesis that does not close suggest improvisatory language and the approximations of sound? Is it the repetition of "spinning" or the phonetic spelling of the phrase "what you mean"? Or is it simply the actual content: the fact that this poem directly addresses a jazz musician and his music? Because all of the questions seem relevant, the antagonistic schools of thought (jazz poetry as form versus jazz poetry as subject) should not be discussed as opposites but rather as part of a larger, more engaging discussion.

Because the poem's title presents a major jazz figure, one way to begin the discussion would be to ask, Why Eric Dolphy? We can begin with general biography: Born in 1928, Dolphy learned the clarinet at age six and by junior high school had learned oboe. "The young Eric liked to play his flute in the backyard," explains John Litweiler, "accompanying the songs of birds" (61). He soon had mastered most of the reed instruments, and in the span of his short life (he died in 1964) became known as a major soloist for some of the greatest leaders in modern jazz, including Charles Mingus, John Coltrane, and Ornette Coleman. He was also a pioneer himself, particularly in Free jazz and in the advancement of two instruments not commonly used in jazz: the bass clarinet and the flute.

Dolphy made many recordings of his flute playing, including several versions of "Hi Fly," a tune written by Randy Weston. For one of his live performances of "Hi Fly," he plays the tune as a duet with bassist Chuck Israels (*Eric Dolphy in Europe*, 1961). Dolphy begins with sustained tones. He then slides into more-complicated phrases, rising ("spinning / spinning / spinning") until he feels it is time to enter the tune itself, which is based on a minimalized, five-note theme. Against the low sounds of the bass lilting its steady beat, the flute soars and circles like clouds in a storm. Dolphy splits some of the notes with his aggressive attack, his staccato faster and faster with spitting rapidity. The sharp wisps of air string the phrases together in conjunction with the actual tones. Dolphy releases flurry upon flurry. His quick gasps for breath become audible, noticeable, part of the solo itself. There is an urgency to the sound, but not urgency in the sense of desperation. These are improvised choruses that fill the air like an enormous field of starlings that, when one or two decide it is time to leave, speckle the air with a miraculous, unified rhythm.

In the poem "For Eric Dolphy," Knight refers to the gyrating quality of Dolphy's flute-playing style and adds extra spacing between the words, almost as though approximating the breath between phrases. The lines of the poem are extremely short, often just one word by itself, and so we read quickly yet emphasize each word much like Dolphy's staccato phrasing. The third stanza breaks that rhythm with the longer line that concludes with the capitalized "LOVE," followed by a still longer line that ends with the vertical spelling of "doing." The verticality of the word creates a corner on the page, like the corner where the speaker must sit, and this technique extends the poem visually and thematically: We have to pause at the line, at the thought, before forcing our eyes to find where we left off and where the new phrase begins. Like Dolphy's musical solo, the poem has no punctuation to direct us, and yet we have little trouble pausing at the end of a phrase and emphasizing the proper stresses in the lines.

When Knight says, "I / know / exactly / whut chew mean / man," he is at the same time expressing his admiration for the music, his personal association with the sound, and his sense of revelatory interpretation. What follows is a description of the speaker's family, and what he achieves is a visual interpretation that, according to the speaker, is "exactly" what Dolphy's improvised musical lines appear to be saying. Knight transcribes sound into a personal narrative, transforming the abstractions of "spinning," "love," and "universe" into family struggles, racial conflicts, and touching implications about how we communicate our most sensitive and complicated emotions. Like Dolphy's music, the little sister's crying is a form of expression almost too complicated for language, so the poet turns to jazz to approximate the emotion.

Curiously enough, the abstractness of jazz has tended to inspire "exact" reflections by poets. Although jazz as an invisible art offers the writer an extremely expansive terrain, converting that response into a poem of merit can be enormously difficult, and some poems that try to capture "the essence" of jazz deteriorate into vague generalities. (This is particularly true for poems that, according to the poet, rely exclusively on jazz accompaniment and that have limited musicality on the page or when read aloud without music.) It is one thing for a poet such as Elizabeth Bishop to describe fireflies in her poem "A Cold Spring" as looking "exactly like the bubbles in champagne" (*Complete Poems*, 56), for here the exactness compares one visual image to another. But when the image is not visual, as with music, "exact" analogy often forces the interpretation to reflect on personal impressions presented in a dramatic narrative.

Like Knight's "For Eric Dolphy," poems addressing jazz often incorporate strong visual images in an attempt to approximate sound. In Aleda Shirley's "Ellington Indigos," for example, music becomes a vehicle for exploring the overwhelming splendor of trees bursting into their autumn colors. Driving in a convertible with the top down, the speaker in the poem melds her own longings for her lover with the images of fall and the sounds of Duke Ellington:

> how is it I sometimes feel as if
>
> I'm waiting for you, even when I'm the one who's late?
> A kind of uneasy indolent longing, it's similar
> to the one evoked in me by Ellington's pastels, or fall.

Though the autumn colors haven't yet peaked,
here and there I see a sweetgum edged in violet,
a maple dying back to pale-yellow. The soft azure

of an alto sax, the jagged red of a growling trumpet,
the raw gold of a clarinet—discussing Ellington's
tone palette, a jazz critic perfectly described

this landscape.

(*JPA*, 198–199)[3]

The word "perfectly" in this case translates to "exactly," and even though
the sounds of Ellington's music may not evoke the same "tone palette"
with all listeners, the personal reflection by this particular speaker allows
us all to unite the sounds of jazz with the lushness of the season. In other
words, her elevated sensitivity for sound and color increases our own appreciation for these natural and man-made wonders.

The interpretation of music, of course, does not necessarily involve confessional or first-person narratives. In "Jazz Drummer," a different poem
from Etheridge Knight's *Belly Song and Other Poems*, the poet celebrates
Max Roach who, with Kenny "Klook" Clarke and others, modernized jazz
drumming. The poem concentrates on the description of drumming, the
associated imagery, and a final gesture that extends far beyond the speaker
of the poem:

MAX ROACH
 has fire and steel in his hands,
 rides high, is a Makabele warrior,
 tastes death on his lips, beats babies
 from worn out wombs,
     grins with grace,
 and cries in the middle of his eyes.

MAX ROACH
 thumps the big circle in bare feet,
 opens wide the big arms,
 and like the sea
    calls us all. (47)

The call to "us all" has the same expansive feeling as Dolphy's sound
"spinning / love / thru / out / the universe," and the repeated image of
crying in both poems emphasizes Knight's responses to jazz as a form of
enormous creative pleasure as well as profound sadness. This thematic
similarity connects the two poems, but "Jazz Drummer" and "For Eric
Dolphy" are anything but minor variations on a familiar theme. They are
celebrations of individual musicians, and the formal elements of the poems
explore these distinct sounds: in contrast to the quick, short lines in the

Dolphy poem, "Jazz Drummer" stops and starts within longer lines, and the two capitalized, monosyllabic words of the drummer's name—"MAX ROACH"—project like the powerful percussion of Roach himself, who became known, in part, for accentuating the rhythm section with explosive shots from the bass drum.

Although these two works and those by many other poets concentrate on one particular instrumentalist, many jazz-related poems refer to great numbers of musicians, such as Marvin Bell's "The Fifties" (*JPA*, 10–11), Hayden Carruth's "Paragraphs" (*JPA*, 28–30), or, to look at an extreme example, Ted Joans's "Jazz Must Be a Woman" (*JPA*, 105–106). Some poems discuss the spirited verve of jazz as performed by anonymous musicians (John Logan's "Chicago Scene" [*JPA*, 132–133], Mina Loy's "The Widow's Jazz" [*JPA*, 133–134], Carl Sandburg's "Jazz Fantasia" [*JPA*, 187]), and others concentrate on the atmosphere of jazz itself (Wanda Coleman's "At the Jazz Club He Comes on a Ghost" [*JPA*, 36], C. D. Wright's "Jazz Impressions in the Garden" [*JPA*, 240]).

Just as jazz musicians interpret standard songs according to their own musical styles and changing moods, so do poets responding to music create verse that reflects their own poetic sensibilities as well as their individual associations with jazz. Duke Ellington, for example, inspired a great number of jazz-related poems, and the poems created offer a range of sound and form that rivals the musical extremes in Ellington's remarkable career. Aleda Shirley's "Ellington Indigos," as noted earlier, transforms the sounds of the Ellington big band into the vibrant colors of fall, but David Wojahn's "Satin Doll" uses Ellington as a touchstone for the Big Band era, the band itself performing for a dance at the Casablanca ballroom: "women floating / in their taffeta, chilly red corsages from/their pencil-mustached men, ivory tuxedos, lotion, / and bay rum" (*JPA*, 238–239). Quincy Troupe's "The Day Duke Raised; May 24th, 1974" (*JPA*, 219–220) addresses Ellington through elegy and focuses on the funeral itself; when reading the poem for a recent recording, however, Troupe shouted out the stanzas like a man with a megaphone announcing the start of a road race.[4] Léopold Sédar Senghor does not discuss the actual funeral service for Ellington, but his poem "Blues" also concentrates on grief and concludes "Just play me your 'Solitude,' Duke, till I cry myself to sleep" (*JPA*, 192). Jayne Cortez's "Rose Solitude," which is dedicated to Ellington, concludes "I cover the hands of Duke who like Satchmo / like Nat (King) Cole will never die / because love they say / never dies" and is filled with disparate imagery that floods together like orchestral voices:

> I tell you from stair steps of these navy blue nights
> these metallic snakes
> these flashing fish skins
> and the melodious cry of Shango

. . . .
of grey and black scissors
of bee bee shots and fifty red boils
yes the whole world loved him.

(*JPA*, 44–45)

And, in another extreme, Paul Zimmer imagines himself in "The Duke Ellington Dream" actually playing with the orchestra. The character Zimmer blows one remarkable tenor sax solo after another, and the admiring voice of Ellington himself concludes the poem: " 'Zimmer,' he said, 'You most astonishing ofay! / You have shat upon my charts / But I love you madly' " (*JPA*, 248).

Despite the variety of responses, all of these poems incorporate Ellington's music or persona; like Knight's poems for Eric Dolphy and Max Roach, the direct reference to the musician makes it relatively easy to refer to these pieces as being jazz-related. The issue becomes significantly more complex, however, when a musician is not named or when the references to jazz are more implicit than explicit, and I find myself feeling uneasy labeling poems "jazz poems" when form alone becomes the sole criterion, when nothing is known about the inspiration for the work. With a poet such as Etheridge Knight—or Amiri Baraka, Sterling Brown, Hayden Carruth, Wanda Coleman, Jayne Cortez, Michael Harper, Langston Hughes, Ted Joans, Bob Kaufman, William Matthews, Larry Neal, Sonia Sanchez, and Al Young, to name a few among many—the aesthetics of jazz has so directly influenced their craft that one can make some plausible assessment of form as well. But even with poets such as those mentioned here, it can be misleading if not unprofessional to use the term "jazz poetry" as a blanketing description for their work.

What about titles that refer to jazz or to famous jazz compositions? Is that enough of a reference to establish a poem as a jazz poem? Again, the answer is complicated and, finally, a matter of personal decision. Often the title of a poem can cue the reader in to the dramatic context and its relationship to jazz. Elegies written for jazz musicians are unquestionably jazz-related simply by the nature of the subject, and poem titles often make that subject clear, as with Yusef Komunyakaa's "Elegy for Thelonious" (*JPA*, 120), William Matthews' "Coleman Hawkins (d. 1969), RIP" (*JPA*, 148), Frank O'Hara's "The Day Lady Died" (*JPA*, 162–163), Michael Stillman's "In Memoriam John Coltrane" (*JPA*, 207), and hundreds of others. Many poems have titles that place the speaker live at the club itself, such as Paul Blackburn's "Listening to Sonny Rollins at the Five-Spot" (*JPA*, 15), George Bowering's "Pharoah Sanders, in the Flesh" (*JPA*, 16–17), or Ira Sadoff's "At the Half-Note Cafe" (*JPA*, 182–183). In these cases, the poet is obviously responding to the music or the musician.

This can be true even if the description or reference is not presented directly. Here is a poem by Ron Welburn called "Gonsalves" from *The Look in the Night Sky* (1977): (p. 81)

crescendoes are indigo scarves
women wear in the new england autumns
diminuendoes the sky overcast
by whisky and evil moods.
rhode island is a whisker
on the chin of obatala
and festivals are light years
in the memory. exiled,
the mood of a song comes into the bay,
a *mornas* all the way from
cabo verde, a place not far
from guinea.

The curious mix of imagery here probably makes little sense, narratively, to someone with no jazz background. Those who are familiar with the music, on the other hand, will associate "Gonsalves" with the tenor saxophonist Paul Gonsalves, who played his most famous solo with the Duke Ellington orchestra. The year: 1956; the place: Rhode Island's Newport Jazz Festival; the tune: "Diminuendo and Crescendo in Blue."

But using the title of a poem as a definitive reason for calling a poem jazz-related can be misleading. Hundreds of poems with "Blues" in the title exhibit no connection whatsoever with the music or even with the common emotions often associated with the blues.[5] These kinds of circumstances have complicated attempts to define jazz and blues poetry, as seen in numerous essays over the years, including Charles S. Johnson's "Jazz Poetry and Blues" from 1928. Johnson begins with a statement regarding race:

"Negro poetry" has two meanings which are constantly confused: in one sense it is poetry of any mood and theme which happens to have been written by Negroes; in another it is poetry bearing a distinct and recognizable flavor of the Negro temperament and his life. (16)

In a more direct commentary on jazz poetry, Johnson calls the title "a misnomer," and states that "Jazz is not so much music as method. The poetry which goes by the name," he says, "is a venture in the new, bold rhythms characteristic of the music. And, although it has come, curiously, to express the fierce tempo of our contemporary life, it is also its vent. For jazz, more than being rhythm, is an atmosphere" (16). Johnson invites us to quibble with his definitions, but his general observations about jazz poetry seem sound; by referring to "the new, bold rhythms" as well the "atmosphere," he acknowledges the attraction to jazz as both an influence in form and subject.

It has been decades since Johnson published his essay, and it certainly seems time to stop arguing over form versus subject, or rhythm versus context. For what emerges from all of the hundreds of poems informed by jazz is a challenging and engaging study of twentieth-century poetry and its relationship to the music of the time.

The history of jazz poetry comprises an enormous range of poems. Some were written by very famous poets who knew almost nothing about jazz; others were composed by obscure writers who have been virtually ignored by the academic community. The styles of poetry seem just as diverse as the writers themselves, and this book tries to embrace the startling variety of verse: portraits of jazz musicians and descriptions of jazz eras; meditations from the jazz club; poems written expressly for performance with live jazz; quiet reflections on the music and passionate political statements; poems that have been written in an improvisatory approach and poems that have been formally structured; poems that illuminate cultural and societal issues for Americans, African-Americans, Native Americans, and Asian-Americans, as well as Africans, Europeans, and other cultures around the world; abstract meditations and pellucid memories; elegies, tributes, celebrations.

When I began working on this book, I found that the history began to divide into various movements. Like most projects, I suppose, this was not planned. I had no sweeping hypothesis that I set out to prove. Instead, I began to place in chronological order the hundreds of jazz poems collected over several years, and I discovered that some broad issues emerged, particularly social and racial issues as seen in American poetry. Here, then, is a general summary of the book.

Chapter 2 describes the racist poetry from the 1920s (as well as work by more-sympathetic white writers), with an emphasis on the racial and sexual anxieties evoked by jazz music. In contrast, the subsequent chapter discusses the poetry of Langston Hughes, Sterling Brown, and, to a lesser degree, Melvin Tolson—poets who embraced the blues and jazz as integral to American and African-American culture. Chapters 4 and 5 concentrate on the 1950s when, to various degrees of success, poets popularized readings with live jazz accompaniment and turned to Charlie Parker as their artistic and spiritual leader. In the late 1960s, the period addressed in Chapter 6, poets focused more on John Coltrane and equated his music with Malcolm X and the Black Civil Rights movement. In short, Chapters 2–6 present a kind of call and response between white writers, who were often unable to get beyond the social and cultural barriers of African-American music, and African-American writers, whose work might be seen in part as a reaction to their white predecessors.

Jazz poetry from the 1970s to the present, which has swelled in its international scope and creative range, has moved further from the issues of racism and, generally speaking, reflects a changing emphasis from polemic and elegiac grief to celebration. Chapter 7 therefore focuses on the remarkable number of jazz innovators who died and the predominant elegiac theme in the jazz poetry from the 1970s. The final chapter, however, concentrates on contemporary poets—particularly William Matthews, Yusef Komunyakaa, Hayden Carruth, and Al Young—who, in the spirit of the human grieving process, write less about the tragedies in jazz and more about its fertility as one of the most important contributions to twentieth-century culture.

This book could have been substantially longer, and it in no way attempts to cover all of the important jazz poems or poets. Instead, I have tried to condense the history of jazz poetry into a digestible presentation. Furthermore, I had hoped to quote more poems in full, but permission costs significantly hampered my prospects for quoting entire poems or even, in some cases, small excerpts. Fortunately, most of the poems discussed in this book have been anthologized in two collections from Indiana University Press, *The Jazz Poetry Anthology* (1991) and *The Second Set* (1996).[6]

My goal in discussing the history of jazz poetry is to present the most engaging jazz-related work while at the same time discussing poets and poems that have played significant roles in the history of this genre. Collecting the material, a process that involved diligent scholarship and pure luck, has been an odyssey of sorts, but a wonderful one. I still feel much like an archeologist who may not know exactly where to dig but who knows nevertheless that treasures remain buried.

More writers are addressing jazz in their work now than at any other time in the twentieth century, and the varied styles remain as splintered and personal as the styles of jazz itself. Contemporary poets have sometimes turned to jazz as a way of expressing their admiration for the music; other times they have expressed sorrow for the musicians who have died, for all the music that will no longer be played. And sometimes they have conveyed a complex union of loss and resilience, as expressed in Etheridge Knight's "Con/Tin/U/Way/Shun Blues":

> They say the blues is just a slave song
> But I say that's just a lie
> Cause even when we be free, baby—
> Lord knows we still have got to die
> >   lovers will still lie
> >   babies will still cry
>
> >   (*Essential*, 93)

I heard Etheridge read his poetry for the last time at Butler University on November 14, 1990, about seven months after the jazz poetry symposium. He was joined that evening by Carolyn Forché, and it happened to be his birthday. I hadn't seen him since the symposium, and although he looked almost the same, it was clear that the cancer had gotten worse and that this might be his last birthday celebration.

He gave a stunning reading, filled with humor, political statements, infectious rhythms, and stylistic ease. When Forché came to the podium after his reading, she felt obliged to recognize what he had done. "Etheridge," she said smiling, "you sure know how to warm up a room." He recited most of his poems by heart, enacting his conviction that the power of poetry is, by nature, oral. (In my copy of *The Essential Etheridge Knight*, he inscribed, "Be / making / sounds / Words / be / beautiful.") Hearing the poems again was like reviewing an autobiography in verse, from "Rehabilitation & Treatment in the Prisons of America" to "Circling the Daughter." When he read "Ilu, the Talking Drum," his bass voice resonated in the refrain. And soon he was rocking to the rhythm of his poetry, shifting his weight left and right, until the pulse of the poem became the pulse of the audience, sounds that we all still hear:

> and the day opened to the sound
> kah doom / kah doom-doom / kah doom / kah doom-doom-doom
> and our feet moved to the sound of life
> kah doom / kah doom-doom / kah doom / kah doom-doom-doom
> and we rode the rhythms as one
> from Nigeria to Mississippi
> and back
> kah doom / kah doom-doom / kah doom / kah doom-doom-doom
>
> (*Essential*, 55–56)

NOTES

1. The symposium took place on April 1, 1990, at the Writer's Center of Indianapolis, which sponsored the event. Later that evening, some of us read at a poetry and jazz performance at the Madam Walker Urban-Life Center.

2. This transcript was taken from a cassette made at the time of the symposium. Unfortunately, the poor recording equipment produced substandard sound quality, and much of this tape simply could not be deciphered. The passages I have summarized are a collage of words from the tape and my own memory of the conversation.

3. Here and elsewhere, I have used the abbreviation *JPA* to represent *The Jazz Poetry Anthology* (1991). For brief examples in this chapter, I have tried to use poems from that anthology for the sake of convenient reference.

4. For Troupe's reading, as well as jazz poetry performances by a number of other poets, listen to *JazzSpeak: A Word Collection*.

5. Steven Tracy, in his book *Langston Hughes and the Blues* (1988), discusses this issue in depth. His book, and several of his articles, also helps elucidate the various forms of the blues that poets have used for structuring the formal elements of their blues-related poetry.

6. In addition to these anthologies, there is also a slim but engaging collection of jazz poetry edited by Jim Stephens, *Bright Moments* (1980), as well as Stephen Henderson's classic collection, *Understanding the New Black Poetry* (1973), which features a number of jazz poems as well as a lengthy introduction that includes a discussion of jazz and poetry. For more general references, *The Jazz Word* (eds. Cerulli, Korall, and Nasatir, 1960) remains a fairly good introduction to jazz-related literature; *Mixed Voices* (1991), edited by Emilie Buchwald and Ruth Roston, offers a selection of poems inspired by different kinds of music, including jazz; and, more recently, Art Lange and Nathaniel Mackey edited a collection of poetry, fiction, and prose titled *Moment's Notice* (1993).

REFERENCES

Bishop, Elizabeth. *The Complete Poems: 1927–1979*. New York: Farrar, Straus, Giroux, 1983.

Buchwald, Emilie, and Ruth Roston, eds. *Mixed Voices: Contemporary Poems about Music*. Minneapolis: Milkweed, 1991.

Cerulli, Dom, Burt Korall, and Mort L. Nasatir, eds. *The Jazz Word*. New York: Ballantine, 1960.

Dolphy, Eric. *Eric Dolphy in Europe Volume 1*. Rec. Sept. 8, 1961. Prestige, OJCCD-413-2, 1989.

Feinstein, Sascha, and Yusef Komunyakaa, eds. *The Jazz Poetry Anthology*. Bloomington: Indiana University Press, 1991.

———. *The Second Set*. Bloomington: Indiana University Press, 1996.

Henderson, Stephen, ed. *Understanding the New Black Poetry*. New York: Morrow, 1973.

Jauss, David. "Contemporary American Poetry and All That Jazz." *Crazyhorse* 42 (Spring 1992): 125–140.

JazzSpeak: A Word Collection. Produced and compiled by Harvey Robert Kubernik, with Amiri Baraka, Wanda Coleman, Ishmael Reed, Quincy Troupe, et al. New Alliance, NAR CD 054, 1991.

Johnson, Charles S. "Jazz Poetry and Blues." *Carolina Magazine* (May 1928): 16–20.

Knight, Etheridge. *Belly Song*. Detroit: Broadside, 1973.

———. *Born of a Woman*. Boston: Houghton Mifflin, 1980.

———. *The Essential Etheridge Knight*. Pittsburgh: University of Pittsburgh, 1986.

———. *Poems from Prison*. Detroit: Broadside, 1969.

Knight, Etheridge, Sascha Feinstein, et al. "Jazz Poetry Symposium." Madam Walker Theatre. Sponsored by the Writer's Center of Indianapolis. Indianapolis, April 1990.

Knight, Etheridge, and Carolyn Forché. Poetry Reading. Butler University, Indianapolis, April 19, 1990.

Lange, Art, and Nathaniel Mackey. *Moment's Notice*. Minneapolis: Coffee House, 1993.

Litweiler, John. *The Freedom Principle*. New York: Morrow, 1984.
Stephens, Jim, ed. *Bright Moments*. Madison, Wis.: Abraxas, 1980.
Tracy, Steven C. *Langston Hughes and the Blues*. Urbana and Chicago: University of Illinois, 1988.
Welburn, Ron. *The Look in the Night Sky*. Kansas City, Mo.: BkMk, 1977.

2

The Sin in Syncopation

What did Judas do with his silver thirty pieces?
Bought himself a saxophone and played "The Beale Street Blues."
  —Vachel Lindsay

Drum on your drums, batter on your banjos,
sob on the long cool winding saxophones.
Go to it, O jazzmen.
  —Carl Sandburg

The origins and early history of jazz remain steeped in myth, improvised histories, and ingenious story telling—fertile material for poets, exasperating details for historians. What we know for certain, however, is that popularity and actual innovation rarely coincided with each other, and with jazz the issue of race tended to divide commercial and artistic success. Most jazz scholars agree that the dominant innovators have been African-Americans, whose musicianship nurtured the development of the blues and jazz. Yet in 1917 it was the Original Dixieland Jazz Band (ODJB), a group consisting entirely of white musicians, who established their place in jazz history by being the first band to make a commercial jazz recording.

"The controversy over the music of the ODJB in its heyday," explains Gunther Schuller, "was nurtured by many extra-musical factors. There was to begin with the very term jazz, only a few years earlier an obscene expression current in red-light districts" (176). Schuller adds:

Finally we must understand that American musical sophistication in 1917 was sufficiently low to allow the ODJB's trombonist Edward B. Edwards to make, unchallenged, statements to reporters such as: "None of us know music." (This was not true, particularly of Edwards, who read music and was well-trained on his instrument.) "Jazz, I think, means jumble." Jazz is "the untuneful harmony of rhythm." (176)

Jazz became celebrated madness, a musical expression of the social tumult resulting from World War I. Both the players, such as Edwards, and the reviewers relished the controversy of sound. Yet, while the media felt safe commercializing an all-white band, the African-American musicians of the time—monumental figures such as King Oliver, Louis Armstrong, and Jelly Roll Morton—were practically ignored, despite their musical superiority.

Like American jazz musicians, American poets at the turn of the century modernized their craft with an almost unimaginable rapidity. The parallel development between the two arts has led to some glib, if not totally incorrect, discussions about the similarities between poetry and jazz, but the fact remains that the new freedoms in American verse—particularly the innovations by T. S. Eliot, Ezra Pound, and William Carlos Williams—coincided with the sounds of American blues and jazz.[1] Aesthetically, poetry and jazz shared the jagged forms of rhythmic syncopation, as well as the explosiveness of urban modernity. American poets struggled to establish their voice, their new idiom; in music, the new American idiom was jazz.

In evaluating the early history of jazz-related poetry, it is not surprising to find many parallels with the history of jazz. The more-popular figures of the time and those first publishing jazz-related poems were white writers, such as Carl Sandburg and Vachel Lindsay. But the great innovators of the genre have been African-American, particularly Langston Hughes and Sterling Brown, who established the integral links between jazz and African-American culture and did their best to promote a national respect for jazz and the blues. They fought both the resurgent racism of the twenties and thirties as well as the attacks by African-American "intellectuals," such as Countee Cullen, who felt that jazz degraded African-American culture by perpetuating lower-class stereotypes. Like the music performed by Louis Armstrong and Bessie Smith, the poetry by Hughes and Brown has outlived the naive criticism of its time.[2]

In fact, there has been an ironic yet appropriate reversal of emphasis: The achievements of Hughes in particular have so overshadowed the other jazz-influenced poets from the twenties that very few people have written about the jazz poetry by white writers of the time. In truth, the poetry tended to have more value as social commentary than as creative achievement. Among those poets, Sandburg and Lindsay became the most popular, although their jazz-related work now sounds more dated and clichéd than the poems by Hart Crane or even Mina Loy, both of whom used abstract imagery to evoke the music's seductiveness. Many of the white poets from the twenties—including Lindsay, E. E. Cummings, Arthur Guiterman, and Clement Wood—savagely attacked these new African-American sounds. Representative of the national if not global panic, their poetry projected the extremes of racial and sexual anxiety that had been incited by jazz music.

On December 3, 1922, Vachel Lindsay wrote two letters to Harriet Monroe, the editor of *Poetry* magazine. The first, a cover note, explained that he was enclosing "a horribly grubby letter" that responded to an article by Edward Shanks titled "An English Impression of American Literature" (*Letters*, 257, n. 1). Lindsay seemed incensed that his entire body of work could be summed up so quickly and, more important, that the emphasis should rest so heavily on jazz music. "I have very much resented being called a 'Jazz' poet," he wrote,

especially by the British Papers, because it was used to mean something synonymous with hysteria, shrieking and fidgets. I abhor the kind of Ball-Room dancing that goes with Jazz, and I abhor the blasphemy that Jazz has made of the beautiful slow whispered Negro Spirituals. The British Newspapers especially assume "The Daniel Jazz" is the one thing I have written. . . . [J]azz is hectic, has the leer of the bad-lands in it, and first, last and always is hysteric. It is full of the dust of the dirty dance. The Saxophone, its chief instrument[,] is the most diseased instrument in all modern music. It absolutely smells of the hospital. (*Letters*, 255)

Lindsay's letter showed not only resentment at being misinterpreted but a genuine fear of jazz music in general. The hectic hysteria, "the leer of the bad-lands," and "the dirty dance" seemed to him an orgiastic frenzy of uncontrolled sound and emotion. His feelings had not always been so extreme; in 1918 he wrote to Katharine Lee Bates, "I insist that Jazz does not discredit America. I think the Jazz element in America is a sure sign of health" (*Letters*, 169). But the public associations made between this music and his own poetry caused him to reassess his opinion of jazz from a "sign of health" to a disease.

In 1920 Lindsay published *The Golden Whales of California*, which featured his most famous jazz-related poem, "The Daniel Jazz" (also known as "Daniel"). This poem, like Lindsay's "The Congo," italicizes musical and theatrical directions to the right of the page; the tunes begin with "a strain of 'Dixie,' " continue with "a touch of 'Alexander's Ragtime Band,' " and conclude with a chorus of "Go chain the lions down" (*Poetry*, 378–379). The poem itself is not terribly interesting, nor does it seem truly informed by the music it invokes, despite the intriguing parallel between the biblical Daniel and the contemporary African-Americans. Rather than gain rhythmic momentum, the repetitions instead become tedious, partic-

ularly at the conclusion of the poem, where each uninteresting line repeats
three times.

Lindsay's "The Apple Blossom Snow Blues," also from *The Golden
Whales of California*, highlights his moldy-fig understanding of the blues
and jazz. The poem begins with an italicized epigraph that describes a
blues as "*a song in the mood of Milton's Il Penseroso, or a paragraph from
Burton's Anatomy of Melancholy*" (87) and concludes with this instruction
for music to be performed with the poem: "*Grand finale of jazz music,
like the fall of a pile of dishes in the kitchen*" (90). Like "Daniel," "The
Apple Blossom Snow Blues" fails to present any innate appreciation for
the music, but the newness of jazz music led to a great deal of misunder-
standing about the music itself and about those who apparently were in
the know. In this case the mere words "jazz" and "blues" were enough
to label Lindsay a "jazz poet," a label that he detested.

Lindsay's contempt for jazz seems directly related to the sexual overtones associated with the music. "Before marriage [in 1925 at age 45],"
explains Ann Massa,

anything aphrodisiac was taboo to Lindsay. Jazz he found an inescapable sexual
incitement. Scott Fitzgerald, the expert of the Jazz Age, described jazz as "first
sex, then dancing, then music," and to Lindsay it was "midnight dirt and a sad
morning after." He . . . was disturbed by what for him were erotic foxtrots and
tangos; he was haunted by the earthy note of the saxophone. He would have
answered in the affirmative the question the *Ladies Home Journal* asked in 1921:
"Does Jazz put the Sin in Syncopation?" and would have agreed with the dry Dr.
Henry Van Dyke that jazz was "a sensual teasing of the strings of sensual passion."
(196)

By 1926, with the publication of *Going-to-the-Stars*, Lindsay did what he
could to rebuke his reputation as a jazz poet; "The Jazz of This Hotel"
and, particularly, "A Curse for the Saxophone" (first published in 1924)
both attacked jazz in no uncertain terms. "The Jazz of This Hotel," a
nonce sonnet, begins by explaining why he cursed jazz, and the thrust of
the poem's argument concerns the velocity of sound: Lindsay prefers "the
slower tom-toms of the sea," "the slower tom-toms of the thunder," "the
slower deeper violin," and "the slower bells that ring for church" (48). In
this poem, at least, he "evaded the sexual issue, and concentrated on the
musical one" (Massa, 196), but the poem implies his deeper distress as
shown in the reference to church bells, which, as a foil for the sounds of
jazz, suggests the heathenism in African-American music.

"A Curse for the Saxophone," the poem that immediately followed
"The Jazz of This Hotel," was a no-holds-barred attack initiated by a far
more damning religious reference. The poem proclaimed, "When Cain
killed Abel to end a perfect day, / He founded a city, called the City of

Cain, / And he ordered the saxophones to play" (49) and continued, "What did Judas do with his silver thirty pieces? / Bought himself a saxophone and played 'The Beale Street Blues' " (50). Just as anachronistically, Nero watches Rome burn to "The Beale Street Blues," and Henry the Eighth, before murdering his last wife, orders more saxophones to play (50). When John Wilkes Booth enters Hell, the Devil himself blows a few choruses to welcome him:

> And they played it on the saxophone, grunting and rasping,
> The red-hot horn in his hot hands clasping,
> And he played a typical radio jazz,
> He started an earthquake, he knew what for,
> And at last he started the late World War. (51)

Lindsay belabored his generality with obsessive, repetitive imagery. He failed to hear any structure in the new modern music. For him, jazz represented the chaos of World War I and, by association, symbolized all the unnecessary violence throughout history.

Where "The Jazz of This Hotel" seemed tempered by form and tone, "A Curse for the Saxophone" blasted the reader with accusations, pleading for society to "forget our jazzes and our razzes and our hates" (52). The poem focused on violence, yet Lindsay's sexual anxieties also appear early in the work. He described Jezebel wearing a tiara and "three-piece pajamas" with a "diamond bosom-band"; when she slaughtered "honest prophets," "She licked her wicked chops, she pulled out all her stops, / And she ordered the saxophones to play" (49).

The endnote to this poem credited Stoddard King, a local journalist and poet, for "offering valuable amendments and suggestions including 'The Beale Street Blues' " (52). Lindsay added, "Mr. King could claim at least half the poem if he chose, not only as an aspiring but also as a constructive artist. In short, he helped me write it" (52). What this tells us, of course, is that Lindsay was not even familiar with the most-popular blues and jazz pieces of the time. But the general naiveté, if not ignorance, about popular American music did not stop him from addressing it in his verse, nor did this limited understanding deter other poets, including Sandburg, from writing about the music in theirs.

The general fear of jazz was not isolated to a few people, and certainly not to poetry circles. On the one hand, jazz music had suddenly exploded in America, both as a form of popular entertainment and as a symbol of the Gatsbyesque romanticism. When Mamie Smith sang "Crazy Blues" on the very first recording of the blues (1920), the sales struck a staggering seventy-five thousand copies within the first month. Soon, hand-cranked victrolas filled neighborhoods with the sounds of Jelly Roll Morton, Louis Armstrong, and many others. "Through Louis Armstrong and his influence," explains Schuller, "jazz became a truly twentieth-century language. And it no longer belonged to New Orleans, but to the world" (88). But with this burst of sound came a fear that these Black musicians, who had crooned, to quote Lindsay again, "beautiful slow whispered Negro spirituals" and who had been allowed to do so as slaves, now were on stage, live—active threats to the bigots and racists in America.

One poet responding directly to this change in sound and dance was Arthur Guiterman, whose poem "Jazz" appeared in his book *The Light Guitar* (1923). The poem begins by hailing jazz as the nemesis of our age and then, in the fourth stanza, offers this rambling, diarrhetic definition of the music:

> What is this Jazz?—A mad inebriation,
>   Vibration, syncopation, agitation,
> Gyration, hesitation, coruscation,
>   Clamation, lamentation, ululation,
> Sensation, titillation, exaltation,
>   Negation, affirmation, dubitation,
> Elation, elevation, cachinnation,
> Damnation, dissipation, degradation! (97)

"I hate the thing," Guiterman continued, "because I think it's ugly; / Its voice is harsh, its motions most uncouth" (98). Like the concern by present-day parents over the sexual and violent influence of hard rock, the possible influences of jazz greatly disturbed Guiterman. "Its dancers nestle cheek to cheek too snugly," he continued; "Perhaps this sort of thing corrupts our youth" (98). The poem concludes with a confession that every age must have some element of immorality that must be judged, and since "We must be damned for something, make it Jazz!" (99).

Although Guiterman's poem may have damned jazz as a form of entertainment, other poems from the twenties were far more directly racist; jazz music, as conceived and developed by African-Americans, brought with it a racial threat that went beyond the usual social trepidation often present when any art form evolves. On January 10, 1925, *Literary Digest* reprinted "The Jazz Cannibal," a poem that had appeared overseas in *Punch* magazine the previous December and that was later credited to Percy Haselden.[3] It begins with this epigraph from a letter printed in *The Daily Graphic*: "The noisy beats of jazz-bands are merely a disguised and modern form of the tom-toms of old, which incited savages to fury and fired the fierce energy of cannibals." The poem itself reads as follows:

> My Phillida, before the jazz
>   Began its devastating boom,
> My thoughts of you were gentle as
>   The tunes that whirled us around the room;

To perfect harmony with grace
   We moved, delighted and content
To smile into each other's face
   With meanings kind and innocent.

Alack! my Phillida, to-day
   The music does not soothe my mind,
In truth I am compelled to say
   My dreams are horrid and unkind;
For, while the bawling niggers biff
   The drums that agitate our feet,
I'm gravely speculating if
   You're really nice enough to eat.

                               (*Literary Digest*, 36)

This disturbing narrative, which attempts to be clever and witty, offers little substance apart, perhaps, from the bizarre point of view. As a poem, "The Jazz Cannibal" should be dismissed, but historically it is of interest because it exemplifies the attitude at that time of many poets who were not unknown. These writers include E. E. Cummings and Clement Wood, whose *The Greenwich Village Blues* (1926) unintentionally revealed just how wretched narrative verse about American jazz could be. Wood socialized with many of the best-known literary figures, and his *Rhyming Dictionary* (now revised) remains in print. But the bulk of his prolific body of writing—from his own poetry and fiction to his overview of American poetry titled *Contemporary Poetry of America* (1925)—remains not only dated but second-rate.[4] Divided into nine sections, *The Greenwich Village Blues* begins with a series of disastrous couplets before introducing the poem's protagonist, Howard F. Dodge, who, "recollecting that he still was single, / . . . took a wife in Derby on departing, / One Minna Merriweather" (9). The marriage, like the writing, quickly grows stale. Imagining himself trapped in wedlock for another twenty-five years, Dodge takes a taxi to downtown Manhattan and enters an "insidiously dusky" nightclub where he meets his soon-to-be mistress, Djuna Lee. Like an adolescent smirking at his own naughty little joke, Dodge asks her, "Shall we jazz together?" (16).

One evening at the cabaret, Dodge spots his wife, Minna, and, though he initially cannot believe his eyes, he quickly finds himself lost in the seductive music, and jazz brings the sexual spark back into their marriage. He delivers lines such as "I know that my desertion was a sin—/ But— Jazz! I didn't mean to let it get me. / It simply did" (44), and Minna, as aroused by the music as her philandering husband, greets him with open arms. She giggles, "Naughty child! / And did it want a dance? Come, take me, man!" (45). The poem concludes with bizarre references to jazz as a global intoxicant, one that will spread from clubs to governments, from the current date (1925) through 1999, from this Earth "To the scandalized, astonished moon, / To Mercury and to envious Mars, / And the final furthest commuting stars" (64). The final cynical couplet announces, "The news that the air will laugh to tell—/ That Jazz is elected—and all is well!" (64).

Like Wood's poetry, the few jazz-related poems by E. E. Cummings associate jazz with sexual immorality and explicit vulgarity. Typical of Cummings' enigmatic style, the poems do not blatantly attack jazz in the way, say, "The Jazz Cannibal" does; instead, he convolutes the syntax to disguise his anxious feelings about jazz. This distress probably began during his formative years as an undergraduate at Harvard. As Richard Kennedy explains,

He continued to explore the seedier side of Boston, to frequent the saloons of Washington Street, to visit Scollay Square with its drunks, its prostitutes, its down-and-outers, its Salvation Army preachers, and to attend the Old Howard, the burlesque theater with its crude parodies of popular songs and its broad comedy sketches (girl with stuffed donkey and cat: "You can pat my ass but you can't stroke my pussy"). (90)

He also began to explore the new arts in general, and the forms of entertainment ranged from circus performers to ragtime piano players (Kennedy, 90).[5] For the youthful Cummings, jazz was not so much a separate art as it was background music for burlesque dance, drunken revelry, and overt sexual displays.

In his poem "[ta]," the third section of "Portraits" in his book & (1925), Cummings offers one of his more generous descriptions of early jazz, in this case a portrait of a ragtime pianist:

      ta
      ppin
      g
      toe

      hip
      popot
      amus Back

      gen
      teel-ly
      lugu-
      bri ous

                          eyes
      LOOPTHELOOP

      as

fathandsbangrag

(Complete, 78)

The only clue to a jazz allusion arrives in the final three letters, and when we unpuzzle the enjambed sentence, our own eyes "LOOPTHELOOP" to the beginning, which in turn urges us to reread the poem with a greater appreciation for the narrative. Rushworth Kidder, in *E. E. Cummings: An Introduction to the Poetry* (1979), spends considerable effort explicating the jazz influence on this short-lined poem. "Just as jazz syncopates rhythms by carrying phrases across the normal divisions of measures and beats," he writes, "so here the accent on 'ppin' comes a little ahead of its expected place in the syllable 'ping,' and the phrase carries over into the next measure before it ends" (51). Kidder's analysis may be a little too pat; even though his statement about jazz music rings true, it is also true that Cummings achieved this syncopation in many of his poems, very few of which concerned jazz. At the last, Cummings probably did not learn this technique from listening to jazz music.

But Kidder's analysis of the poem offers many engaging moments. First, he explains the portrait: "breaking the word 'hippopotamus' so that *hip* and *pot* are revealed, and capitalizing the word 'Back,' Cummings swiftly defines the image of a corpulent pianist seen from the rear" (51). He continues:

Where the sincere blues singer or jazzman would abandon himself to a compelling mournfulness, the pianist here can only muster a polite and hyperbolic gloom. True to the stereotypes of jazz pianists, his eyes roll; but the phrase used to describe them—"LOOP-THE-LOOP" [*sic*]—has more than a tinge of the carnival-ride atmosphere about it. Like the many musicians in Cummings' paintings and drawings of Harlem dance-halls and burlesque theaters, this one is depicted in a tone that registers something less than complete approbation. (51–52)

In addition, one should not dismiss the implied relationship between the "hippopotamus" and the jazz figure himself. Like the many animal images used in other, more racist poems, Cummings offers an animalistic portrait of a man sluggish and fat, a player removed from any artistic and disciplined expression, ungoverned in comparison to modern classicists such as Schönberg, Satie, and Stravinsky.

Other poems from & criticize jazz far more blatantly. The entire section titled "Sonnets—Realities," for example, emphasizes what Cummings saw as the disgusting obviousness of modern sexuality. His depictions of women and young lovers leave little for the imagination; the sonnets in this sequence become dominated by a sense of fleshliness, with overtones of his embarrassment and queasiness. In this bordello of imagery, Cum-

mings introduces the theme of jazz as a music that thrives on the obscenity
of exposed sexuality and the pulse of shameless sexual awareness.

The eleventh sonnet in this series, "[god pity me whom(god distinctly
has)]," shares this spirit. Cleverly disguised with a nonce rhyme scheme
(*abca cddb e fgg ef*) and a snaking syntax, this sonnet reveals unspoken
anxieties about America's new music:

> god pity me whom(god distinctly has)
> the weightless svelte drifting sexual feather
> of your shall i say body?follows
> truly through a dribbling moan of jazz
>
> whose arched occasional steep youth swallows
> curvingly the keenness of my hips;
> or,your first twitch of crisp boy flesh dips
> my height in a firm fragile stinging weather,
>
> (breathless with sharp necessary lips)kid
>
> female cracksman of the nifty, ruffian-rogue,
> laughing body with wise breasts half-grown,
> lisping flesh quick to thread the fattish drone
> of I Want a Doll,
>   wispish-agile feet with slid
> steps parting the tousle of saxophonic brogue.

(Complete, 125)

If the poem is any reflection of Cummings' own response to jazz (and I
think it is), his associations with this music are anything but flattering. The
poem implies that jazz assaults our senses with "a dribbling moan" and a
"fattish drone."[6] The appeal of this music is strictly limited to adolescents
who are just becoming sexually aware of their "crisp boy flesh" or of "wise
breasts half-grown." Their dancing ("whispish-agile feet with slid / steps")
tries to organize the chaos of jazz ("the tousle of saxophonic brogue"),
which epitomizes for the speaker the obviousness of this sexual expression.

The following sonnet in the "Sonnets—Reality" series (the twelfth,
"[even a pencil has fear to]") begins with a statement about the visual
arts—about the fragility of trying to capture a temporary moment on paper—and then introduces the theme of jazz almost as an afterthought,
although this afterthought acts as direct commentary: ",did you ever hear
a jazz / Band? / or unnoise men don't make soup who drink" (*Complete*,
158). Cummings equates the sounds of jazz (dribbling moans and saxophonic brogues) with the slurps of men drinking soup, and the poem asks,
why make such an effort to organize slurping sounds through music when
we can hear such noise in our own kitchens?[7] Like the drunken sounds of
men and women in the cabarets that Cummings frequented in the 1910s

and early 1920s, the descriptions of jazz in these two sonnets from & dwell on the chaos of sound and the sexuality of the atmosphere.[8]

Not all of the twenties' poets writing about jazz, of course, focused on hatred and fear, and one of the more sympathetic voices was Carl Sandburg, whose interest in jazz music probably developed from his appreciation for folk music, as well as the modernist aesthetic in general.[9] Even his earliest poems reflect a keen attraction to sound, particularly the new sounds by African-American musicians. In his first collection of poetry, *Chicago Poems* (1916), the poem with the disturbing title "Nigger" nevertheless celebrates the importance of the blues and Negro spirituals by virtue of their links to slavery and depth of emotion. The poem describes the "Lazy love of the banjo thrum" as well as a singer "Brooding and muttering with memories of shackles" (*Complete*, 23). Two years later, in "Potato Blossom Songs and Jigs" from *Cornhuskers* (1918), Sandburg wrote "Niggers play banjos because they want to. / The explanation is easy" (*Complete*, 97), suggesting again, albeit much too glibly, that these African-Americans create sound from an artistic drive ironically nurtured by a sinister history. In "Singing Nigger," also from *Cornhuskers*, Sandburg states this still more clearly; the poem addresses Jazbo, a figure, as I will explain later, often associated with the origins of jazz music:

> I know where your songs came from.
> I know why God listens to your, "Walk All Over God's Heaven."
> I know you shooting craps, "My baby's going to have a new dress."
> I heard you in the cinders, "I'm going to live anyhow until I die."
> I saw five of you with a can of beer on a summer night and I listened to the
>   five of you harmonizing six ways to sing, "Way Down Yonder in the
>   Cornfield."
> I went away asking where I come from.
>
> (*Complete*, 108)

Again, Sandburg too easily announces his profound sympathy and personal appreciation for African-American sensibilities, but the final line of the poem does, in fact, imply at least two positive interpretations. First, there is the speaker's recognition of America's deplorable past, and second, the speaker clearly envies the richness of the music and admires the remarkable resilience that in turn produced the haunting spirituals.

In his own musical efforts, Sandburg attempted to achieve the "Lazy love of the banjo thrum" and by 1919 began to perform his poetry, accompanying himself on guitar, more in the American folk song tradition than the blues or jazz.[10] The biographer Penelope Niven describes one such reading from December 21, 1919:

Billed as the Poet of the City, Sandburg read his poems and, to his own guitar accompaniment, sang folk songs he had collected in his travels. He could play only two or three chords, and his mellow baritone voice, like his guitar playing, was

self-taught. He crooned his songs to an enthralled audience and discovered a new
way to express himself and earn money at the same time. (347–348)

But music for Sandburg did not seem to require the same amount of
discipline as poetry or other arts (as seen in his bold presentation of his
own limited skills on the guitar). And, in fact, the poems from *Chicago
Poems* and *Cornhuskers* imply that African-Americans simply had "natural" performing talent, that jazz music was an extension of that ease.
Spirited and uplifting, jazz was a musical pleasure that should in no way
be intellectualized or treated with the same seriousness as classical music.
    The freewheeling structure of jazz, as Sandburg saw it, can be seen in
the poem "Honky Tonk in Cleveland, Ohio" from *Smoke and Steel* (1920).
Here Sandburg sketches a combo much like the ODJB that incorporated
whistles, various blaring sounds, and braying horns: "It's a jazz affair,
drum crashes and cornet razzes. / The trombone pony neighs and the tuba
jackass snorts. / The banjo tickles and titters too awful" (*Complete*, 164).
Sandburg cynically describes four "white hopes" who "mourn with inter-
spersed snickers: / 'I got the blues. / I got the blues. / I got the blues' " as
well as "cartoonists [who] weep in their beer" (164). The poem accuses
white audiences of either mocking jazz music or overintellectualizing their
responses. Sandburg may not have been the most informed jazz listener,
but his social commentary seems appropriate for the time.
    Smoke and Steel also included Sandburg's most popular jazz-related
poem, "Jazz Fantasia," which emphasized the exuberance of jazz, the
spirit of its rhythms.[11] The musicians in the poem batter banjos, sob
through saxophones, knuckle the tin pans, bang on drums. Like William
Carlos Williams's poem for Bunk Johnson, written about twenty-five years
later but surprisingly similar in its tone, this poem by Sandburg has been
ridiculed in recent criticism for its corny use of language and poorly conceived metaphors. Various passages seem to be improvisatory notes scrib-
bled on cocktail napkins, and the flux of images clashes like the sound of
a drumset thrown from a second story window. But it seems too easy and
unfair to dismiss this poem entirely. "Jazz Fantasia" deserves praise for
its energy and, even more so, for its endorsement of this controversial
form of expression. In an effort to conjure the images of slavery and southern blues, Sandburg weaved in the line "now a Mississippi steamboat
pushes up the night river with a hoo-hoo-hoo-oo," but he also implied
how violence has inspired the music and encouraged that sound: "make
two people fight / on the top of a stairway and scratch each other's eyes
/ in a clinch tumbling down the stairs" (*Complete*, 179). The violence of
jazz reflected the age of urban upheaval, and Sandburg, as he did in so
many of his poems, tried to celebrate and not flinch from these revolutionary changes.
    In that regard, "The Windy City" from *Slabs of the Sunburnt West*

(1922) stated in no uncertain terms Sandburg's associative responses to jazz and modern society in general:

> Forgive us if the jazz timebeats
> Of these clumsy mass shadows
> Moan in saxophone undertones,
> And the footsteps of the jungle,
> The fang cry, the rip claw hiss,
> The sneak-up and the still watch,
> The slant of the slit eyes waiting—
> If these bother respectable people
>   with the right crimp in their napkins
>   reading breakfast menu cards—
>   forgive us—let it pass—let be.
>
>   (*Complete*, 276)

Sandburg's jazz poetry has not been recognized as fully as it should be. Many critics—too many to cite—have focused their attacks on his famous "Jazz Fantasia," noting what seem to be corny phrases; others ironically dismiss Sandburg's efforts in favor of Lindsay yet fail to acknowledge that Lindsay hated jazz. Sandburg was, in fact, one of the few white poets of the time to endorse jazz, and he was not alone. At least three others merit recognition: DuBose Heyward, Mina Loy, and Hart Crane.

Heyward's *Jasbo Brown and Selected Poems* first appeared in 1925, and the title poem, which opens the collection, demonstrates his sympathies for the spirituality of the blues. Heyward footnoted the poem with this explanation: "According to tradition, jazz has taken its name from Jasbo Brown, an itinerant Negro player along the Mississippi, and later, in Chicago cabarets" (9). Whatever "tradition" this citation attempts to invoke, it has no more authority than the myriad of other possible sources that claim the etymology of the term "jazz."[12] At the same time, the explanation also gives the character Jasbo Brown a specified history, and the geographic movement in the poem, from the rural South to the more urban North, echoes the mythology of Brown traveling from Mississippi to Chicago.

The poem begins with mysterious sounds emerging from a dark nightscape. The sounds become a gumbo of flavors, "Loose heady laughter" mixing with the ring of a whistle "as lonely as a soul in flight" from along the river. (This whirling mixture of laughter and loneliness, one of the many oxymoronic unions in this poem, relates directly to the sound of the blues later sung by Jasbo Brown.) A riverboat emerges in the second stanza, which, like the poem as a whole, is suffused with beautiful lines ("paddles threshing phosphorescent blue") as well as vague and awkward descriptions ("A sudden world swam into view").

Enter Jasbo Brown, whose first words in this initial scene reflect the proposed tension between joyous celebration and depressing realities:

" 'Gawd, I's tired,' he said, and then far down / Among the shacks: 'Heaben, Heaben' " (11). At the sound of distant voices, he feels somewhat
comforted ("he was not alone"), but all the anxieties of moving from the
South to the North become immediately pressing upon him. The discrepancy between religious spirituals versus "heathenistic" blues lyrics, as well
as his personal insecurities about being too rural, all seem to be evoked
in the relatively simple line "Churches were no place for muddy jeans"
(11). Brown worries about his ability to adapt to the new environment
("He was not good enough for city ways"), and his concerns parallel the
split in social acceptance between Church spirituals and the blues:

> When they whined
> Their mournful hymns a trigger in his mind
> Would click, and he would yearn to shout
> Queer broken measures that his soul flung out
> Of some recess where joy and agony
> Whirled in a rhythm that he could feel and see. (12)

The description of the blues as "Queer broken measures that his soul flung
out" sounds much like the opening second and third lines of the poem,
"Bells jangled shrilly, and a whistle flung / A note as lonely as a soul in
flight" (9). Like the connection between the slave work-songs and the
blues, here the bells and whistles of the riverboat are compared to the
spontaneous, cathartic release of blues singing.

When a woman recognizes Brown, he is brought to a piano; glasses of
gin fill and refill, and he sings into the night. At dawn, when the party
finally comes to a close, he wonders where he will stay until a woman,
responding to the sexually hypnotic quality of his blues singing, admits,
"I'd die for you / Most anytime yo' say when yo' are playin'!" (16). She
invites him home with her, and on the way, again lost in the trance of
music, his lips loose again and his eyes looking somewhere beyond, he
mumbles a song in a low, minor key:

> "Take me home an' res' me
> In de white folks' town.
> But I got to leabe yo'
> When de boat comes down.
>
> "De boat, an' de niggers
> What love my song.
> Life is jus' hello
> An' so-long." (16–17)

At 176 lines, "Jasbo Brown" remains one of the longest of jazz-related
poems. It is by no means one of the best; Heyward's use of dialect often
sounds forced, and ridiculous lines such as "The river clucked and sobbed"

(12) damage the movement and tone of the piece. But the poem has many positive elements to it, particularly in relation to other poems from the period. Whatever the aesthetic problems, "Jasbo Brown" can be seen as a sincere attempt to express the religious nature of African-American music and to bridge the gap between the accepted Church spirituals and the blasphemous blues.

The book *Jasbo Brown* became Heyward's farewell to poetry; with the publication of his novel *Porgy*, he established himself more as a fiction writer than a poet. And in retrospect, the most successful white writers addressing jazz were probably not Heyward, or even Sandburg, but rather Mina Loy and Hart Crane, whose work captured the urban intensity often associated with jazz. In addition to being one of the stronger poets to embrace jazz, Loy may very well be the first woman writer to incorporate the music in her poetry—no small statement, given the dominant male influence on jazz and jazz poetry—but her attraction to jazz had more to do with Fitzgerald's jazz age than it did with the actual music.[13] Still underrated as a writer, and certainly not known for her writing on jazz, Loy's poems have received new attention in recent years. Yet her own life remains a puzzle of sorts: In the twenties, Loy established herself as an integral member of elite Parisian circles, and then she suddenly withdrew entirely from her social life.

Although several poets and critics, including William Carlos Williams and Kenneth Rexroth, considered her to be among the more important modernist writers, "Loy remains a largely unknown poet," explains Virginia Kouidis, "undermined by early public indifference and confusion as well as her own lack of discipline and the attitude that, for her, poetry was only an avocation" (25). Her primary collection of poetry, *Lunar Baedeker*, appeared in 1923 and was then reprinted in 1958 in a slightly larger edition as *Lunar Baedeker and Time-Tables*. She died in 1966, and her collected poems, appropriately titled *The Last Lunar Baedeker*, appeared posthumously in 1982.

For the most part, Loy's poetry refers to jazz music only in passing, as brush strokes to highlight the verse. But her attraction to jazz makes eminent good sense in the context of her life and work. For one, Loy had a predilection both for the socially elite and the outcast members of society, a paradox perfectly analagous to jazz in the twenties: It was considered chic to be seen at such performances, yet virtually no one would consider bridging the gap between the audience and the musicians. Furthermore, her own work exhibited daring abstract imagery and jagged meter, and her aesthetic sense of poetry undoubtedly enabled her to appreciate similarities in jazz.

In "Crab-Angel," a poem from her book of 1923, she presents "the fantasy world of the dwarf as well as his helplessness and sexual ambiguity" (Kouidis 115) and emphasizes the ironic opposites with this stanza:

> The jeering jangling
> jazz
> crashes to silence (16)[14]

A slightly later poem, "Lady Laura in Bohemia" (1931), uses jazz to jux-
tapose a different set of opposites—the purity of Catholicism versus the
seedier, sinful elements of jazz:

> This abbess-prostitute
> presides
> Jazz-Mass
>
> The gin-fizz eucharist dispenses
> —she kisses and curses (183)

Her earliest reference to jazz appears in "Mexican Desert" (1921), and
the reference itself seems still further removed from the actual music:

> The belching ghost-wail of the locomotive
> trails; her rattling wooden tail
> into the jazz band sunset (17)

Color and form have often been used as a synthesthetic reference for the
sounds of jazz, but here music acts as the basis for visual description.

Despite the vibrant image of a "jazz band sunset," most of "Mexican
Desert" concentrates on loneliness and the need to prevail against depression. "The mountains in a row / set pinnacles of ferocious isolation,"
and yet the "Vegetable cripples of drought / Thrust up the parching appeal
/ cracking open the earth" (17). Vaguely disguised by metaphor, this poem
must have been an act of catharsis: In Mexico City, during the first month
of 1918, Loy married the poet Arthur Cravan, whom she loved passionately and who disappeared mysteriously in October of that same year.[15]
"After Cravan's disappearance," explains Kouidis,

Loy searched for her missing husband in Europe and America. Eventually she
learned from the U.S. State Department that his body had been found beaten and
robbed in the Mexican desert. . . . The depth of her loss appears . . . in her response
to the *Little Review* "Questionnaire" of 1929: "What has been the happiest moment of your life?"—"Every moment I spent with Arthur Cravan." "The unhap-
piest?"—"The rest of the time." (12)

Loy titled the most ambitious poem about her lost love "The Widow's
Jazz" (1931). Divided into two sections, the poem does not begin with
references to Cravan or Mexico but instead describes the sounds that inspired her sad reflections: the Chicago-style jazz that could be heard in

numerous Parisian nightclubs in the twenties. The poem begins with a cynical description of the white dancers:

> The white flesh quakes to the negro soul
> Chicago! Chicago!
>
> An uninterpretable wail
> stirs in a tangle of pale snakes
>
> to the lethargic ecstacy of steps
> backing into primeval goal
>
> White man quit his actin' wise
> colored folk hab de moon in dere eyes (200)

Loy, who was always attracted to abstraction and the avant-garde, and who fell in love with Cravan partly because of his bohemian characteristics, focuses on the women in the poem, the "maiden saplings," who are "encroaching Eros / in adolescence." Like the symbiosis of an old woman comforted by feeding bread crumbs to grateful birds, "impish musics / crumble the ecstatic loaf / before a swooning flock of doves" (201). "The black brute-angels" playing jazz wield the magic; they "hab de moon in dere eyes," and their instruments extend their physical bodies into inhuman form (saxophones, for example, become "a monstrous growth of metal trunks"). Yet the dancers "slant" their bodies to the music and in this form of creative response become entranced themselves. Unlike so many of her contemporaries, Loy managed not merely to transcend the fear of jazz's sexual allure but to celebrate it.

And yet, it is precisely this exultation of jazz that becomes the catalyst for Loy's depression; rather than revitalize her spirits, the youthfulness of the forms and sounds force her to compare this jazz scene to her own life, particularly her severed romantic relationship. Section II of the poem begins with the single word "Cravan" and continues "colossal absentee / the substitute dark / rolls to the incandescent memory / of love's survivor" (201). The abstract "flames of sound" and jazz dancing allow her mind to drift into painful memory, while the union of the dancers and the musicians seems to mock her lost marriage:

> Husband
> how secretly you cuckold me with death
>
> while this cajoling jazz
> blows with its tropic breath
>
> among the echoes of the flesh
> a synthesis
> of racial caress (201)

As the music merges with the dancers in an "everlit delight," Loy's speaker, like Orpheus searching for Eurydice, thinks only of her loss and concludes the poem with personal despair:

> my desire
> receded
> to the distance of the dead
>
> searches
> the opaque silence
> of unpeopled space. (202)

The glorious sounds of Chicago-style jazz recede to silence, and the lithe dancers only emphasize her own unpopulated, black-hole of sadness.

Mina Loy gave several poetry readings in the twenties at Natalie Barney's salon and, on at least one occasion, read this particular poem. "She read her own work," said Barney, "and in English, an unpublished poem she had just finished: 'The Widow's Jazz' " (Loy 326).[16] The reading must have been impressive, for years later, at the age of eighty-three, Barney wrote to Loy in thanks for receiving her "wonderful book," adding "what, please, has become of a poem written by you which took place at a jazz-band supper, where you exclaimed: 'husband, why have you cuckold me with death?' " [sic] (Loy 326). The answer is that it had appeared with one other poem of hers in *Pagany* magazine, 1931, but these poems virtually concluded her publishing career. Very self-aware and fiercely independent, she chose to replace the spirit of the jazz age with opaque silence.

The abstractness of Loy's verse suggests the abstractness of jazz, and in that respect her work most closely resembles Hart Crane's. As with Loy, the relationship between jazz and Crane's poetry remains both integral and elusive. On the one hand, Crane admired the sounds of modern jazz and, according to his letters and essays, tried to emulate some of the qualities of the music in his poetry; on the other, the direct references to jazz are rare, and trying to decide what was necessarily jazz-influenced has sometimes led to weak arguments. Maria F. Bennett's *Unfractured Idiom: Hart Crane and Modernism* (1987), for example, tries to link aesthetic crossovers between the music and his poetry, but too often the prose succumbs to cloudy generalities:

The modern ear, like the modern eye, must interpret the physical nature of the "new" music as well as its aural effect; syncopated beat, crescendo, unresolved tension and many other technical foci of jazz placed a highly physical element in composition, creating the sense of a totality of experience. (58–59)

Some of Bennett's other direct parallels between Crane and jazz seem equally spurious, such as the suggestion that all repeated themes, rhythmic cadences, syncopated rhythms, and unresolved tensions (62, 63, 65, 67) necessarily correspond to jazz influences.[17] Although both the poetry and the music share these general characteristics, it is virtually impossible to distinguish musical influences as opposed to poetic sensibilities. Did Crane respond to jazz because he had an acute ear for sound and rhythm? Did jazz change his poetic style?

Both may be true. What we know for certain is that Crane did indeed enjoy the music and that the relationship between the two arts—in terms of rhythm and imagery—fascinated him. The second section of "For the Marriage of Faustus and Helen," first published in 1924, may well be the best example of Crane's synesthetic union of jazz and poetry:

Brazen hypnotics glitter here:
Glee shifts from foot to foot,
Magnetic to their tremolo.
This crashing opéra bouffe,
Blest excursion! this ricochet
From roof to roof—
Know, Olympians, we are breathless
While nigger cupids scour the stars!

A thousand light shrugs balance us
Through snarling hails of melody.
White shadows slip across the floor
Splayed like cards from a loose hand;
Rhythmic ellipses lead into canters
Until somewhere a rooster banters.

Greet naïvely—yet intrepidly
New soothings, new amazements
That cornets introduce at every turn—
And you may fall downstairs with me
With perfect grace and equanimity.
Or, plaintively scud past shores
Where, by strange harmonic laws
All relatives, serene and cool,
Sit rocked in patent armchairs.

O, I have known metallic paradises
Where cuckoos clucked to finches
Above the deft catastrophes of drums.
While titters hailed the groans of death
Beneath gyrating awnings I have seen
The incunabula of the divine grotesque.
This music has a reassuring way.

The siren of the springs of guilty song—
Let us take her on the incandescent wax
Striated with nuances, nervosities
That we are heir to: she is still so young,
We cannot frown upon her as she smiles,
Dipping here in this cultivated storm
Among slim skaters of the gardened skies.

(*Complete*, 30–31)

Crane incorporates polarities, such as "the divine grotesque," as a way of celebrating jazz, rather than denigrating the music. His use of "nervosities" does not condemn the sound, as with Lindsay and Guiterman, nor does the imagery of birds seem as racist as the associations of monkeys and other screaming beasts. (Of course, the line "nigger cupids"—which now reads as bad poetry written in bad taste—significantly detracts from his good intentions.) The sexual nature of the music, implied in the phrase "guilty song," and the "Rhythmic ellipses" of dancing figures do not conjure up the same seediness as seen in the work by Cummings or Wood. Instead, the "Brazen hypnotics" of jazz, with all its "snarling hails of melody," create an atmosphere to be embraced, wholeheartedly: "The music has a reassuring way."

Crane wrote the second section of "Faustus and Helen" significantly faster than either I or III (Weber, 176), possibly a sign of his natural appreciation for the rhythms of jazz, and his ecstatic tone resounded not merely in the poem itself but in his letters about the work. To Allen Tate, on May 16, 1922, Crane wrote:

The poetry of negation is beautiful—alas, too dangerously so for one of my mind. But I am trying to break away from it. Perhaps this is useless, perhaps it is silly—but one *does* have joys. The vocabulary of damnations and prostrations has been developed at the expense of these other moods, however, so that it is hard to dance in proper measure. Let us invent an idiom for the proper transposition of jazz into words! Something clean, sparkling, elusive! (*Letters*, 89)

Less than a month later, on June 4, he wrote to Gorham Munson about his newly written second section:

I have been at it for the last 24 hours and it may be subjected to a few changes and additions, but as I see it now in the red light of the womb it seems to me like a work of youth and magic.

At any rate, it is something entirely new in English poetry, so far as I know. The jazz rhythms in that first verse are something I have been wishing to "do" for many a day. (*Letters*, 89)

One of the arguments over the actual poem concerns the success of these "jazz rhythms" in "Faustus and Helen." Whereas Bennett argues in favor of the achievement, other critics disagree. For instance, Herbert Leibowitz explains how Crane, in an attempt to capture the jazz rhythms, turns to iambic tetrameter and creates a rather steady beat; images syncopate the movement more than meter. "['Faustus and Helen'] is jazzy," writes R. W. B. Lewis, "only as language can be jazzy but not as jazz is jazzy" (104). Between tongue twisters and vague parallels, the argument becomes cloudy at best, and one can sympathize with Warner Berthoff when he concludes

Crane's success in this has been rather pointlessly disputed. If you already have jazz rhythms in your head, or an idea of them, it will be easy enough to think of them in reading lines in which the aim is to simulate these rhythms directly as well as to describe their psychic impact. (49)

But Crane definitely achieved a dance of images that evoked the sexual freedoms often associated with jazz, and the drunken vibrancy of the cabaret atmosphere. For Crane, the "strange harmonic" sounds from the "cornets" and other horns created a "metallic paradise" that beat against the wild chant of drum rhythms. Here was a "cultivated storm" to rival Cummings' men slurping soup.

In December 1925, almost three years to the day after Vachel Lindsay wrote his distressed letter to Monroe about being labeled a Jazz Poet by so many critics (including, no doubt, Clement Wood), Lindsay traveled to Washington, D.C., for a scheduled reading in a small theater at the Wardman Park Hotel. Because he had already established himself as an important American poet, his reading had been fairly well publicized. That evening, when he sat down for dinner prior to his reading, an African-American busboy slipped Lindsay three handwritten poems, offered some brief words of praise for the poet's work, and quickly left the room for the kitchen area. Lindsay read the poems immediately. All three resonated with the rhythms of blues and jazz, but this did not seem to bother Lindsay at all. In fact, he became quite taken by them. At his reading, he told the story of this busboy and claimed, as Arnold Rampersad puts it, "That he had discovered a poet, a bona fide poet, a Negro poet no less" (117). In triumph, Lindsay read the three poems to his audience, and the following morning the busboy found a number of reporters eager to learn more about his life and to take photographs of him surrounded by pots and kitchenware. What Lindsay and the reporters did not realize, however, was that this "new discovery" had already published work in a number of magazines, and that his first book of poems, *The Weary Blues*, was immediately forthcoming from Knopf. The poet's name: Langston Hughes.

NOTES

1. This book does not address the influence of jazz music on the poetry of Eliot simply because the connection seems general at best, but several publications have attempted to prove otherwise, including David Chinitz's essay "T. S. Eliot and the Cultural Divide" and Robert Gaspar's dissertation "Everyone and I Stopped Breathing" (38–43).

2. I have limited my discussion to poems that address jazz music directly (positively and negatively), but other writers seemed indifferent towards the subject. For example, in 1929 Charles Henri Ford edited *Blues: A Magazine of New Rhythms*, but most of the poems had little or nothing to do with African-American music. As Steven Tracy explains, "The nine issues of *Blues* contained only two poems that referred explicitly to blues music: Herman Spector's 'These Are Those Back-Again, Once-Before, Home-Again Blues,' the title a play on the occasionally lengthy and humorous titles of vaudeville blues songs, and William Closson Emory's 'Theme for a Blues Song,' about an urban prostitute who is mocked by the concrete around her" (265, n. 183). But even these two poems seem extremely removed from the form or spirit of the music.

3. The *Punch* publication appeared on December 10, 1924, and is uncredited; however, the index to the July–December volumes lists Percy Haselden as the author. The *Literary Digest*, misinterpreting a line wrap for a line break, reprinted the poem in three stanzas instead of two; it also assumed, because there was no credit on the original page, that no credit was ever given. As a result, several sources, including Alan P. Merriam's *A Bibliography of Jazz* (1954), refer to this poem as an anonymous publication.

4. *Contemporary Poetry of America*, a book panned by the critics from the twenties and long since forgotten, presents a chapter on Vachel Lindsay titled "Vachel Lindsay: Jazz and the Poet," yet Wood never explores that parallel with any depth. Wood probably shared Lindsay's admiration for Negro spirituals (he edited a pocket-sized anthology titled *Negro Songs* in 1924), but even though he celebrated Lindsay's use of rhythm, he spent most of the essay criticizing the weaknesses in the poet's work, particularly his use of trite rhymes and unimaginative syntax. When he cites the actual texts, his points ring true.

5. During this time, Cummings submitted an essay titled "The New Art," in which he addressed a number of the avant-garde arts, including music, although in this area Cummings only mentioned classical composers (Stravinsky, Debussy, Satie, Schönberg) and made no references to jazz music.

6. The reference to "I Want a Doll" certainly suggests the name of a particular dance number, but no such song seems to have existed at that time. Cummings was, perhaps, inventing a name that would approximate the names of other jazz tunes; or, possibly, he was quoting from memory and misquoted a title such as "I Want a Girl," which was quite a popular song at the time.

7. Robert Gaspar's explication of this poem avoids the double negative at the poem's close and offers an interpretation opposite to my own: "The fact that these are 'unnoise men,' in Cummings's linguistic world, is a compliment, suggesting that jazz musicians create the very opposite of noise, i.e. music of high order" (55).

8. Cummings created a similar union in "Gert," the third section of his poem

"Five Americans" from *is 5* (1926). Here his vulgar descriptions of the woman dissolve into each other like the changes in the poem from "joggle" to "jounce" to "jazz," and then, after the visual descriptions, concentrates on sound. The ugliness of the woman's voice in the final lines emphasizes the vulgarity of the preceding visual imagery ("corpsecolored body," "twitching lips"), as well as the progression from "jazz" to the "grusome" [sic] Brooklyn accent.

9. My discussion of Sandburg, Heyward, Loy, and Crane does not attempt to cover all of the poets or poems that endorse jazz. Maxwell Bodenheim, for example, wrote many jazz poems (such as those in his book *Bringing Jazz!* from 1930) and even performed his poetry to jazz long before poetry-read-to-jazz became popularized in the late fifties; though I find his poetry trite, he might be of interest to those studying jazz poetry from this period. Henry Crowder's collection, *Henry-Music* (1930), sets six poems to music, including work by Richard Aldington and Samuel Beckett, as well as Nancy Cunard's "Memory Blues." In 1934 Cunard herself edited a collection titled *Negro*, which anthologized the poem "Louis Armstrong," written by the Belgian poet and playwright Ernst Moerman and translated by Samuel Beckett. In short, my sweeping coverage of this period (and others) has inevitably left room for more-detailed discussions.

10. When I use the term jazz in this case, I am talking specifically about the early style of jazz from the 1910s and early 1920s. The word jazz, at that time, had different connotations that reflected the spirit of the time as much as it did the actual music—for example, Ben Hecht's review of *Cornhuskers* in 1918 for the *Chicago Daily News* in which he wrote of Sandburg, "He's the only genuine jazz motif in the letters of the day—a motif sonorous and quick, brazen and elusive" (Niven, 336).

11. Sandburg claimed that "Jazz Fantasia" was the first jazz poem to be written and, for whatever it is worth, he may be correct. But numerous poets began writing about jazz at that same time, including Raymond Dandridge whose jazz-related, dialect poem "De Drum Majah" also appeared in 1920 (*The Poet and Other Poems*).

12. Bill Crow, in the second chapter of *Jazz Anecdotes* titled "The Word 'Jazz,'" discusses some of the many possible variants, including one anonymous source that "claims that a Chicago musician called Jasbo Brown was the genesis of the term" (19). But this small claim is overshadowed by the wealth of alternatives, including the influence of African and Arabian roots; the derivation from the French verb *jaser*, meaning "to gossip" or "to chatter"; the various sexual implications stemming from "jass," "gism," "jasm"; and so on.

13. Amy Lowell's "Jazz Dance" appeared posthumously in 1927. This racially condescending poem is of marginal interest in terms of poetic achievement, but it is, perhaps, of historic importance given the limited number of women poets writing about jazz in the first half of this century.

14. All quotations from Loy's poetry come from *The Last Lunar Baedeker* (1982).

15. Loy's failed first marriage and tragic history as a parent made this loss all the more devastating. For a more thorough appreciation of her life, see the various essays and reflections in *The Last Lunar Baedeker*, as well as Virginia Kouidis' *Mina Loy: American Modernist Poet*.

16. The actual quotation is in French and reads: "elle lut elle-même, et en anglais, un poème inédit qu'elle venait de terminer: *la Veuve et le Jazz*."

17. There are other maddening features to the book, including an index that does not correspond to the proper page numbers and a flood of typographical errors, some of which initially stump interpretation: for example, "Louis Armstrong was cheating [*sic*] his own form of 'swing' or 'hot jazz' " (59). The "h," I believe, should be an "r."

REFERENCES

Bennett, Maria F. *Unfractured Idiom: Hart Crane and Modernism*. New York: Peter Lang, 1987.

Berthoff, Warner. *Hart Crane: A Re-Introduction*. Minneapolis: University of Minnesota, 1989.

Bodenheim, Maxwell. *Bringing Jazz!* New York: Horace Liveright, 1930.

Chinitz, David. "T. S. Eliot and the Cultural Divide." *PMLA* 110 (March 1995): 236–247.

Crane, Hart. *The Complete Poems and Selected Letters and Prose of Hart Crane*. Ed. Brom Weber. London: Oxford University Press, 1968.

———. *The Letters of Hart Crane 1916–1932*. Ed. Brom Weber. New York: Hermitage House, 1952.

Crow, Bill. *Jazz Anecdotes*. New York: Oxford University Press, 1990.

Crowder, Henry. *Henry-Music*. Paris: Hours, 1930.

Cummings, E. E. *The Complete Poems 1904–1962*. Ed. George J. Firmage. New York: Liveright, 1991.

Cunard, Nancy, ed. *Negro*. London: Wishart, 1934.

Dandridge, Raymond Garfield. *The Poet and Other Poems*. Cincinnati: Powell and White, 1920.

Ford, Charles Henri, ed. *Blues: A Magazine of New Rhythms*. Vol. I (February–July 1929).

Gaspar, Robert Peter. "Everyone and I Stopped Breathing: Jazz in American Poetry." Diss. University of Connecticut, 1992.

Guiterman, Arthur. *The Light Guitar*. New York and London: Harper and Brothers, 1923.

Haselden, Percy. "The Jazz Cannibal." *Punch* CLXVII (December 10, 1924): 651. [Reprinted, anon., in *Literary Digest* (January 10, 1925): 36.]

Heyward, DuBose. *Jasbo Brown and Selected Poems*. New York: Farrar, Rinehart, 1931.

Kennedy, Richard. *Dreams in the Mirror: A Biography of E. E. Cummings*. New York: Liveright, 1980.

Kidder, Rushworth. *E. E. Cummings: An Introduction to the Poetry*. New York: Columbia University Press, 1979.

Kouidis, Virginia M. *Mina Loy: American Modernist Poet*. Baton Rouge: Louisiana State University Press, 1980.

Leibowitz, Herbert A. *Hart Crane: An Introduction to the Poetry*. New York: Columbia University Press, 1968.

Lewis, R.W.B. *The Poetry of Hart Crane: A Critical Study*. Princeton: Princeton University Press, 1967.

Lindsay, Vachel. *The Golden Whales of California*. New York: Macmillan, 1920.

———. *Letters of Vachel Lindsay*. Ed. Marc Chenetier. New York: Burt Franklin, 1979.

———. *The Poetry of Vachel Lindsay: Volume 1*. Ed. Dennis Camp. Peoria, Il.: Spoon River, 1984.

Lowell, Amy. *Ballads for Sale*. Boston and New York: Houghton Mifflin, 1927.

Loy, Mina. *The Last Lunar Baedeker*. Highlands: Jargon Society, 1982.

Massa, Ann. *Vachel Lindsay: Fieldworker for the American Dream*. Bloomington: Indiana University Press, 1970.

Merriam, Alan P. *A Bibliography of Jazz*. Philadelphia: American Folklore Society, 1954.

Niven, Penelope. *Carl Sandburg: A Biography*. New York: Scribners, 1991.

Rampersad, Arnold. *The Life of Langston Hughes. Vol. 1: 1902–1941*. New York: Oxford University Press, 1986.

Sandburg, Carl. *Complete Poems*. New York: Harcourt, Brace, 1950.

Schuller, Gunther. *Early Jazz*. New York: Oxford University Press, 1968.

Tracy, Steven. *Langston Hughes and the Blues*. Urbana and Chicago: University of Illinois, 1988.

Weber, Brom. *Hart Crane: A Biographical and Critical Study*. Corrected Edition. New York: Russell and Russell, 1970.

Wood, Clement. *The Greenwich Village Blues*. New York: Henry Harrison, 1926.

———. *The Complete Rhyming Dictionary Revised*. Rev. by Ronald Bogus. New York: Doubleday, 1991. [Originally published in 1936.]

———. *Contemporary Poetry of America*. New York: Dutton, 1925.

———. *Negro Songs: An Anthology*. Girard, Kansas: Haldeman-Julius, 1924.

3

Weary Blues, Harlem Galleries, and Southern Roads

But jazz to me is one of the inherent expressions of Negro life in Amer-
ica: the eternal tom-tom beating in the Negro soul—tom-tom of revolt
against weariness in a white world, a world of subway trains, and work,
work, work; the tom-tom of joy and laughter, and pain swallowed in a
smile.
                    —Langston Hughes

An' all dat Big Boy axes
   When time comes fo' to go,
Lemme be wid John Henry, steel drivin' man,
   Lemme be wid old Jazzbo,
      Lemme be wid ole Jazzbo....
                    —Sterling Brown

The poems that Hughes chose to show Lindsay were "The Weary Blues,"
"Jazzonia," and "Negro Dancers," the same three poems that open the
first section of *The Weary Blues* (1926). Hughes had gambled with the
gesture. He knew that the auditorium would not admit African-American
people and that he would have to act before the reading if he was to have
any chance of meeting Lindsay or showing him his work. Still, the odds
stood in his favor: At worst, Lindsay could have ignored the verse. But
Hughes must also have known the strength of those three poems, and a
brief glance would probably be enough to keep Lindsay's attention. Like
a card player drawing three aces, Lindsay would be hard pressed to fold.
    The irony, though, had to do with timing. Although the early twenties
found Lindsay ranting against the title "Jazz Poet," it was also a time when
Hughes had begun to find his poetic voice, a voice nurtured by the sounds

of the blues and jazz. At the end of 1924, Lindsay wrote, "I used the word [jazz] once or twice when it meant spice. But just after that the world, the whole world went jazz-mad . . . and the saxophone, which I hate—was read into everything I ever did" (*Letters*, 331). Hughes, meanwhile, seemed to thrive on the "jazz-mad" world, haunting various cabarets and replaying those sounds on his victrola, which, along with various blues and jazz records, he had lugged with him to Europe in his various travels. Reading Hughes's poetry would not, certainly, diminish Lindsay's reputation as a jazz enthusiast, but the rhythms in the varying poetic lines and the active jazz imagery must have overshadowed whatever personal qualms he may have had.

Langston Hughes must be considered the first major jazz poet. His earliest poems, in *The Weary Blues* and other books from the twenties and thirties, were primarily influenced by the blues. But Hughes's career as a poet reflects his increasing interest in the jazz aesthetic. Even *The Weary Blues* includes several poems that, particularly in contrast to Lindsay and others, demonstrate his understanding of jazz as a necessary expression of African-American culture. With Sterling Brown and Melvin Tolson in the thirties, Hughes offered a new poetic to counter the racism so prevalent in jazz poetry from the turn of the century.[1]

Hughes began the poem "The Weary Blues" in 1922, when he found himself on board a ship that was not (contrary to his hopes) traveling to foreign lands but was instead anchored with others near West Point; ghostly remnants of the war, these ships had to be maintained despite their stagnancy, and Hughes, blindly eager to travel, did not realize his fate. Although he learned to enjoy his shipmates and some of the surrounding landscapes, he nevertheless became utterly isolated, finding solace primarily in his writing.[2] He particularly found inspiration in his memories of Harlem, and despite his solitude the sounds of jazz and blues remained fresh in his ears. "That winter [on board the ship]," Hughes explained,

I wrote a poem called "The Weary Blues," about a piano-player I heard in Harlem, but I didn't send it anywhere because I wasn't satisfied with it. . . . I could not achieve an ending I liked, although I worked and worked on it—something that seldom happens to any of my poems. (*The Big Sea*, 92)

The poem quickly became a lucky charm for Hughes. Shortly after his encounter with Lindsay in late December 1925, Hughes received the poetry prize at the first literary contest sponsored by *Opportunity* magazine; the judges included James Weldon Johnson and Clement Wood.[3] When Johnson read the poem out loud as part of the ceremony, Carl Van Vechten approached Hughes about publishing a full-length volume of poetry, which Hughes would later title after the poem that had opened these doors.

"['The Weary Blues'] was a poem about a working man who sang the blues all night," Hughes wrote, "and then went to bed and slept like a rock. That was all. And it included the first blues verse I'd ever heard way back in Lawrence, Kansas, when I was a kid" (*The Big Sea*, 215). When Hughes wrote "That was all," he meant that was the primary image and impulse behind the poem; but in some respects he belittled both the poem and his personal association with the work. For Hughes, "The Weary Blues" gave him some solace in his lonely time on the ship.

The relationship between his own depressions and his creative impulses became a recurring theme in his autobiography, *The Big Sea*, in which he repeatedly explained how, creatively, he thrived on sadness and hard times. Here is one example among many:

I felt very bad in Washington that winter [in 1924], so I wrote a great many poems. (I wrote only a few poems in Paris, because I had had such a good time there.) But in Washington . . . I didn't like my job, and I didn't know what was going to happen to me, and I was cold and half-hungry, so I wrote a great many poems. I began to write poems in the manner of the Negro blues and the spirituals. (205)

The blues became an inspiration rooted in sadness, but with a complex mixture of humor and spiritual uplift. Writing about the blues allowed Hughes, as the poet, to respond to musicians, to their music, and to the wonderful dance of cultural varieties associated with the sound. "On Seventh Street in 1924," Hughes wrote,

they played the blues, ate watermelon, barbecue, and fish sandwiches, shot pool, told tall tales, looked at the dome of the Capitol and laughed out loud. I listened to their blues:

Did you ever dream lucky—
Wake up cold in hand?

And I went to their churches and heard the tambourines play and the little tinkling bells of the triangles adorn the gay shouting tunes that sent sisters dancing down the aisles for joy.
I tried to write poems like the songs they sang on Seventh Street. (*The Big Sea*, 208–209)

Hughes soon recognized the importance of uniting poetry with jazz. His goal: that poetry would offer respectability to jazz and that the music would in turn give poetry a larger audience.

Much has been written about "The Weary Blues" (including Steven Tracy's fine discussion of the poem in *Langston Hughes & the Blues*, 219–223), and for good reason: Apart from its importance to Hughes's career, "The Weary Blues" might be seen as a landmark in the history of jazz poetry. The indented passages in the poem—from the couplet "He did a lazy sway" that repeats like the movement of an ocean, or the punctuated, almost-exuberant "O Blues!"—allowed the lines themselves to have a rhythmic sway that Lindsay had failed to achieve in rather contrived poems such as "The Congo." The call-and-response quality to these lines invoke the spirit and form of the blues, but they also act as a bridge to Hughes's jazz-related poems, which, while steeped in the blues, seem freer in form and often more impressionistic. Hughes personalized the sorrow he heard in the blues, a complicated moodiness too neatly summarized by poets such as Sandburg ("sob on the long cool winding saxophones"), and brilliantly evoked the anonymous blues musician through sepia visuals, musical refrains, and syncopated pulses.

If "The Weary Blues" tried to capture the moaning sounds of a lonely blues musician, "Jazzonia" emulated the rhythmic imagery of a twenties cabaret in which jazz and dance, sound and sight, become one aesthetic response:

> Oh, silver tree!
> Oh, shining rivers of the soul.
>
> In a Harlem cabaret
> Six long-headed jazzers play.
> A dancing girl whose eyes are bold
> Lifts high a dress of silken gold.
>
> Oh, singing tree!
> Oh, shining rivers of the soul!
>
> Were Eve's eyes
> In the first garden
> Just a bit too bold?
> Was Cleopatra gorgeous
> In a gown of gold?
>
> Oh, shining tree!
> Oh, silver rivers of the soul!
>
> In a whirling cabaret
> Six long-headed jazzers play.

(The Weary Blues, 25)

Like sparse musical notes that begin to evoke a full melody, the mysterious opening couplet teases the reader into the musical scene. The phrase "silver tree" fuses semiprecious metal with organic growth, a wonderful synesthetic metaphor for a trumpet or cornet. The couplet shimmers with its "silver" and "shining rivers," and, like our own responses to music that can never be articulated exactly, draws an abstract parallel between the sound of jazz and the stirrings in one's soul, a concept explored throughout *The Weary Blues*, particularly in Hughes's famous poem, "The Negro Speaks of Rivers:" "I've known rivers: / I've known rivers ancient as the world and older than the flow of human blood in human veins. / My soul has grown deep like the rivers" (51).

The second stanza of "Jazzonia" sets the scene of the Harlem cabaret and emphasizes the importance of group sound, a quality central to twenties' jazz that changed in the following decade to an emphasis on individual soloists. The relationship between jazz and dance—and the sexual connotations of that relationship—are boldly sketched here with none of the moral insinuations that appeared in the poems by Cummings, Wood, Guiterman, and others.[4] Here, the bold eyes suggest the consciousness of the actions; there is nothing pathetic or degrading about this dancer who "Lifts high a dress of silken gold," an image that again unites precious, regal metals with the art itself. Like the dancer Josephine Baker, who began her career in the twenties and performed with Sidney Bechet as well as other important jazz musicians of the time, this dancer nonchalantly exposes herself as part of the performance. Her sexuality is as natural as the rhythms of a silver cornet or surging, shining rivers.

Hughes subtly melds sight with sound through his imagistic sketches and then emphasizes this transition in the third stanza, which changes the "silver tree" from the opening couplet to a "singing tree." In variations on its theme, the poem plays with these adjectives until, in the final couplet, the original description has reversed: "Oh, shining tree! / Oh, silver rivers of the soul!" The repetition of the words, like musical phrases and riffs, evokes the blues without relying on blues forms, and these rhythms propel the poem to its close.

When Hughes describes the exotic dancers, he offers, through historical references, a way of contextualizing this cabaret that makes it significantly less shocking and unquestionably moral by nature. Just as Hughes wanted poetry to give jazz respectability, so too are his references to Eve and Cleopatra designed to elevate our respect for these jazz dancers, and for the music itself. The poem implies that we are all naturally attracted to the splendor of shimmering gold and the sensuality of rhythmic dance. And this entire jazz world, this "Jazzonia," encompasses a provocative tension between what is desired and what is forbidden.

The final couplet echoes the second stanza almost exactly, but here, as with the modifications of "silver," "singing," and "shining," Hughes replaces "Harlem cabaret" with "whirling cabaret," and "whirling" becomes the operative word for this poem, which swirls from one dancing image to the next, interweaving the sound of jazz with the movement of the dancers. Silver glints of light refract from trumpets as a reflection of the soul. The histories and myths of the past become commentary for the history and mythology being created on the bandstand. The parallels now seem natural and necessary, but it would take many years for critics and writers to accept the dignity and complexities of jazz that Hughes worked so adroitly to evoke in "Jazzonia" and other poems.

The same kind of endorsement can be seen and heard in "Negro Dancers," the third poem in the first section of *The Weary Blues* and the third poem slipped to Vachel Lindsay that December afternoon in 1925. In this poem, Hughes creates speed and rhythm not so much from the rhyme as from repetition:

> "Me an' ma baby's
> Got two mo' ways,
> Two mo' ways to do de Charleston!"
>   Da, da,
>   Da, da, da!
> Two mo' ways to do de Charleston! (26)

There is a sense of freedom to these lines but also strong control over the rhythms—a far cry from Lindsay's sense of hysteric, atavistic chaos.[5] The fact that Hughes placed the opening lines in quotation marks raises several questions, such as: Is this part of a song? If so, are the Negro dancers singing this song, or is music in the background? (As with "Jazzonia," this poem raises questions and then answers them.) Hughes then describes the cabaret with "Soft light," lively jazz, and "Brown-skin steppers" performing in front of a receptive white audience: "White folks, laugh! / White folks, pray!" The commas after "folks" point toward an intentionally understated observation that the white people can respond to the music and the dance with cynical or condescending laughter, in moralizing prayer for these lost souls, but the fact remains that the music and the rhythms will outlive the critical responses. Both "the dancers and the dance go on," writes Arnold Rampersad, who then quotes Hughes directly:

"Do you like it? Do you get it?" Hughes asked [Countee] Cullen excitedly. "We'll dance! Let the white world tear itself to pieces. Let the white folks worry. We know two more joyous steps . . . C'est vrai?" (*Vol. I*, 89)

The poem directly attacks social fads and juxtaposes the craze of the "Charleston" with the jazz dancing of these "Brown-skin steppers." Did Lindsay recognize this social commentary when he enthusiastically read the poems aloud? Probably not.

Did Cullen? If he did not, then it was made clear to him by Hughes. Hughes had submitted the poem in 1924 to Cullen and Jessie Fauset for *Crisis*, but "Both Countee and Fauset . . . preferred rhymed, sentimental verse, marinated in pathos" and chose "Song for a Suicide" instead (Rampersad, *Vol. I*, 89). Their disapproval of Hughes's work, however, echoed the feelings by many other African-American writers of the time, who felt that emphasizing cabaret life (the dancing, drinking, live jazz and blues, sexuality, and so on) degraded their race and perpetuated stereotypes. Cullen's review of *The Weary Blues* in *Opportunity* magazine questioned if these or any jazz poems could ever join that "select and austere circle of high literary expression which we call poetry" (73). He objected to the emphasis on race, making the distinction between "racial artists" and "artists pure and simple." Thus, in Cullen's view at least, Hughes, in trying to give jazz the dignity of poetry, had actually widened the gap for many of his African-American contemporaries.

The white reviewers did not attack the book on similar grounds, although their praise for Hughes's use of jazz tended to compare his work with that of Lindsay or Sandburg rather than recognize his unique voice. DuBose Heyward's review of the book for the *New York Herald Tribune* was quite favorable but claimed that Hughes had done "nothing particularly revolutionary in the field of rhythm" (4). *The New York Times Book Review* referred to the jazz-related poems as the worst in the collection but begrudgingly admitted that they were "superior to the jazz poetry that is peddled on Broadway" and "not inferior to Vachel Lindsay's jazz poems" ("Five Silhouettes," 16). In short, most reviewers agreed that the author of "The Negro Speaks of Rivers" deserved to be celebrated as an important new voice, but they also did not find any merit in addressing the blues and jazz. Failing to convince either the African-American or the white intellectuals of the time that jazz should be treated as seriously as classical music, Hughes rebutted such contempt throughout his career with essays such as "The Negro Artist and the Racial Mountain" published in *The Nation* in 1926: "Let the blare of Negro jazz bands and the bellowing voice of Bessie Smith singing Blues penetrate the closed ears of the colored near-intellectuals until they listen and perhaps understand" (694). Yet, much like the response to jazz itself, his first significant attempts to develop jazz poetry had been treated with condescension and dismissal.

His next book of poems, *Fine Clothes to the Jew* (1927), disappointed many of the critics who favored *The Weary Blues* and added fuel to the fire of those who had previously tried to discredit Hughes's poetry.[6] But this second collection contains numerous blues-related poems that deserve attention, including the poem "Hey!" that asks, "Wonder what de blues'll bring?" (17). The answer to that question helps explain why the constricting form of the blues maintains its freshness in Hughes's poetry, which ranged in its tone from light verse to tragic narratives. Rampersad goes so far as to claim that "*Fine Clothes to the Jew* was also his most brilliant book of poems," adding that it "falls deliberately within the range of authentic blues emotion and blues culture" (*Vol. I*, 141). But if *Fine Clothes to the Jew* extended his mastery of the blues as a significant form of poetry, then his next two books further developed those sensibilities, particularly with regard to humor. "The blues," Hughes once wrote, "are mostly very sad songs about being without love, without money, or without a home. And yet, almost always in the blues, there is some humorous twist of thought, in words that make people laugh" (*Famous Negro Music Makers* 94). Both "Homesick Blues" from *The Dream Keeper* (1931) and "Morning After" from *Shakespeare in Harlem* (1942) use humor as a safeguard against sadness, yet the tone of the two poems differs as much as the voices of a chained slave and a vaudeville artist. In "Homesick Blues," the speaker cannot see any break from his relentless depression and wanders the streets like the embodiment of hopelessness. Finally, he laments,

> Homesick blues, Lawd,
> 'S a terrible thing to have.
> Homesick blues is
> A terrible thing to have.
> To keep from cryin'
> I opens ma mouth an' laughs.

> > > > > > > > > (*The Dream Keeper*, 24)

"Morning After" also has three stanzas, identically structured in the classic blues style, but in this case the speaker's mind aches because he has consumed a massive quantity of cheap booze and cannot bear to hear any loud noises:

> I said, Baby! Baby!
> Please don't snore so loud
> Baby! Please!
> Please don't snore so loud.
> You jest a little bit o' woman but you
> Sound like a great big crowd.

> > > > > > > (*Shakespeare in Harlem*, 44–45)

Both poems share the blues rhyme scheme, a particular visual appearance on the page, and certain thematic concerns. But tonally they remain utterly contrary to each other, and, as only two among a great many blues-related poems, they act as touchstones for Hughes's sensibilities as a poet coming to terms with the essence of the blues, a union of grief and joy.

The Dream Keeper and *Shakespeare in Harlem* emphasize Hughes's passion for the blues rather than jazz, and this generality holds true for all of his early books of poems. Two significant jazz-related poems, however, appeared later in the forties: "Trumpet Player: 32nd Street" (*Fields of Wonder*, 1947) and "Song for Billie Holiday" (*One-Way Ticket*, 1949). Together, they prefigure some of Hughes's poetic achievements of the fifties, including his deft faculties for transforming abstractions into concrete expression and using the rhythms of jazz to influence a freer hand with metrics and form. "The Trumpet Player" repeats a stanzaic introduction ("The Negro / With the trumpet at his lips") in order to create cadence and motifs within the poem the way a jazz musician repeats phrases in order to achieve continuity and highlight variations within a solo. Like Mina Loy's musicians in "The Widow's Jazz" who "hab de moon in dere eyes," this player's face features "dark moons of weariness / Beneath his eyes." As a creative writer, Hughes could appreciate how jazz musicians lose themselves in song; by giving in to the creative act of jazz, this trumpeter "Does not know / Upon what riff the music slips / Its hyperdermic needle / To his soul."

Because of the intimate connection between emotion and created sound, this musician, like most, necessarily becomes vulnerable to his present emotions as well as those from his past. As he plays, he recalls the "smoldering memory / Of slave ships" and suddenly must confront those feelings through his instrument. Yet the trumpeter transforms his slave memories and failed desires into the sound of salvation—"Trouble / Mellows to a golden note"—and the poem therefore offers a positive message of inspiration that transcends other forms of coping, such as the "laughter" in "Homesick Blues." In this sense, this anonymous trumpet player represents many African-American jazz musicians from the thirties and forties, including Louis Armstrong, one of Hughes's heroes.[7]

Many if not most creative acts have as their source emotional upheaval, and for Hughes the negative extremes (sadness, depression, despair) not only inspired him to write more but also acted as the foundation for "The Trumpet Player" and many of his other poems. Although he tended to celebrate the blues and jazz as creative forces used to counter oppression, some works questioned the efficacy of that concept. "Song for Billie Holiday" (1949), for example, begs the reader to meditate on this issue with an urgency and metric cadence reminiscent of Holiday's own pleading songs: Where Holiday often sang about lost love, this poem relentlessly asks how to purge such sadness.

Holiday, who died in 1959 at age 44, has since been the subject of more jazz-related poems than any other singer, but Hughes's poem may indeed be the first. (In fact, I can think of no other Holiday-inspired poem written prior to her death.) Most poems for her have been elegiac and have emphasized the now well-known tragedies of her life. Even though Hughes's poem does not specifically confront many of her personal struggles (heroin addiction, poverty, the extremes of racism), it nevertheless captures a profound sense of loss: "The sorrow that I speak of / Is dusted with despair." He describes Holiday as a "Voice of muted trumpet, / Cold brass in warm air" and, in the concluding couplet, suggests that song can indeed cut through this haze of depression ("Bitter television blurred"). But the song, the "sound that shimmers," is not specified, and the poem closes with a one-word question that still searches for an answer: "Where?"

Hughes's career through 1950 laid the groundwork for some exceptional jazz-related poetry collections (*Montage of a Dream Deferred*, 1951, and *Ask Your Mama: 12 Moods for Jazz*, 1961), several books of prose about jazz (including *The First Book of Jazz*, 1955), and a career-within-a-career as a poet performing with live jazz accompaniment.[8] But his writing prior to this period, from *The Weary Blues* (1926) through *One-Way Ticket* (1949), represents the majority of his work as a poet. Like the history of jazz in general, Hughes's poetry progressed from blues-oriented verse to the freer structures of jazz-related poetry.

In retrospect, Hughes's earliest publications, including *The Weary Blues* (1926) and *Fine Clothes to the Jew* (1927), substantiate his status as the most successful poet from the twenties to achieve a union between poetry and jazz. For the thirties, that honor probably belongs to Sterling Brown. Like Mina Loy's publishing history, Brown's career is marked by one major collection of poems, a volume titled *Southern Road*, which appeared in 1932.[9] Most of the tributes for Brown have labored to assert the importance of his writing, each one announcing that his time has finally come. One hopes that it has. But his limited number of publications has often allowed the sheer wealth of work by his contemporaries (particularly Hughes) to distract critics from his vitality as a poet.

In order to appreciate—indeed, celebrate—Brown's poetry, one must also recognize the influence of jazz and the blues that resound throughout his verse. The title poem to *Southern Road*, for example, emphasizes both the classic form of the blues and his use of phonetics to capture the poetic voice; Brown's choice of blues form evokes the relentless hardships of slaves and shackled chain gang members:

> Swing dat hammer—hunh—
> Steady bo';
> Swing dat hammer—hunh—
> Steady bo';
> Ain't no rush, bebby,
> Long ways to go. (46)

The feelings of hopelessness and remorse reappear in several other poems from the collection, including "Old King Cotton" where the speaker laments,

> Cotton, cotton,
> All we know;
> Plant cotton, hoe it,
> Baig it to grow;

What good it do to us
Gawd only know!" (66)

or the section titled "Low Down" from "New St. Louis Blues," which concludes,

Dice are loaded, an' de deck's all marked to hell,
Dice are loaded, de deck's all marked to hell,
Whoever runs dis gamble sholy runs it well. (72)

These are among the darkest poems in Brown's collection, for they offer little salvation, little hope against white oppression.

Yet *Southern Road* does offer uplifting messages to the reader. Brown realized that all people, to quote a different passage from "New St. Louis Blues," are "known fuh to have dark days" (70), but his depictions of such dark days actually enhance the expressions of perseverance and prevailing strength, particularly as witnessed in the blues. Although the poem "Southern Road" is the penultimate poem to Section One of the book, the section's concluding poem, "Strong Men," addresses oppressed slaves not as spiritually gutted human beings but as people who find salvation in song:

You sang:
  Bye and bye
  I'm gonna lay down dis heaby load....

You sang:
  Walk togedder, chillen,
  Dontcha git weary....
      The strong men keep a-comin' on
      The strong men git stronger. (51)

It may be a cliché to discuss the blues as a conversion of hopelessness into creativity, but it happens to be steeped in truth, and Brown never tired of celebrating that fact. *Southern Road* offers a number of possible ways to overcome the burdens of racism—from the sheer escapism of alcohol, to the ultimate refuge of suicide—but the predominant poetic form of the book, and the most memorable philosophies of survival, have to do with the blues and the people who continue to sing those songs of rebirth.

The repetition and musical refrain inherent in the blues make the blues form both easy to write poorly and extremely difficult to execute well.[10] Brown's mastery of this form has to do in part with the variations of his repeated lines (technically called "worrying" the line) in which the repeated statement changes in meter or sound, like the second line in the previous quotation from "New St. Louis Blues." Equally impressive is

Brown's use of the refrain, which keeps the momentum driving through poems such as "Southern Road," "Strong Men," or "When De Saints Go Ma'ching In," a portrait of a wandering musician. In this last poem, the actual lyrics keep reappearing and weave the piece together, not merely referentially but also in terms of form (repetition as refrain) and sound (syntactical variations on the lyric). Like a jazz musician cleverly modifying an established phrase, Brown restates his lines with small changes, as with this italicized couplet, *"Oh when de saints go ma'chin' home, / Oh when de sayaints goa ma'chin' home"* (12), which contracts and expands words to create a musical voice. Similarly, the lyric *"Lawd I wanna be one in nummer"* (13) repeats as *"Lawd I wanna be one o'dat nummer"* (13) and once again as *"Oh kain't I be one in nummer?"* (17). Brown recognized the importance of varied repetition (vital to blues musicians) and implemented this technique in order to keep the repetition sounding fresh while at the same time maintaining the statement's sentiment.

As a social commentator, Brown used jazz and the blues to charge his verse politically. In "Cabaret," for example, he presents a scene similar to that in Loy's "The Widow's Jazz," but Brown's poem does much more to highlight the vulgar distinctions in social class. "Hebrew and Anglo-Saxon" patrons "with their glittering darlings" arrive at the club in anticipation of authentic Negro culture: jazz from the muddied waters of the South. The white audience dances to the rhythms of the stage dancers, and everyone watching continues to drink excessively and spout their ignorant, "cultured" observations (*"O, le bal des belles quarterounes!"* and "There's peace and happiness there / I declare" [116]).

But irony plagues the entire scene, a fact that no one in the audience recognizes but one profoundly understood by the musicians and dancers. The dancers realize that they will later have to prostitute themselves (*"What am I offered, gentlemen, gentlemen"* [117]), and the musicians know that what they play for this group of upper-class socialites has nothing to do with their creative abilities. The perceived "peace and happiness" is, in reality, *"The stench of the drying mud,"* *"a bitter reminder of death"* (118). The performers mock authenticity in an effort to please club owners and their clientele. As the poet says: *"that's a nice doggie, / Show your tricks to the gentlemen"* (115).

Brown's understanding of this dispassionate performance helps to put in perspective the anxiety-ridden, jazz-related poetry by many of his white contemporaries. Aware of the many misconceptions about jazz, Brown intentionally degraded the musicians in his poem by describing the jazz band as something animalistic that "unleashes its frenzy":

> The trombone belches, and the saxophone
> Wails curdlingly, the cymbals clash,
> The drummer twitches in an epileptic fit (115)

The phrases bear a remarkable resemblance to those by white poets (such as Lindsay, Guiterman, and Cummings) who feared this music, and by mocking such stereotypical descriptions, Brown asserts himself as a poet of acute artistic and political observation. This was a direct assault on the critics who felt that cabaret jazz represented the mindless ramblings of former slaves. Brown targeted racism and ignorance in America, and African-American music became, as it did for many in the sixties, one of his strongest vehicles.

If "Cabaret" represents the falseness of many jazz performances at the turn of the twentieth century, then "Ma Rainey" presents the blues as an essential, spiritually uplifting form of expression. More specifically, the poem celebrates the Mother of the Blues, whose voice influenced scores of others, including Bessie Smith. In the vast history of jazz-related poems, "Ma Rainey" remains a touchstone as the first significant poem to celebrate a major blues or jazz artist. But more important, the merits of the poetry itself demand close explication; all Sterling Brown scholars have recognized this poem as being among his very best.[11]

To emphasize the mass appeal of Rainey's voice, Brown opens the poem with a stanza of Southern geography, where "Folks from anyplace / Miles aroun' " (62) pack the trains and boats, strain the horses and mules, simply to hear her song. We watch the world at cloud level, and in the second stanza zoom closer to the event, to the arrival of the audience ("Dey stumble in de hall, jes' a-laughin' an' a-cacklin' " [63]) and then to the arrival of Ma Rainey herself: "Ma comes out before dem, a-smilin' gold-toofed smiles / An' Long Boy ripples minors on de black an' yellow keys" (63). Like Hughes's use of gold in "Jazzonia," the strength of the couplet focuses on the sparkle of that precious metal. (It is also an accurate portrait of Rainey's most noted facial feature.) Yet the yellow of gold and the yellow in the piano keys do not shine the same light; unlike the splendor of gold, which will not tarnish, white keys discolor to yellow from age and neglect, like the sadness in the "minors" performed by Rainey's accompanist. This central couplet accurately describes the singer herself while at the same time evoking the most profound emotions associated with the blues.

The omniscient speaker in the third stanza implores the singer both to "Sing us 'bout de hard luck" and to "Keep us strong" (63)—in short, to "Sing us 'bout de lonesome road / We mus' go" (63)—and in the fourth stanza she actualizes the hope of her audience. Much of the stanza quotes the "Backwater Blues," which invites us to imagine her sound, and unites the achievement of Ma Rainey with the formal qualities of the poem itself.[12] In response to the singing, the people "shut dey moufs up tight an' cried" (64); the poem tells us no more about the music or the reaction. It concludes: "She jes' gits hold of us dataway" (64).

The phrase might incorrectly seem anticlimactic (as though the speaker gives up, "I just can't explain myself"), yet it is precisely this loss of words that makes the poem so moving, much like Frank O'Hara's famous conclusion to "The Day Lady Died": "and everyone and I stopped breathing" (325). Brown recognized the inescapable distinctions between poetry and music, and he made no attempt to force analogies that might limit the music by this artist, or the blues in general for that matter. The poem admits to the limitations of language when it comes to describing the abstraction of music, and, by doing so, it pays homage to all of the best blues and jazz musicians.

Sterling Brown in many ways remains an unsung hero, and he is one of many African-American writers who deserve a far broader readership, including Melvin Tolson, who never received great recognition. Only recently have there been serious efforts to evaluate his achievements as a poet.[13] During his lifetime (1898–1966), Tolson failed to find a publisher for his first major work, *A Gallery of Harlem Portraits*, a project he began in 1932, the same year Brown published *Southern Road*. Like the poetic concerns of Hughes and Brown, Tolson's passion for the blues courses throughout the collection.

As Robert Farnsworth explains, "*A Gallery* is only a nascent or loosely conceived epic compared to the much more deservedly famous *Harlem Gallery*, published in 1965" (43). Yet most of Tolson's portraits in *A Gallery* seem no less crafted or moving than those in Brown's *Southern Road* (such as "Maumee Ruth," "Effie," or "Market Street Woman") or Hughes's *The Weary Blues* ("Nude Young Dancer," "Aunt Sue's Stories," "Mexican Market Woman"). In the central stanzas of "Peg Leg Snelson," for example, Tolson integrates the character's personal history with blues commentary:

> Snelson lost his left leg in Houston, Texas,
> When a truckload of white strikebreakers
> Crashed into a Ford containing
> Six Negro longshoremen.
>
> *Heart's so heavy cain't raise a song,*
> *Heart's so heavy cain't raise a song,*
> *Gonna catch de first train comin' along.*
>
> Mr. Heinrich Zangwill discovered Peg Leg Snelson
> At a cheap beer garden on Market Street in St. Louis. (30)

Like many of Tolson's portraits, this narrative weaves the emotions commonly associated with the blues (particularly the search for hope amid despair) with the figure being discussed. In this case, and in many others, the actual blues form accentuates that union. For Tolson, the blues as song and as social commentary remained necessarily integrated with African-American culture.

The continual rejections for his manuscript *A Gallery of Harlem Portraits* demoralized Tolson, and yet he continued to write plays, columns, and other poems.[14] By the sixties, he began work on *Harlem Gallery*, a proposed five-part project of which he completed only the first section. (The full title as published by Twayne in 1965 was *Harlem Gallery: Book I, The Curator*.) If *A Gallery of Harlem Portraits* was more inspired by the blues than by jazz, the opposite was true for this later work; *Harlem Gallery* not only addressed jazz as an inspiring subject but, on a more general level, embodied the spirit of jazz improvisation.

Accurately assessing the various inspirations for *Harlem Gallery*, Ronald Walcott once described the book as "an epic undertaking owing as much to Eliot, Pound, Yeats, Crane and Stevens as it does to Billie Holiday, Bessie Smith, Satchmo, Langston Hughes, and Ol' Red Taylor" (27). Of the twenty-four sections in *Harlem Gallery*, "Lambda" and "Mu" appear to be most governed by jazz, at least in terms of subject. "Lambda" introduces the character Hideho Heights, a poet of strong opinion (" 'In the beginning was the Word,' / he challenged, 'not the Brush!' ") who, with a swig of whiskey to loosen his lips, enjoys preaching the gospel of jazz. Indeed, the entire second half of this section consists of his speech praising Louis Armstrong, "old Satchmo." Hideho Heights concludes:

> *Old Satchmo's*
> *gravelly voice and tapping foot and crazy notes*
> *set my soul on fire.*
> *If I climbed*
> *the seventy-seven steps of the Seventh*
> *Heaven, Satchmo's high C would carry me higher!*
> *Are you hip to this, Harlem? Are you hip?*
> *On Judgment Day, Gabriel will say*
> *after he blows his horn:*
> *"I'd be the greatest trumpeter in the Universe,*
> *if old Satchmo had never been born!"* (70)

The words may seem overblown, perhaps even trite, yet they seem appropriate coming from such a character who had begun "to rhetorize in the grand style / of a Doctor Faustus in the dilapidated Harlem Opera House." Rather than submit to the overwhelming emotions inspired by music (like Brown's line about Ma Rainey's voice, "She jes' gits hold of us dataway"), Hideho Heights tries to use his rhetoric as accurate description, and he fails.

But this is by no means Tolson's failure, for when Tolson steps back as an omniscient narrator, his descriptions of music prove significantly more

seductive. In "Mu," the poem that follows "Lambda" and continues with
Hideho Heights as the central figure, Tolson compares the music by Frog
Legs Lux and the Indigo Combo to the glistening fins of feeding fish:

> Out of the Indigo Combo
> flowed rich and complex polyrhythms.
> Like surfacing bass,
> exotic swells and softenings
> of the veld vibrato
> emerged. (73)

Later in the poem, when the band kicks into a quicker beat, Tolson, improvising with a collage of imagery, writes,

> Frog Legs Lux and his Indigo Combo
> let go
> with a wailing pedal point
> that slid into
> *Basin Street Blues*
> like Ty Cobb stealing second base:
> Zulu,
> King of the Africans,
> arrives on Mardi Gras morning;
> the veld drum of Baby Dodds'
> great-grandfather
> in Congo Square
> pancakes the first blue note
> in a callithump of the USA. (75)

The poem concludes with the band's sound dissipating like a drummer's
cymbal shimmering to silence:

> With a dissonance
> from the Weird Sisters,
> the jazz diablerie
> boiled down and away
> in the vacuum pan
> of the Indigo Combo. (76)

The language in "Lambda" and "Mu" sounds considerably more modernist than anything written by Brown, Hughes, or many of the other
writers from the twenties and thirties, and I should re-emphasize the discrepancy in time: Three decades separate Tolson's publication of *Harlem
Gallery* (1965) and his completion of *A Gallery of Harlem Portraits* (circa
1935). Yet, although this work may indeed be a more mature and emotionally complex collection of poems than *A Gallery of Harlem Portraits*,
the characters in the later work owe much to those created in his first

attempt at an epic. Like Armstrong and all of the best musicians from the twenties, Tolson used the blues as a foundation for his ventures with jazz.

Written in a style reminiscent of Eliot and Pound, *Harlem Gallery* received praise by some who admired his stylistic abstractness in conjunction with African-American themes. Eugene Redmond, for example, wrote that "it provides one of the most powerful and authentic links between the Harlem Renaissance and the Black Arts Movement of the 1960's and 1970's" (258). But the general rejection of modernist verse also caused Sarah Webster Fabio to complain that "while Tolson busied himself outpounding Pound, his fellow poets forgot to send him the message that Pound was out" (57). When Tolson died in 1966 of cancer (diagnosed in 1964, shortly before the publication of *Harlem Gallery*), few made the effort to point out the awards he had received and the many successes in his career. For that matter, so many barbs had been thrown at the Beat writers from the fifties that no one bothered to recognize Tolson as someone who had achieved a marvelous union between poetry and jazz. Typical of so many artists, including most jazz innovators, Tolson's recognition as a writer has been primarily posthumous.

As African-American writers responding to music by other African-Americans, Hughes, Brown, and Tolson achieved an intimacy with jazz and the blues unparalleled in the efforts by their white predecessors and contemporaries. And though the racism in poems such as "The Jazz Cannibal" seems no less shocking or disgusting, such works when criticized as poems—as creative works—simply appear uninteresting. Even the poems by Sandburg and Heyward, well-intentioned though they may have been, do not sustain the complexities of emotion found particularly in the poems by Hughes and Brown. Just as the extraordinary African-American musicians and singers from the turn of the century through the forties made the Original Dixieland Jazz Band and the dance bands from the thirties seem obvious and relatively uninteresting, so did the jazz-related poems by African-American writers from this period dominate the genre.

Still, jazz poetry, even by the forties, received little attention—certainly nothing comparable to the forthcoming explosion in the late fifties. The use of jazz and blues in poetry remained controversial, even in the strongest writing by Hughes and Brown. And yet, whether or not critics favored the new verse, jazz poetry had been embraced by some of the strongest African-American writers of the time. Silver trees, shining rivers of the soul: The world of jazzonia was no longer confined to the air.

NOTES

1. Hughes, Brown, and Tolson may have been the most important or influential poets of this period, but there were others as well. A case could be made, for example, that Frank Marshall Davis deserves equal recognition.

2. For a thorough discussion of this time in Hughes's life, see Arnold Rampersad's *The Life of Langston Hughes, Volume 1*, pp. 59–66.

3. It would be very interesting to know what Hughes thought of Clement Wood's *The Greenwich Village Blues*, which appeared not long after his own book, *The Weary Blues*, in 1926. At the time, of course, it would have been politically suicidal to attack Wood. One of the few times that Hughes cites Wood is in a personal letter to Arna Bontemps, written on December 6, 1955. Responding to a manuscript by J. Saunders Redding, Hughes wrote: "I LOATHE the title 'The Glory Road' as it reminds me of Clemment [*sic*] Wood and that synthetic spiritual of his that George Dewey Washington used to bawl from L.A. to Paris, in rags and with the loudest voice of the century" (*Bontemps-Hughes Letters*, 339).

4. Among those who could be added to this list is Joseph Moncure March, a relatively unknown poet who published *The Wild Party* in 1928. Louis Untermeyer's introduction to the work described it as "Masefield's Daffodil Murder translated into postwar, night-clubbed, bootlegged, sex-ridden, tabloid-jazzed New York" (ix). Written in verse, *The Wild Party* cascades onward in an orgiastic frenzy (culminating in murder), all to the throbbing sounds of jazz.

5. The phonetic spelling in lines four and five present various options for accent and rhythm. My own ear tends to sing line four as two short notes with space in between (much like the opening two notes to the song "Charleston") and line five like two eighth notes followed by a short quarter note (more like "Dada-da").

6. For an accurate summary of these reviews, see Rampersad (*Vol. I*, 145). In fact, Rampersad synthesizes the critical reviews for all of Hughes's major publications.

7. Hughes wrote in *Famous Negro Music Makers* (1955), "Louis heard jazz all his life, played it most of his life, and became the greatest jazz man of the twentieth century" (117). He listened to Armstrong's music constantly, even on lengthy, overseas journeys; on a trip to Russia in 1932, for example, he carried along with him "his victrola and his records of Louis Armstrong and Ethel Waters, which were a hit as the train headed toward Central Asia" (Rampersad, *Vol. I*, 254). He gave Armstrong a special acknowledgment in *The First Book of Jazz* (1955), and in 1961 Hughes dedicated *Ask Your Mama* to him.

8. A discussion of this period of his life, from 1950 until his death in 1966, seemed more appropriate for the subsequent chapters in which I concentrate on poets from the fifties.

9. Brown did, however, continue to publish in various literary magazines, and in 1980 he published *The Collected Poems of Sterling Brown*.

10. For an engaging essay on the difficulties of writing blues poetry, see Hayden Carruth's "The Blues as Poetry" from *Sitting In*.

11. Among the numerous explications of this poem, two stand out. The first is in Joanne V. Gabbin's *Sterling A. Brown: Building the Black Aesthetic Tradition* (157–161) in which she discusses Brown's fusion of the blues and ballad forms (a unique collage of form first noted in Stephen Henderson's *Understanding the New Black Poetry*.) The second is in the dissertation written by Patrick James Brown (no relation to the poet), which includes "Ma Rainey" among the six explicated in depth as representative jazz poems. His emphasis is on the oral nature of the work, as well as the performance elements that the poem avails; of the two approaches, I found the former particularly valuable.

12. In his essay "Spirituals, Blues, and Jazz: The Negro in the Lively Arts" (1945), Brown stated that most blues "express sorrow in love" and that others "tell of rambling, of leaving an oppressive place" (64). As a third category, he notes, "And some, such as 'Back Water Blues' by Bessie Smith, about the Mississippi in flood, deal starkly with the tragedies of nature" (65).

13. With regard to Tolson's recent recognition, Robert M. Farnsworth has been invaluable, not merely for his excellent biographical study titled *Melvin B. Tolson 1898–1966* (1984) but also for editing the uncollected newspaper columns written by Tolson (*Caviar and Cabbage*, 1982) as well as Tolson's lengthy series of poems, *A Gallery of Harlem Portraits* (1979).

14. There have been some discrepancies about the full effects of Tolson's rejection. Although Tolson himself told Joy Flasch that he had "put his 'man-wrecked' manuscript in a trunk" and had not written for many years afterwards, Farnsworth explains that, in actuality, "The late thirties and early forties, the years during and immediately following publishers' rejections of *A Gallery*, were in fact particularly productive years in Tolson's career" (62).

REFERENCES

Bontemps, Arna, and Langston Hughes. *Arna Bontemps-Langston Hughes Letters 1925–1967*. Ed. Charles H. Nichols. New York: Dodd, Mead, 1980.

Brown, Patrick James. "Jazz Poetry: Definition, Analysis, and Performance." Diss. University of Southern California, 1978.

Brown, Sterling A. *The Collected Poems of Sterling A. Brown*. New York: Harper & Row, 1980.

———. *Southern Road*. New York: Harcourt, Brace, 1932.

———. "Spirituals, Blues, and Jazz: The Negro in the Lively Arts." *Tricolor* 3 (1945): 62–70.

Carruth, Hayden. *Sitting In: Selected Writings on Jazz, Blues, and Related Topics*. Iowa City: University of Iowa, 1986.

Cullen, Countee. "Poet on Poet." *Opportunity* 4 (March 4, 1926): 73–74.

Fabio, Sarah Webster. "Who Speaks Negro?" *Negro Digest*. 14 (September 1966): 54–58.

Farnsworth, Robert M. *Melvin B. Tolson, 1898–1966: Plain Talk and Poetic Prophecy*. Columbia: University of Missouri, 1984.

"Five Silhouettes on the Slope of Mount Parnassus." *The New York Times Book Review* (March 21, 1926): 6, 16.

Gabbin, Joanne V. *Sterling Brown: Building the Black Aesthetic Tradition*. Westport, Conn.: Greenwood, 1985.

Heyward, DuBose. "The Jazz Band's Sob." *New York Herald Tribune* (August 1, 1926): 4.

Hughes, Langston. *Ask Your Mama*. New York: Knopf, 1961.

———. *The Big Sea*. New York: Knopf, 1940.

———. *The Dream Keeper and Other Poems*. New York: Knopf, 1932.

———. *Famous Negro Music Makers*. New York: Dodd, Mead, 1955.

———. *Fields of Wonder*. New York: Knopf, 1947.

———. *Fine Clothes to the Jew*. New York: Knopf, 1927.

————. *Montage of a Dream Deferred*. New York: Henry Holt, 1951.

————. "The Negro Artist and the Racial Mountain." *The Nation*. 122 (1926): 692–694.

————. *One-Way Ticket*. New York: Knopf, 1949.

————. *Shakespeare in Harlem*. New York: Knopf, 1942.

————. *The Weary Blues*. New York: Knopf, 1926.

Lindsay, Vachel. *Letters of Vachel Lindsay*. Ed. Marc Chenetier. New York: Burt Franklin, 1979.

March, Joseph Moncure. *The Wild Party*. New York: Covici, Friede, 1928.

O'Hara, Frank. *The Collected Poems of Frank O'Hara*. Ed. Donald Allen. New York: Knopf, 1971.

Rampersad, Arnold. *The Life of Langston Hughes*. 2 Volumes. New York: Oxford University Press, 1986, 1988.

Redmond, Eugene B., ed. *Drumvoices*. Garden City: Doubleday, 1976.

Tolson, Melvin B. *Caviar and Cabbage: Selected Columns by Melvin B. Tolson from the "Washington Tribune," 1937–1944*. Edited by Robert M. Farnsworth. Columbia and London: University of Missouri, 1982.

————. *A Gallery of Harlem Portraits*. Edited by Robert M. Farnsworth. Columbia and London: University of Missouri, 1979.

————. *Harlem Gallery: Book I, The Curator*. New York: Twayne, 1965.

Walcott, Ronald. "Ellison, Gordone, and Tolson: Some Notes on the Blues, Style, and Space." *Black World*. 22 (December 1972): 4–29.

4

From Obscurity to Fad: Jazz and Poetry in Performance

Poetry and jazz is not a gimmick, a freak gig, something for the sockless cats and the unwashed chicks of the marijuana circuit.
—Kenneth Rexroth, 1958

Poetry read to jazz had only a brief popularity in America. It was ruined by people who knew nothing about either jazz or poetry.
—Kenneth Rexroth, 1978

Bebop, which began in the early forties and fully matured at the end of that decade, stunned American audiences like no other form of jazz before or since. It divided modernists and traditionalists to such a degree that its only parallel in poetry might be the critical reaction to T. S. Eliot's *The Waste Land*. Bop arrived after the chaos of World War II, after the commercialization of dance bands. It arrived with the popularization of heroin as the "in" drug, and bebop's chief innovator, alto saxophonist Charlie "Bird" Parker, became a cult hero as much for his suicidal life-style as for his magnificent playing. Whatever the opinion of bop, no one could deny its impact: Bebop radically modernized the sound of jazz and set new standards for all future musicians.

Although a fertile decade for jazz music, the forties produced very few jazz-related poems. The Harlem Renaissance appeared to be over, suddenly considered to be a sensation of the thirties. The jazz bands of that decade had become vehicles for upper-class outings, and the commercial values of the Swing Era, shallow and superficial when compared to the horrors of World War II, did not, for obvious reasons, inspire the poets of the time.[1] No collection of jazz-related poetry from the forties matched the innovative importance of Hughes's *The Weary Blues* or Brown's *South-ern Road*.

Yet, references to jazz as the prevailing sound in the United States permeated a wealth of poems from the forties, including, of course, those in Hughes's *Shakespeare in Harlem* (1942), *Fields of Wonder* (1947), and *One-Way Ticket* (1949). Frank Marshall Davis published *Black Man's Verse* (featuring poems such as "Jazz Band") in 1935, and he continued to write jazz-related poems throughout the forties.[2] Muriel Rukeyser, whose work was not necessarily steeped in any of the jazz idioms, nevertheless showed an awareness of the music in poems such as "George Robinson: Blues" (a section of "The Book of the Dead") and "Homage to Literature" (both from *U. S. 1*, 1938) and "Suicide Blues" (*Beast in View*, 1944); her poem "Bunk Johnson Blowing," though not published until 1968, reflects her experience hearing that jazz trumpeter from the early forties. Beatrice Murphy edited an anthology in 1948 titled *Ebony Rhythm* that featured a number of jazz-related poems.[3] Gwendolyn Brooks published her first volume of poems, *A Street in Bronzeville* (1945), which included "Queen of the Blues." Even Ezra Pound, by no means a jazz aficionado, made mention of the music in Canto LV from *Cantos LII–LXXI* (London, 1940).[4]

The threat of African-American jazz and jazz musicians, as witnessed in poems from the twenties, persisted in work from the forties. In 1940, *The New York Times Magazine* published Ethel Jacobson's "Air de Bar-relhouse," a poorly crafted poem about the "jim-jam-jiving generation." She describes jazz as "rhythm run riot," but the final couplet exposes the terror and anger in her message: "Oh, the addicts can swing till Kingdom Come— / If they'd just find a gibbet to do it from" (19). The same image of lynching concludes Anderson Scruggs' poem, "Meditation on Swing," published the following year in *Hygeia*, ironically a health magazine: "How can I grudge these boys their sway? / Long may they swing, is my earnest hope, / Accompanied by a tree and rope" (195). The curious illustrations that surround the poem depict white musicians playing various instru-ments, but the blatant racism in the poem proves that jazz, for Scruggs, was nothing more than animalistic chaos, performed by "Two pairs of monkeys, ranged in rows." He describes jazz musicians as inhuman and brainless—all the worst stereotypes of African-Americans:

> Two trombone players, tall and brown,
> Blow out their brains and then sit down.
>
> Somebody's boy—believe it or not—
> Gets in a groove and then gets hot
> On an agony pipe that is also known
> Among primitive tribes as a saxophone. (195)

The poems by Scruggs and Jacobson highlighted the same emotions from "The Jazz Cannibal": Jazz was the expression of freed slaves, emotions to be feared, a threat to take seriously.[5] It evoked all the paranoia and anxiety of racism. Was jazz a warning to white America, a pounding of the drums that the savages were loose and waiting to avenge themselves? Was this Langston Hughes's deferred dream now exploding?

The Second World War dominated this decade, and the relationship between jazz and war may at first seem obscure at best, yet here too the sounds of jazz appear in some of the war literature of the time.[6] In Peter Bowman's *Beach Red* (1945), a novel written in broken prose that reads like poetic lines, he managed to integrate the two cultural phenomena, as with this passage:

Heavy guns blare out their syncopated jazz and abruptly stop
and there is a short pause while the warring spirits
terminate their jitterbugging and stand around to applaud the number.
Then someone puts another nickel in the same old jukebox
and havoc selects a partner and the dance goes on. (17)

Bebop became associated with the general, splintered world view, and the phenomenal speed of Charlie Parker's alto became, for many who could not appreciate his genius and misinterpreted his intent, the musical manifestation of a society thrown into a tailspin. Like the earlier forms of jazz in their embryonic stages, this new style of playing was bound for rejection before acceptance.

In response, a countermovement in jazz began, one that celebrated traditional Dixieland jazz. From September 1945 to January 1946, for example, the Stuyvesant Casino in New York City spotlighted Bunk Johnson, a New Orleans trumpet player, as one of the great jazz legends still living.[7] This return to jazz roots did not interest most modern poets of the time, many of whom became consumed by the evolution of bebop, but twice during the fall of 1945, Johnson's audience included the poet William Carlos Williams, and the second evening inspired the poem "Ol' Bunk's Band" as well as an unfinished novel called *Man Orchid*.[8]

Williams's interest in jazz began during the twenties, and around 1927 he wrote a postcard to his friend Fred Miller. Williams expressed his wish to write a book about the music. The card reads vertically with the heading "Jazz": "A book. The whole life of it = America and the full evokations [*sic*] of it all. Full as the short articles on it have been faint, pale. It's fullness. It's all jazz."[9] Unfortunately, Williams never acknowledged that he would not be the proper choice to correct the "faint" and "pale" interpretations, and his writing about jazz—which he began almost twenty years after writing this postcard to Miller—has been criticized in virtually every evaluation of the writing.

In the poem "Ol' Bunk's Band," Williams tried to capture verbally the jagged, energetic trumpet lines: "These are men! the gaunt, unfore- / sold, the vocal, / blatant." After the bass string slap ("Pick, ping!"), the poem introduces Johnson's own sound:

> The horn, the
> hollow horn
> long drawn out, a hound-deep
> tone—
> Choking, choking!

(Collected Poems II, 149)

Williams tried to accentuate the rhythmic qualities of jazz, but instead he enthusiastically scripted some disastrous lines, among them "drum drum drum drum drum / drum, drum!" and "torn, tears, term, / town, tense." Like many poets to follow, he seemed unaware of the limitations of language to capture sound, and because the primary goal was to capture the rhythmic spirit of jazz, the poem as a whole fails to engage.

Hayden Carruth, whose poetry and critical work have often concerned jazz, finds Williams's poem about Johnson not merely inaccurate but offensive. In an essay titled "Influences: The Formal Idea of Jazz," Carruth states that "Some people can hear jazz, and others, by far the greater number, cannot." He then adds:

The worst poem Dr. Williams ever wrote was "Ole Bunk's Band" (I give the title from memory), in which he treats Bunk Johnson and the other old-time musicians playing with him as if they were some unintelligible anthropological specimens, people from another and distant culture making noises for the mere hell of it or out of animal exuberance. That they were artists like him never crossed his mind. (24)

Carruth's essay does not address *Man Orchid*, but his reservations about the poem seem that much more appropriate for this unsuccessful work of fiction. Fred Miller, who had coaxed Williams to the Stuyvesant Casino, proposed the jazz-inspired project in December 1945, stating that the only rules were no rules, "everything short of flukiness":

We start sans plot. You write chap. I, send it to me, I do the 2d Chap., send mess back to you, you do 3—and so on, until one of us has a brain blowout, or we get short of stamps. (Mariani, "Novel," 69)

Williams jumped at the offer and wrote the first installment ten days later.[10] Commenting on their protagonist—an intellectual jazz musician who was black but passing for white—Williams naively bragged, "I don't know a damned thing about him so that ought to give me a good start" (Mariani, "Novel," 69).[11] Like a musician unable to retract notes from the stage, Williams spewed out phrases and tried to manipulate his "mistakes" into statements:

Why should life have an objective? Og—there you are—I would have written "of" and I wrote "Og". What's the difference? Does one mean more than the other? Not at all. My meaning was the same, only the word was different. In one of the Russian dialects it is probably "og". It can't possibley [*sic*] be otherwise. (100)

Seemingly blinded to the lack of sophistication in this prose and insisting on the freshness of its improvisational qualities, Williams never fully understood how formal constructs, such as established chord changes, root all jazz improvisations. Nor did he realize that his poetry exhibiting the essential qualities of jazz—a mixture of dynamic rhythm with moving lyrical statements—was more successful in *Patterson*, for example, than in any of his jazz-related works.

About poetry in general, he felt that "Each piece of work, rhythmic in whole is then in essence an assembly of tides, waves, ripples" (Wagner, 67), and he tried to describe Bunk Johnson's music analogously:

alone, ripples, screams
　　　slow to fast—
to second to first! These are men!

"We poets," he said in 1957, "have to talk in a language which is not English. It is the American idiom. Rhythmically, it's organized as a sample of the American idiom. It has as much originality as jazz" (Wagner, 74). In a sense, Williams had tried to endorse Hart Crane's enthusiastic suggestion that American poets should "invent an idiom for the transposition of jazz into words!" (Crane, 89). But in 1961, when asked about jazz and the Beat movement, he contradicted his feelings:

The Beat generation has nothing to do with beat, and they should if they're interested in jazz because jazz is always percussive. But in jazz music even the saxophone sounds are not advanced enough from the primitive to interest me at all. I don't like jazz. The artists in Paris rave about jazz, but it's too tiresome, it's too much the same thing. (Wagner, 55)

Williams's radical shift in perspective probably had more to do with the jazz-enamored hipsters of the late fifties than with jazz itself. Bebop became an integral part of being hip or cool, and the writers of the time, particularly those on the West Coast, responded passionately to the music. These well-known lines from Allen Ginsberg's *Howl* (1956), for example, observe the trend:

angelheaded hipsters burning for the ancient heavenly connection to the
starry dynamo in the machinery of night,
who poverty and tatters and hollow-eyed and high sat up smoking in the
supernatural darkness of cold-water flats floating across the tops of cities
contemplating jazz

(*Collected*, 126)

If "Howl" was the signature poem of the time, Jack Kerouac's *On the Road* (1957) became its prose counterpart, with jazz resounding throughout that text as well. Jazz was suddenly part of the lingo, the image. After a lengthy hiatus, jazz poetry began to flourish.

Williams's freedom of the line made him a principal archetype for many Beat writers, yet he rejected their interpretations of that freedom, particularly as it related to jazz. In fact, scores of critics after Williams, including strong advocates of jazz poetry, have criticized the poetry by the San Francisco writers from the fifties. Recently, for example, David Jauss's review of *The Jazz Poetry Anthology* included this statement about "the Beat aesthetic":

All too often, these poems suffer from a "hipper-than-thou" attitude and the pseudo-profundity that attitude inspires ("Life is a saxophone played by death," Bob Kaufman tells us). And, of course, there are the usual strained metaphors, the abstractions yoked to concrete images like U-Haul trailers, the hyperbolic claims of spiritual enlightenment, and the word "angel," without which, it seems, no self-respecting Beat can write a poem. . . . Despite all their talk of iconoclasm and originality, the Beats have produced an astonishingly homogenous poetry. . . . Even the most recent Beat poems seem far more dated than such artful and unmannered poems as Langston Hughes' "[The] Weary Blues," which appeared the year Allen Ginsberg was born. (139)

But even Jauss admits "The Beats deserve credit for many things—not the least of which is calling our attention to jazz" (139). Whatever their shortcomings, the Beat poets most certainly concerned themselves with the jazz beat and tried to immerse themselves into the jazz, hipster culture of the fifties. And they are also responsible for the popularization of jazz poetry as a performance art.

"The boppers' recognition that the conditions which produced traditional and standard styles had been rendered obsolete was an analogy for the new poetry," wrote the poet Michael Horovitz, adding,

Jazz—deeply ingrained in the American idiom, was a discovery for us—the secret universal language of our upbringing, and remains a crystallization of the *avant gardes* that preceded it—the esperanto of the subconscious accented by Joyce and the surrealists, the dada internationals of the spirit made palpable. The resultant oral progressions constitute a group enterprise, our voices directly dovetailed with the indigenous free-form jazz of London's new-wave modernists. (Corso, *Riverside*, 63)

The critic Michael Skau agrees with this generalization. "The Beats," he wrote, "saw jazz as a predominantly colloquial medium, its spontaneity and improvisation suggesting personal freedom rather than formal confinement, and their poetry modeled on jazz attempts to project the same qualities" (69). What the Beats also managed to do, for better or for worse, was to transform the public awareness of poetry and jazz. By the end of the fifties, jazz poetry had become not merely an acknowledged interest but a movement.

In 1957, two years after Parker's premature death, many of the finest musicians of that era produced marvelous, lasting recordings. A highly selective listing of artists would include the two most influential tenor saxophonists of the time, John Coltrane and Sonny Rollins, as well as Miles Davis, Gerry Mulligan, Charles Mingus, and Thelonious Monk.[12] Non-modernist players who had developed in the twenties and thirties—such as tenor players Ben Webster and Coleman Hawkins, or trumpeter Red Allen—also flourished in that year, and on December 8, 1957, CBS television broadcast a performance featuring many of the outstanding musicians from the Swing era, as well as Mulligan and Billie Holiday.[13]

The year 1957 also marked the start of the Poetry-and-Jazz movement in which poets not merely wrote about jazz but read their work to live accompaniment. Several poets had experimented with this technique over the years.[14] "But the jazz-poetry sessions at The Cellar [in San Francisco]," explains Barry Silesky,

became by far the most popular of all these performances. Rexroth had invited Ferlinghetti to join him in the 1957 performances, and they filled the club from the beginning. Only about a hundred could fit into the room, but on the very first night, some five hundred more lined up outside to get in and a fire marshal had to be called to clear the hallway. (89)[15]

The remarkable popularity of the Rexroth/Ferlinghetti performances became the impetus for a recording, *Poetry Reading in "The Cellar"* (1957), and spurred a series of poetry-read-to-jazz performances on the West Coast, most notably Kenneth Patchen's readings at the Blackhawk, also in San Francisco. On the East Coast, well-known New York clubs such as the Five Spot and the Village Vanguard experimented with performances featuring Rexroth, Patchen, Howard Hart, and Jack Kerouac.[16] The popularity did not last long, and far more writers have criticized rather than supported its conceptual validity as an art form. But in 1957, sparked by Rexroth, Ferlinghetti, and a house band willing to experiment with the new medium, jazz and poetry brought the house down on The Cellar.

Of the two poets, Rexroth received far more attention by the press, possibly because his status as a translator and literary intellectual did not, intriguingly, concur with the image of a Bohemian Beat writer (an image that Rexroth himself rejected). At The Cellar, he performed works primarily by other writers and, contrary to the popular conceptions of poetry-read-to-jazz, spent a good deal of time rehearsing for the performances. For Carl Sandburg's "Mag," Rexroth instructed the band to play Duke Ellington's "Things Ain't What They Used To Be," and as the band traded solos, from tenor sax to trumpet to trombone, he read the stanzas already marked for his performance. (On the right-hand side of the page, he wrote "TENOR," "TRUMPET," and "TROMBONE"). His notations for a Pablo Neruda translation were slightly more detailed: For the first two stanzas, he simply wrote "GUITAR SOLO," but he elaborated his instructions for the final two: "TENOR ENTERS VERY SOFTLY / FEW WIDELY SPACED TOOTS AT FIRST / BASS ENTERS / VERY PENSIVE CHORALE" (Roskolenko, 150).

Rexroth feared, and rightfully so, that his performance would be cast off as being careless, undignified, and trite. He demanded structure. Unlike many of his contemporaries, Rexroth at least appreciated the fact that improvisation did not mean spilling notes in a frenzy of wishful thinking.[17] In 1969, reflecting on the failures of those who followed his lead, Rexroth pointed the finger at his generation's naiveté of jazz in general, and jazz poetry in particular:

in every Greenwich Village coffee shop and bar for about two years, all kinds of bums with pawnshop saxophones put together with scotch tape, and some other guy with something called poetry, were, like, you know, blowing poetry, man, dig? And it was absolutely unmitigated crap. . . . You went down there where the first miniskirts were worn, and the miniskirted chicks were waitresses, and you got yourself a free grope, and you listened to bums who weren't being paid anything, and it killed the whole thing. (Meltzer, 25)

But despite the crowds and the publicity from various publications including *TIME* magazine, the better-than-average musicianship, and the rehearsals, Rexroth himself was not entirely successful. Discussing Rexroth's performance of Neruda's poem, Harry Roskolenko wrote that "it was impossible to hear either the romantic poetry or the fusions between the words and the music" (150–151). John Ciardi, also a friend of the poet, similarly objected that "the sextet [was] coming up over (rather than under) the voice, with the result that one begins to lose the words" (57).

Of Rexroth and Ferlinghetti's recording, *Poetry Reading in "The Cellar"* (1957), the publisher James Laughlin said that he had "enjoyed it very much," but added, "The only thing I didn't like was the monotony of the verbal tone" (Cherkovski, 88). Ferlinghetti, on the other hand, praised

Rexroth's achievement on this same record as being among the very best poetry-read-to-jazz in the history of the movement:

Once in a while by happy chance they [the musicians and the poet] came together. The most successful I think was Kenneth Rexroth on his side of an old Fantasy L.P., where he did his elegy on the death of Dylan Thomas called <u>Thou Shalt Not Kill</u>. The music on that complemented the words completely and didn't dominate them. (*Riverside*, 6)

The poem to which he refers may very well have been Rexroth's most cohesive work in this genre. When isolated from jazz accompaniment, "Thou Shalt Not Kill" does not read like a jazz poem: It does not include direct references to jazz or experimental techniques in rhythm, meter, or form that might call attention to the music's influence. Yet the piece succeeded more than his others partly because of its length, which enabled the players to interact more organically with the reader. More important, the use of repetition as a refrain (such as the repeated phrase "He is dead" in Section IV) allowed the musicians to anticipate the rhythm of the poem and therefore respond accordingly, much like a jazz drummer who, when hearing an instrumentalist repeat a phrase, changes the drum rhythm to match the statement.

The anti-establishment theme in "Thou Shalt Not Kill" also appealed to the hipster crowd who frequented Rexroth's performances. Section I begins, "They are murdering all the young men. / For half a century now, every day" (*Collected Shorter*, 267), and later unveils the murderer: The "YOU" to whom he points his finger is corporate America. Section II lists a litany of poets who have died prematurely or in obscurity, and by Section III, the poem angrily asks, "How many stopped writing at thirty? / How many went to work for *Time?*" (272). The final section screams to a close: "You killed him! You killed him. / In your God damned Brooks Brothers suit, / You son of a bitch" (275).

As with Rexroth, Ferlinghetti's most successful poem performed to jazz was also one of his longest, "Autobiography." Ferlinghetti included this poem with six others to establish the second section of his classic collection, *A Coney Island of the Mind* (1958). Section 2, titled "Oral Messages," begins with this note:

These seven poems were conceived specifically for jazz accompaniment and as such should be considered as spontaneously spoken "oral messages" rather than as poems written for the printed page. As a result of continued experimental reading with jazz, they are still in a state of change. (48)

Both Rexroth and Ferlinghetti preferred the jazz from the thirties and forties to the modern sounds of bebop (which Ferlinghetti actively disliked), and, significantly, the only direct reference to jazz in "Autobiography" invokes the music of Dixieland: "I have heard Kid Ory cry. / I have heard a trombone preach" (62). Like the repetition in "Thou Shalt Not Kill," the concentration on first person ("I have," "I saw," "I am") builds rhythm in the poem and makes it more conducive to musical accompaniment. The jazz critic Ralph Gleason must have realized the integral relationship between "Autobiography" and jazz music—the direct references, certainly, but also the established rhythms in the poem as well as its success as a vehicle for poetry and jazz performances—for in 1958 Gleason included part of the poem in *Jam Session: An Anthology of Jazz*, published the same year as *A Coney Island of the Mind*.

The poetry readings by Rexroth and Ferlinghetti shared several themes, particularly the anti-establishment statements. But while Rexroth railed against society in "Thou Shalt Not Kill," Ferlinghetti treated such social and political issues with satire and sarcasm. "[Sometime during eternity]," the fifth poem in *A Coney Island of the Mind*, inverts Rexroth's formal diatribe into a piece animated by humor but no less thought provoking. Written in cascading lines reminiscent of Williams's style, the poem satirizes Christ as a jazz hipster:

You're hot
            they tell him

And they cool him

They stretch him on the Tree to cool

            And everybody after that
                              is always making models
                  of this Tree
                              with Him hung up
      and always crooning His name
                  and calling Him to come down
            and sit in
                        on their combo
            as if he is the king cat
                        who's got to blow
      or they can't quite make it (15–16)

With "king cat" lingo and terrible puns ("Him just hang there / on His Tree / looking real Petered out"), the poem closes with humorous cynicism in which Christ appears to be "real cool / and also / according to a roundup / of late world news / from the usual unreliable sources / real dead" (16). "[Sometime during eternity]" manifests a rhythm that might be compared to jazz music in terms of form, sound, and syntax. "Vocabulary and grammatical structure in Ferlinghetti's poems," explains Michael Skau, "are popular rather than formal, vernacular rather than academic, as the poet attempts to create a form of oral expression which accurately reflects contemporary spoken American English" (69). At his best, Ferlinghetti achieved what Williams termed "improvisations in slang."

Like Hughes in the twenties, Rexroth and Ferlinghetti aspired to enlarge the audience for poetry, and Larry Smith argues that they concentrated on this desire more than any need to further the virtues of this experimental art form. Smith criticizes their performances as being poetry read to jazz accompaniment, as opposed to a synthesis of the two media, and on this basis he distinguishes the efforts by Kenneth Patchen as transcending the limited efforts by his contemporaries. James Shevill agrees:

Other poets were unable somehow to work with jazz musicians and shape words and music into a unified web of sound. Only Patchen achieved this effect and, fortunately, it's there to hear on the record—a marvelous voice balanced between a grave, compassionate tone and a defiant, satirical attack. (Clodd, 26)

Once described by Diane di Prima as "singing like Miles Davis" (Clodd, 38), Patchen became interested in jazz during the thirties. In his poem "[AND IN ANOTHER PLACE USES THE SAME PHRASE]" from *First Will and Testament* (1939), he intermingled various literary figures with jazz musicians. Presented in the form of a brief drama, the poem includes this amusing exchange centered on a performance by the trumpeter Bix Beiderbecke:

GLORIA DAWN: Let's ride em, Bix. Point that ole horn at Mr. God. (*Bix puts his trumpet through "Wabash Blues," "Tin Roof" and good old "Basin Street"; one by one Red Allen, Teddy Wilson, Coleman Hawkins, Earl Dipper Hines, Jack Teagarden, Cozy Cole, Ziggy Elman and Louis The One And Only put that big train on through the night.*)

NATHANIEL HAWTHORNE: I don't see much in that.

HERMAN MELVILLE (*easily*): You wouldn't. (115)

Memoirs of a Shy Pornographer (1945) offers a list of jazz and blues recordings necessary, according to the character Mr. Berg, "if you want a basic jazz library" (56), and the recommendation includes works by King Oliver, the ODJB, Louis Armstrong, Bix Beiderbecke, Jelly Roll Morton, Bunk Johnson, and George Lewis—an impressive selection of musicians reflecting Patchen's own acute appreciation for jazz.

According to Jonathan Williams, by 1951 Patchen began to make tapes of his poetry as read to records by Johnson and Lewis.[18] In a statement about the origins of Patchen's *Fables and Other Little Tales* (1953), Williams parenthetically noted,

(A little later [after May, 1950], it was these LPs [of Johnson and Lewis] that Patchen used in making private tapes of the fables. All kinds of homemade noises and jazz were interpolated back of the voice. I don't know what's become of these tapes, made by two young Patchen enthusiasts from Harvard, Alden Ashforth and David Wykoff. They were, to my knowledge, the first instances of the later poetry/jazz experiment.) (*Aflame*, 86–87).

Patchen's first professional recording, *Kenneth Patchen Reads with the Chamber Jazz Sextet* (1958), set pre-recorded poetry to pleasant background music but does not achieve, as Smith suggests, "an engaging synthesis" (*K.P.*, 132). Patchen's more significant achievement appeared the following year on the album *Kenneth Patchen Reads with Jazz in Canada*, which Smith acclaims as "the highest and truest achievement of the poetry-and-jazz synthesis" (*K.P.*, 128). Unlike the *Chamber Jazz* recording or his experiments reading with records, this session featured the poet reading simultaneously with a jazz quartet led by pianist Alan Neil, who also wrote the notes for the album.[19] Whether or not this can be considered "the highest and truest" form of jazz poetry, the synthesis of voice with music unquestionably surpassed the previous recording by Patchen, as well as that by Rexroth and Ferlinghetti.

The opening blues sequence, in which Patchen reads four poems while the band plays Charlie Parker's "Laird Baird," sounds more standard (poetry with jazz in the background) than the second series of poems, titled "Four Song Poems," in which the piano and alto sax respond more directly to Patchen's voice. Here Patchen begins to take more chances with the stretches and slurs in his pronunciation, making his spoken word recording more musical than the monotone that James Laughlin objected to in *Poetry Reading in "The Cellar."* (Sometimes Patchen uses this technique to emphasize the humor of the poem; in the comic "As I Opened the Window," his delivery sounds like a drunk impersonating John Wayne.) The fourth and final section, "Glory, Glory," unites Patchen's speeches from *Don't Look Now* with the musicians improvising over the chord changes of Charlie Parker's "Confirmation."[20] Even though the musicians frame the performance with a corny arrangement of Dixie (at one point joined by Patchen's horribly out-of-tune humming), the central passages energize the set. Patchen actually shouts his speeches, and the emotional surge made Neil conclude that this was their consummate achievement. But for me, the second series of poems ("The Everlasting Contenders," "Do I Not Deal with Angels," "The Sea Is Awash with Roses," and "Not Many Kingdoms Left") integrates the voice with jazz more than any of Patchen's other recorded work. Here the jazz does indeed transcend mere background music, and many of the passages resonate in our ears and imagination.

In 1959, the same year as *Kenneth Patchen Reads to Jazz in Canada*, World Pacific Records released *Jazz Canto: An Anthology of Poetry and Jazz, Vol. 1*, which included various readers and musicians performing poetry by Ferlinghetti, Hughes, Philip Whalen, and Lawrence Lipton, as well as Walt Whitman, William Carlos Williams, and Dylan Thomas. Like the surprising inclusion of Whitman, Williams, and Thomas, the choice of readers was also untraditional; Hoagy Carmichael, for example, read the two Williams poems ("Tract" and the brief "Young Sycamore") and John Carradine performed Whitman's "Poets to Come" and Lipton's "Night Song for the Sleepless." The selection of the poetry and performers, however, may be the most engaging element to this project: Most of the pieces sound like poets reading to a phonograph. Even the resonant bass voice of Roy Glenn seems utterly separate from the music performed by the Gerry Mulligan Quartet—proving that excellent readers and superb musicianship do not necessarily create dynamic unions of the two.

Nevertheless, Bob Dorough's interpretation of Ferlinghetti's "Dog" distinguishes itself from all the other performances on this record, and, I might add, from the other jazz poetry recordings of the time. Dorough's musical arrangement and his own thin voice emphasize the humor in the poem—very intentionally—and he orchestrates moments where the voice fills in rhythmic riffs exactly like a jazz instrumentalist. The musical theme to Dorough's blues echoes his interpreted rhythm in the poem, and as he bops Ferlinghetti's description of the dog prancing through the city neighborhood, the band keeps changing key, each chorus rising in tone, pushing the action of the poem forward. Put simply: It's a lot of fun, thanks to an unpretentious performance.

The surging interest in jazz poetry readings in the fifties sparked a renewed appreciation for Langston Hughes's jazz-related work. Hughes, in fact, capitalized on this renaissance to such a degree that he amazed even himself with his proliferation of writing about jazz as well as jazz poetry performances. In 1958, Verve Records released *Weary Blues*, a jazz poetry recording that begins with a New Orleans sextet led by trumpeter Red Allen and trombonist Vic Dickenson trudging through an arranged chorus of twelve-bar blues based on a repeated four-bar theme. Before they finish the final phrase, Hughes's voice cuts in with the first words from the poem "Hey!" Then the band stops playing, the voice now solo:

Sun's a settin',
This is what I'm gonna sing.
Sun's a settin',
This is what I'm gonna sing:
I feels de blues a comin',
Wonder what de blues'll bring?

Well-orchestrated, on cue, the band kicks in at the penultimate line ("I feels de blues a-comin' "), and, thankfully, Red Allen's airy trumpet mute, improvising over the blues chords, significantly lightens the tone. In mid-chorus, Hughes re-enters with "I got those sad old weary blues," and now the poet and band synchronize like the old spoken-word blues recordings from the turn of the century.[21] The concentration on blues music and blues poetry unites the recording in ways that made other albums (such as *Poetry Readings in "The Cellar"*) seem too diffuse by comparison.

The second half of the record features modern jazz musicians led by the bassist Charles Mingus, and the shift in personnel would be still more interesting if the music sounded more modern. But most of the arrangements (probably written by the critic Leonard Feather rather than Mingus) are steeped in the Swing tradition, so Mingus's band does not contrast the first group as much as it might. Still, Hughes much preferred working with Mingus because he felt that the modern players responded more to the poetry, and there are moments—particularly when Mingus himself bows his solo in an improvised response to the poetry—when the distinction becomes more apparent.[22] In terms of sheer presentation, Hughes reads better on *Weary Blues* than he does on his other spoken word recordings.

Hughes recorded *Weary Blues* in 1958, his most prolific year in terms of reading poetry to jazz: He packed the Village Vanguard in New York City; performed in Stratford, Ontario, for the Shakespeare Festival; and at the end of the year flew to read in California. Like the range of musicians on *Weary Blues*, Hughes's jazz accompaniment varied from modern players (Mingus and Phineas Newborn) to players in the Swing tradition (Allen, Cozy Cole, Ben Webster, Earl Hines). His popularity swelled to monumental proportions:

A vast audience, spread over forty cities, saw and heard him read poetry on NBC backed by the jazz pianist Billy Taylor and followed by discussions with the critics Gilbert Seldes and Harold Taylor. This television appearance sparked so many requests that Langston at one point simply unplugged his telephone. (Rampersad, *Vol. II*, 284)

What had caused this remarkable shift in media attention? In part, the Beat poetry-and-jazz sessions had laid the groundwork, an ironic commentary on race and cultural acceptance given the fact that Hughes had been experimenting with poetry-read-to-jazz in the twenties. "Looking with a mixture of amusement and disdain on the largely white 'Beat' movement," explains Arnold Rampersad,

Langston nevertheless wanted to have his primacy in the field acknowledged. He begged Knopf to call him the "original jazz poet" on the cover of his coming *Selected Poems*. (Soon, the poetic "guiding star" of his youth, Carl Sandburg, a showman himself, hustled to point out that his 1919 poem "Jazz Fantasia" gave *him* primacy in the field.) (*Vol. II*, 280)[23]

On the one hand, Hughes had no interest whatsoever in being associated with the Beats; but on the other, the attention given to them as the innovators of this genre must have left him feeling neglected, if not appalled.

In 1959, one year after Hughes's recording, Jack Kerouac made three records, two of which involved his own writing backed by musicians.[24] The first, *Poetry for the Beat Generation*, featured Steve Allen on piano accompanying Kerouac reading fourteen of his poems. Each cut had only one take, with Allen playfully improvising cocktail jazz in the background. The opening piece, "October in the Railroad Earth," is the longest on the record, and one of the most successful; Kerouac allows each unpunctuated turn in his language to guide his phrases—packing the words tightly together, then stretching them out. He manipulates pitch and rhythm that change in tone from bursts of song, to a put-on Joe Friday accent, a let-me-tell-you-what-happened-to-ME-on-Saturday-night intimacy, and concluding with the humorous "I should have played with her shoo-do-do-do-dook-a-dooky."

The pleasure with rhythms in "October in the Railroad Earth" makes most of the subsequent poems sound stilted by comparison, as with the dated, hip slang in "Deadbelly" ("Deadbelly modern cat / Cool! / Deadbelly, man, / Craziest!"), or the attempts to write phonetically the sounds of Bird's saxophone in "Charlie Parker" ("Wail! Whap!" and "Toot!"). In 1960, one year after the release of *Poetry for the Beat Generation*, the editors for *The Jazz Word* commented, "The poetry read on the recording, like Kerouac's synopsis above [which explained how each cut had only one take], is more notable for its humor than its incisiveness" (Cerulli, 125). Unfortunately, Kerouac had not intended the project to be dismissed as jocular or whimsical.

For Kerouac's next recording, *Blues and Haikus*, he insisted on having his two favorite tenor saxophonists, Al Cohn and Zoot Sims, as accompaniment.[25] "His work on record with Al Cohn and Zoot Sims," wrote David Meltzer, "displayed some lovely possibilities" (Silesky, 90), and Allen Ginsberg reflected, "*Blues and Haikus* remain[s] for me the classic of all Beat era jazz poetry recordings, yet to be matched for delighted recitation—verve of pronunciation, deep color of vowels & consonantal bite, exquisite consciousness in crossing T's & tonguing D's against the teeth with open lips" (*Jack Kerouac Collection*, 8).[26] But despite Ginsberg's valid praise for Kerouac's delivery, this recording of saxophones with voice often sounds disjointed, and uncomfortably so. (Even Meltzer emphasizes the "possibilities" for success rather than commenting on the actual material). The album begins with Kerouac reciting a short passage; [pause]; [brief saxophone line]; [pause]. Kerouac still does not enter, waits, wonders if it is his cue, then: [another brief saxophone line]; [pause]; "Well here I am." Cohn must have sensed the inherent problems of the format and, for the next two pieces, switched to the piano on which he could comp adequately, but his musical limitations on that instrument make the performances unintentionally comical. The most successful (and by far the longest) piece on the record was "Poems from the Unpublished 'Book of Blues,' " which featured Cohn and Sims playing their tenors together, non-stop, in the background. Here, at least, the musicians could each play fluid lines on their primary instrument.

Kerouac never again recorded with musicians, perhaps because he realized that the performance element required more rehearsal rather than improvisation in the recording studio. Furthermore, the session with Cohn and Sims left him demoralized: Typical of jazz musicians, the two tenor players walked out of the building without hearing the session tapes, but Kerouac did not understand this behavior and took it personally. "At the conclusion of the session," explains the producer Bob Thiele,

Zoot and Al packed their horns and departed. When it came time for playbacks, I couldn't find Jack. I finally found him squatted in the corner of the studio, crying—"How could they leave me without listening?"

I consoled Jack as best as I could and we hit an 8th Avenue bar for a few beers.

Jack, after a while, hit 8th Avenue—throwing empty beer bottles onto the pavement. (*Jack Kerouac Collection*, 16)

Readings by Jack Kerouac for the Beat Generation, Kerouac's third recording, focuses more on his prose than poetry and, as Gerald Nicosia points out, it is "Kerouac's only album without actual musical accompaniment, [and yet] it's perhaps the best demonstration of the musicality of Kerouac's art" (*Jack Kerouac Collection*, 9). Relying entirely on his own voice to create rhythm, Kerouac achieves cadences and a jazz feel that surpasses anything from either of the two previous recordings. His recitation of "Fantasy: The Early History of Bop" (almost eleven minutes long) rarely lags or lulls and in fact gains momentum with muscular sentences such as, "Monk punched anguished nub fingers crawling at the keyboard to tear up foundations and guts of jazz from the big master box." The opening piece, "The Beat Generation," begins with a flurry of sentences describing a wild fifties jazz club scene: "Now it's jazz, the place is roaring, all beautiful girls in there, one mad brunette at the bar drunk with her boys." The band arrives in the smoky ambiance. Sensational music turns on the crowd, and Kerouac himself picks up speed as he describes from a collage of memorable nights his passion for this music and its people.

Kerouac's varying successes and failures with poetry-read-to-jazz seem generally representative of jazz poetry experiments by the San Francisco poets. Eventually, many of the poets themselves rejected the efforts. Ferlinghetti, for example, criticized the misconceptions of jazz poetry ("You can't take just any old poem and strum to it in the background") and denounced the entire jazz poetry movement:

Nothing was worse than most of the poetry and jazz in the fifties. Most of it was awful. The poet ended up sounding like he was hawking fish from a street corner. All the musicians wanted to do was blow. Like, "Man, go ahead and read your poems but we gotta blow." (Meltzer, 169)[27]

According to the poet Michael McClure, Meltzer himself "had an advantage over Lawrence and the Kenneths" because, as a musician, he "could compose his poems for poetry and jazz with the idea that he was another instrument in a combo" (Silesky, 90), but McClure adds,

On the whole, however, Meltzer didn't think any of the experiments particularly effective. "Jazz and poetry was an interesting attempt that failed to advance beyond its hybrid and awkward propositions," he wrote. (Silesky, 90)

Rexroth, discontented with the misconceptions of jazz poetry (and later of the genre itself), also criticized the marketing of the performances. With regard to the publicity for Patchen's recordings, he wrote, "They didn't know how to sell it. The only thing that was selling at all was this Ken Nordine record [*Word Jazz*] ... which was to us what Rod McKuen is to Ginsberg. A strictly commercial scene" (Meltzer, 24).[28] Poets, musicians, recording labels, publishing houses: All parts of the movement became subject to hostile rejection.

But not everyone, of course, has damned the jazz poetry movement from the fifties. Although Michael Skau admits "These experiments were not entirely successful," he points out the strengths as well:

However, the importance of these jazz-poetry experiments cannot be ignored: the poets—and the audiences of these readings—were straining against the restrictions of the printed page.... Jazz suggested a new direction, with one of its most attractive features being its improvisatory quality. (65)

Larry Smith shares this optimism and promotes the jazz poetry performances as among the most significant achievements in twentieth-century poetics. Unlike Skau, Smith does not temper his enthusiastic statements but instead allows his praise to remain unqualifiably favorable.[29] Another critic, Ralph Gleason, who once wrote, "At any moment ... I expect to see [Coach] Abe Saperstein announce T. S. Eliot in a coast-to-coast tour with the Harlem Globe Trotters" (*TIME* 71), later reversed his cynicism:

The experiments in jazz and poetry at The Cellar, the investigations of new forms
by Bruce Lippincott and the use of the jazz culture as a subject for poetic writing
by [Kenneth] Ford all mark, for me, steps in a new direction in American literature; steps that will bring it closer to its audience and farther from the formalized
atmosphere of the classroom and the lecture hall. (Gleason, 230)

By 1960, however, the jazz poetry fad had dissipated almost to the point
of extinction.[30] Rexroth must have realized that his best poetry had nothing to do with his jazz-related efforts, and Ferlinghetti, as noted, could
only reflect on jazz poetry with contempt and embarrassment. Patchen's
degenerative ailments made it physically impossible for him to perform.
Kerouac, perhaps too demoralized by his experience with Cohn and Sims,
never recorded with musicians after those 1959 dates; he died just ten
years later. Hughes distanced himself from the San Francisco poetry circles, and his performances of jazz poetry were, at the last, vocational projects.

The pretentiousness of many jazz-and-poetry performances has inspired
many spoofs, including Lenny Bruce's "Psychopathia Sexualis" (1958), arguably the best of all. In 1959 Kenneth Koch and Larry Rivers began an
engagement at New York's Village Vanguard, ostensibly to parody the
experiment.[31] To this day, the term "jazz poet" generally conjures up images of the hipster figures with dated jargon and self-conscious personas.
Ironically, the stereotypes linked with the least successful jazz poetry performances from the late fifties still constitute the general image of jazz
and poetry, as though no other relationship exists.[32] For over thirty years,
the most-pretentious qualities of jazz poetry have remained representative
and have hurt rather than helped the diverse efforts by poets from the
sixties to the present who have been interested in the union between poetry and jazz.

Nevertheless, there have been since 1960 a number of poets and musicians working with jazz and poetry as a performance art, and many of
these performances, unlike the ground-breaking efforts from the late fifties, achieve a greater union between the poet and the instrumentalist. In
the sixties, many of the jazz poetry recordings acted as forms of black
nationalism, as statements of protest. Archie Shepp's poem for Malcolm
X, "Malcolm, Malcolm, Semper Malcolm" (*Fire Music*, 1965), for example,
unites his feelings of loss and anger with appropriately unsettling jazz—
music that responds to the poetic lines. By weaving his knowledge of music
(its emotional impact on the ear) with his personal understanding of the
poetic lines, Shepp forces the listener to pay attention, to feel the loss with
a profundity that the poem read by itself might not demand.

Like Shepp, Amiri Baraka (then Leroi Jones) recorded jazz poems as
part of a national protest against white oppression. For Sonny Murray's

Sonny's Time Now! he read his poem "Black Art," and the musicians thunder their dissonant sounds while Baraka shouts his demands:

> We want "poems that kill."
> Assassin poems, Poems that shoot
> guns. Poems that wrestle cops into alleys
> with tongues pulled out and sent to Ireland.

With the saxophonist David Murray, Baraka recorded *New Poetry—New Music,* a collaboration poorly received by jazz critics despite the formidable musicianship. One of the most prolific writers on jazz and poetry, Baraka continues to record poetry about jazz musicians, inspired by the music, and read to live accompaniment. Given his prominence as a performing poet in the sixties, however, he remains a peculiar omission from *New Jazz Poets,* a 1967 recording that featured numerous writers, including Paul Blackburn, Howard Hart, David Henderson, Joe Johnson, Percy Edward Johnston, and Ishmael Reed.

Although the poetry and jazz movement virtually ended by 1960 in the United States, a similar movement began in England in 1961, but the concerts there tended to be a staggered offering of poetry followed by jazz rather than a synthesis of the two. Many of the poets from the sixties who performed their work in England have been chronicled in Jeremy Robson's *Poems from Poetry and Jazz in Concert* (1969).[33] "Poetry and Jazz in Concert," explains Robson, "began, rather anarchically, at the Hempstead Town Hall on February 4th 1961" (10). For the next concert, in June of that year, three thousand people attended, and for the rest of that decade there were several hundred concerts, with crowds averaging around four hundred people (11). In his introduction to the anthology, Robson emphasizes the performers' need to shake prejudices that formulated during the Beat generation and their desire to create something better: "Although we have worked for the opposite, the journalist's image of long-haired, ranting, beatnik poets, of beer-spilling, drug-taking, key-pounding musicians, is not easily shaken" (12). Robson makes an effort to promote the "relaxed and unpretentious atmosphere" of this format and, like many poets from the United States, maintains that jazz allows for a much larger poetry audience (12). His impressive list of jazz poetry concerts in England from 1961 to 1969 proves his point, at least for that decade.

Apart from the many poets inspired by jazz, there have also been several important musicians who have instigated the collaboration between poetry and jazz. John Coltrane, arguably the most significant jazz innovator from the sixties, incorporated poetry into the title tune of his album *Kulu Sé Mama* (1966), but, unlike Shepp or Baraka, the poem acts more like a chant than a political message.[34] In the seventies, the trumpeter

Freddie Hubbard experimented with jazz played to texts by foreign writers, including Ilhan Mimaroğlu, Fazil Hüsnü Dağlarca, ÑHA-KHÊ, Ché Guevara (*Sing Me a Song of Songmy*, 1971), and the alto saxophonist Marion Brown performed "Karintha," Jean Toomer's poem in *Cane* (*Geechee Recollections*, 1973). In addition, there have been many jazz musicians who have been writing poetry for years, most notably Sun Ra, Ahmad Jamal, and Cecil Taylor.

Of Kerouac's many admirers, the singer Mark Murphy continues to pay homage. Perhaps his two most singular efforts are his version of "Parker's Mood" from *Bop for Kerouac* (1981), which incorporates appropriate passages from Kerouac's *The Subterraneans*, and his song "November in the Snow" (*Kerouac, Then and Now*, 1989), which includes the description of George Shearing from *On the Road*. Murphy avoids Kerouac's poetry, and his vocal training makes the reading of the prose less gritty than Kerouac's inflections and, arguably, smooth to the point of being slick.

A great variety of writers in the last ten years has continued to perform poetry to jazz. In 1986, for example, James Baldwin recorded *A Lover's Question*, a tightly orchestrated performance of poems read to jazz accompaniment and featuring such respected musicians as Slide Hampton on trombone and Toots Thielemans on harmonica. Bassist and critic Vernon Frazer continues to explore jazz poetry (as heard on his album, *Sex Queens of the Berlin Turnpike*, 1988). A number of contemporary poets, most notably Ntozake Shange, Jayne Cortez, David Meltzer, the Last Poets, and Barry Wallenstein, frequently perform and record with live jazz. And New Alliance Records, thanks to the efforts of Harvey Kubernik, concentrates on the spoken word; in 1991 the company released *Berserk on Hollywood BLVD* (poetry by Wanda Coleman, music by Marv Evans) as well as the ambitious *JazzSpeak*, featuring a variety of jazz poems written and read by Amiri and Amina Baraka, Wanda Coleman, Michael Lally, Michael McClure, Ishmael Reed, Archie Shepp, Quincy Troupe, and many others.

The bassist Charlie Haden's *Dream Keeper* (1991) extends the possibilities of merging jazz with the poetry of Langston Hughes. With Carla Bley, Haden orchestrated Hughes's poetry, and the choral singing against the jazz ensemble sounds different from any previous recordings of Hughes's work—and there have been many, including Nina Simone's interpretation of Hughes's "Backlash Blues." (Kenneth P. Neilson's *The World of Langston Hughes*, published in 1982, documents Hughes's own recordings, records that interpret Hughes's poetry, as well as films that relate to Hughes.) Like Duke Ellington's experiments with orchestration, a combination of classical sensibilities with jazz arrangements, Haden's *Dream Keeper* travels through various modes, the choral verses threading the movements with their refrain.

But perhaps the most haunting contemporary performance of poetry and jazz can be heard on the clarinetist Don Byron's debut session as a leader, *Tuskegee Experiments* (1992). The title refers to the horrors that took place at the Tuskegee Institute in which, for the sake of scientific study, hundreds of African-American men were intentionally not treated for syphilis. Byron's title track incorporates a poem written and read by the poet Sadiq, and the combination of the two shocks the listener into awareness: Where many jazz poetry performances from the fifties and sixties failed to synthesize the two forms of expression or suffered from poor musicianship, the players on this recording (Byron in particular) respond with mature and passionate musicality. As the tone in the poem changes (from shock, to despair, to anger and anguish), so do the musical phrases uncurl and jettison their varied lines against the verse:

> bring them to autopsy
> with ulcerated limbs,
> with howling wives,
> bring them in, one coon corpse at a time.

With music, the lines gain rhythm that they might lose on the page, and by the end of the performance Byron plays faster, his thoughts unfolding with remarkable speed. Sadiq begins his chant—"No treatment! No treatment!"—his voice strained until, in a startling moment of silence, the entire band stops playing. Only the poet now, "No treatment."

NOTES

1. Patrick James Brown's thesis, "Jazz Poetry," suggests a still more massive gap from the mid-thirties through the mid-sixties, "and the major reason," he explains, "is the popularity of swing, a big-band ensemble type of jazz, with less emphasis upon solo improvisation. Evidently, the types of jazz music that inspire poets to write [are] those that are improvisationally-based, and this type of jazz is more apt to be heard in small groups" (107–108).

2. John Edgar Tidwell's continuing work on Davis helps to substantiate his importance as a poet. Although his influence cannot accurately be compared to the careers of Langston Hughes and Sterling Brown, he may very well deserve more attention than I have offered in this book.

3. In 1940 Charles O. Harvey edited an anthology of jazz-related fiction, unfortunately titled *Jazz Parody*. It is to my knowledge the first significant anthology exclusively about jazz-related literature.

The visual arts also reflected a growing interest in jazz. In December 1946, the Samuel Kootz Gallery in New York displayed a show titled "Homage to Jazz" featuring work by William Baziotes, Romare Bearden, Byron Browne, Adolph Gottlieb, Carl Holty, and Robert Motherwell. The exhibition pamphlet included a brief but engaging essay by Barry Ulanov on painting and jazz.

4. The line in the canto reads, "Y TSONG his son brought a jazz age HI-TSONG" (*The Cantos*, 292). Alexander Schmitz's article, "Ideogram-Audiogram,"

tries to establish an integral association between Pound and jazz. He cites this particular Canto as evidence, but the thrust of his argument concentrates on the constructs of improvisation: how Pound's poetry might be understood in terms of twentieth-century jazz aesthetics. Robert Gaspar makes similar claims in his dissertation (35–37). Their appreciation for this parallel exceeds my own, but their discussions address some general aesthetics shared by the modern arts in this century.

5. Alan P. Merriam's *A Bibliography of Jazz*, published in 1954 but still considered one of the authoritative indexes for the literature of jazz, lists eleven jazz-related poems (one of which is actually an essay). Of this select few, he includes "The Jazz Cannibal," Jacobson's "Air de Barrelhouse," Scruggs' "Meditations on Swing," as well as Arthur Guiterman's "Jazz," and he lists only two African-American poems (Brown's "Ma Rainey" and Hughes's "Jazzonia"). Merriam created his bibliography to serve those interested in the literature about the music. Given his jazz poetry selection, however, the bibliography emphasizes the popular opinion among several poets that jazz should be abolished.

6. As noted in Chapter 2, Vachel Lindsay's "A Curse for the Saxophone" implied that the spirit of jazz was the cause of World War I. Carl Sandburg, on the other hand, united the themes of jazz and World War I more ambiguously in his poem "Crimson Changes People" (*Smoke and Steel*, 1920), which confronts "the red death jazz of war" (*Collected*, 168).

7. In 1932, when Johnson played as a member of Evan Thomas's Black Eagle jazz band, a fight erupted during a performance and Thomas was murdered. Johnson's trumpet was crumpled, and his teeth were knocked out, making it impossible for him to play. Then in 1937 two scholars discovered him in New Iberia, Louisiana. Given a new horn and false teeth, Johnson began to perform New Orleans Revival jazz, the music of his youth.

8. It is likely that Williams knew the general history of Bunk Johnson, for during an interview with Mike Wallace from 1950 Williams gave a brief account of Johnson's rediscovery. In that same interview, when asked to "Find one of your poems there that has a lot of good American in it," Williams responded, laughing, "Well! Ah yes, let me see, let's take 'Ol' Bunk's Band' " (Wagner, 20–21).

One of the few poems besides Williams's to address Johnson with any depth is Muriel Rukeyser's "Bunk Johnson Blowing," published in 1968, which recounts her experience from 1943 or 1944 when Johnson performed in San Francisco. Curiously enough, Jonathan Williams explains that Kenneth Patchen's first experiments with poetry-read-to-jazz (circa 1951) involved records by Bunk Johnson and George Lewis (Patchen, *Aflame*, 86–87).

9. The year 1927 has been approximated by Neil Baldwin and Steven L. Meyers in *The Manuscripts and Letters of William Carlos Williams in the Poetry Collection of the Lockwood Memorial Library*. On the postcard itself, which is not reproduced in Baldwin and Meyers's reference book, each scripted phrase extends to the end of the card; it does not appear to be in verse.

10. In "Advent of the Slaves," the chapter on African-Americans from *In the American Grain* (begun in 1923 and published in 1925), Williams discussed the great pleasure he received from listening to the dialect of his African-American patients. Referring to one man in particular, he wrote: "I wish I might write a book of his improvisations in slang" (211). Twenty years after he published *In the*

American Grain and shortly after listening to Johnson at the Stuyvesant Casino, he finally had the opportunity to create a book about such "improvisations in slang," albeit with a white collaborator.

11. A detailed account of this exchange, as well as a thorough description of Williams's experience in the Stuyvesant Casino, can be found in Paul Mariani's excellent article, "Williams' Black Novel" in *The Massachusetts Review* (Winter 1973). This same issue, which appeared ten years after Williams's death, includes the only published version of *Man Orchid*. Mariani's scholarship in *William Carlos Williams: A New World Naked* (1981) is helpful with regards to some of Williams's earliest introductions to jazz. Most recently, the *William Carlos Williams Review* dedicated an entire issue (Fall 1989) on "Williams and Music, Particularly Jazz"; of the three pertinent essays, Aldon L. Nielsen's "Whose Blues?" particularly stands out for its intelligent and probing discussion of Williams's limited perspectives on jazz.

12. Some of the records from 1957 that immediately come to mind are *Blue Train* and *Traneing In* (Coltrane); *A Night at the Village Vanguard, Newk's Time*, and *Way Out West* (Rollins); *Miles Ahead* (Davis with Gil Evans); *The Gerry Mulligan-Paul Desmond Quartet, Mulligan Meets Monk, Getz Meets Mulligan in Hi-Fi*, and *Reunion with Chet Baker* (Mulligan); *Thelonious Monk with John Coltrane* and *Monk's Music* (Monk with Coltrane); *East Coasting* and *Tijuana Moods* (Mingus); and so on.

13. A few of the representative records include Webster's *Soulville*; Hawkins's *The Genius of Coleman Hawkins*; Allen's *World on a String*; and *The Sound of Jazz*, which documents the television broadcast.

14. In discussing poetry-read-to-jazz for an article in the *New Yorker* (1958), Kenneth Rexroth said, "Maxwell Bodenheim did it in the twenties and Langston Hughes in the thirties, and even I did it in the twenties, at the Green Mask, in Chicago, with Frank Melrose, a K.C. pianist" (30). Similarly, in an interview with David Meltzer (1969), he claimed to have started reading when he was a teenager, adding, "Maxwell Bodenheim (who couldn't write for sour owlshit) and Langston Hughes and myself used to do poetry and jazz with a Chicago group, the Austin High Gang" (Meltzer, 23). Hughes himself claims to have been the first to experiment in the twenties with poetry read to live jazz accompaniment.

15. *TIME* magazine reported the same phenomenon, with slightly different figures: "When Rexroth first read ... 500 fans stormed The Cellar (seating capacity: 43) to hear him" (71).

16. For a detailed account of the widespread performances, see Larry R. Smith's essay "The Poetry-and-Jazz Movement of the United States" (*Essays on California Writers*, 1978) or his chapter titled "Poetry-and-Jazz" in *Kenneth Patchen* (1978); virtual clones of each other, the essays offer with brevity and accuracy a sweeping review of the movement.

17. In an interview with David Meltzer, he said, "See, the great problem, is that to do a thing really well in the first place, the poet has to know a great deal about music, either play an instrument or be able to write music or both. He should have some idea about what is happening. Then the band has to rehearse. You don't just get up and blow" (24).

Rexroth fumed over the article in *TIME*, claiming that he had been misquoted. But he must have also detested their cynical opening, which perpetuated the stereotype of jazz poetry as nonsense. Reporting on a rehearsal, *TIME* quoted Kenneth Ford as saying, " 'In *Artifacts* we want a sax solo, like the thrill is gone.' 'You mean,' said the jazzman, pointing to the text, 'we goof around here.' 'Yeah,' said the poet. 'Have a ball' " (71).

18. For a brief overview of Patchen's jazz-related publications and recordings, see Smith's chapter "Poetry-and-Jazz" in *Kenneth Patchen.*

19. Alan Neil's notes are well worth reading, if for no other reason than the story of Patchen undergoing major dental surgery the morning of the recording session.

20. The poetry listing for this record is quite misleading. It begins, "FOUR BLUES POEMS (Comp. by Charlie Parker)," which suggests that Parker wrote the four poems from this section. This could have been clarified if the producers had named Parker's blues ("Laird Baird") but Neil, who concludes his notes by saying how delighted he is "that the opening blues on this record was written by the late, great Charlie Parker" (4), never mentions the actual title. Critics such as Larry Smith have also overlooked the title, and, still more surprising, have failed to note that the music from the final section is based on the chord changes to Parker's "Confirmation"—changes unique to that particular composition.

21. There is an important distinction between reading poetry that is in blues form and singing blues lyrics. Hughes himself was keenly aware of the difference, and tells an amusing anecdote in *The Big Sea* about himself trying to sing his verse. "Son," asks a stranger, "what's the matter? Are you ill?" Hughes explains that he was "Just singing," and the man replies, "I thought you were groaning." After that incident, according to Hughes, "I never sang my verses aloud in the street any more" (217).

22. Part of the success was due to Mingus's own appreciation for poetry. In 1957, just one year prior to his session with Hughes, he released *The Clown*, and the title tune from this record featured an improvised, narrative poem. (Two of the key musicians on *The Clown*, saxophonist Shafi Hadi and trombonist Jimmy Knepper, also play on *Weary Blues*.) Mingus's *Hear My Children Speak* includes Mingus reading his own poetry (which, sadly, is not very good). A recent tribute to Mingus, titled *Weird Nightmare* (1992), features several poems read to jazz.

23. In a letter to Hughes in 1958, Arna Bontemps wrote about Sandburg on the Milton Berle show: "Poetry with Jazz. Even he [Sandburg] has gone for it. He gave 1919 as the date of his first jazz poem: 'Jazz Fantasia' " (376). Rampersad must be alluding to this same appearance, but "Jazz Fantasia," although probably written in 1919, first appeared in the *Dial* in 1920, the same year that Sandburg included the poem in *Smoke and Steel.*

24. In 1990, Rhino Records reissued all three in a box set titled *The Jack Kerouac Collection.* The collection also includes an excellent booklet with essays and reflections by Steve Allen, William Burroughs, Ann Charters, Allen Ginsberg, Jan Michele Kerouac, Harvey Kubernik, Michael McClure, Gerald Nicosia, David Perry, Bob Thiele, and others.

25. Unlike Mingus's unquestionable interest in poetry, Cohn and Sims may simply have accepted the date for the money. The producer Bob Thiele noted in 1989, "If Zoot and Al were really sensitive to Jack's poetry, we'll never know. Somehow, I believe, in retrospect, that they just 'blew' without listening. I think they figured, 'just another record' " (*Jack Kerouac Collection*, 16).

26. Ginsberg himself has recorded with musical accompaniment on records such as *First Blues*. These sessions, however, have never equaled his poetry at its best.

27. Similarly, in a different interview, he said, "Well, generally it [poetry and jazz] was a bad experiment. Usually the musicians wanted to blow—like 'Go ahead and read your poems man but we've got to blow'—and the poet ended up like he's trying to make himself heard on the street corner" (*Riverside*, 6).

28. Nordine recorded *Word Jazz* (Dot Jazz Horizons) in 1957. On the same label and in the three subsequent years, Nordine also recorded *Son of Word Jazz, Next! (Word Jazz)*, and *Word Jazz Vol. II*, which were not so much poetry-read-to-jazz as they were short vignettes (some of which were accompanied by capable but relatively uninspired jazz musicians). Selections from these long-out-of-print records have been reissued by Rhino Records as *Word Jazz Vol. 1* (1990).

29. A closer look at Smith's primary sources, however, shows that some of his supportive evidence is not nearly so strong as it may seem. For example, he accurately quotes John Ciardi as writing, "Patchen's poetry is in many ways a natural for jazz accompaniment" (Ciardi, 57), but does not mention that most of Ciardi's article admits to an inability to understand the merits of jazz poetry and criticizes the union because the poetry tends to get lost in the louder sounds of the band.

30. As early as February 1958, *The Jazz Review* printed an essay by Bob Rolontz titled "Whatever Became of Jazz and Poetry?" (an essay reprinted in *The Jazz Word*, 1960). By 1960 the survival of the Beat movement seemed utterly questionable, as expressed in James Truitt's *The Washington Post* column, "The Beats (Who Really Never Were) Are Gone."

31. Interestingly enough, both Koch and Rivers found themselves trying to work with, rather than against, the new techniques afforded by the union of poetry and jazz. "Last year [in 1959]," Koch explained, "Larry Rivers and I tried to kill poetry-and-jazz by parodying it; our first session at the Five Spot, however, turned out to be so enjoyable (for us, at least) that we repeated the experience several times. I don't think we killed it" (440).

32. Filmed in black and white, a recent television commercial for GAP jeans capitalized on the black-suited, hipster-poet reading in a smoky club to the sounds of jazz in the background: "Sky fits heaven so ride it. Child fits mother so hold your baby tight. Lips fit mouth so kiss them. And the face they adorn reminds you of someone you once knew some hot night, long ago, familiar as these blue jeans."

33. The anthology comprises twenty-four poets, including Pete Brown, Anselm Hollo, Christopher Logue, Spike Milligan, and Adrian Mitchell, as well as Ted Hughes, Jon Silkin, and Stevie Smith.

34. Coltrane's *A Love Supreme* (1964) includes the chant, "A Love Supreme, A Love Supreme," but it would be a misnomer to call the refrain a poem. However, for the liner notes on the record, Coltrane did include a printed poem that he wrote, titled "A Love Supreme." Unfortunately, the poem is terrible: a vague, obtuse homage to God that has none of the profound spirituality evoked by the music itself.

REFERENCES

Anonymous. "The Cool, Cool Bards." *TIME*. 70 (December 2, 1957): 71.

Baldwin, James. *A Lover's Question*. Les Disques du Crepuscule, TWI 928-2, 1986.

Baldwin, Neil, and Steven L. Meyers. *The Manuscripts and Letters of William Carlos Williams in the Poetry Collection of the Lockwood Memorial Library, State University of New York at Buffalo: A Descriptive Catalogue*. Boston: G.K. Hall, 1978.

Baraka, Amiri. *New Music—New Poetry*. India Navigations, 1981.

Berserk on Hollywood BLVD. Poetry by Wanda Coleman, music by Marv Evans. New Alliance, NAR CD 059, 1991.

Bontemps, Arna, and Langston Hughes. *Arna Bontemps-Langston Hughes Letters 1925–1967*. Ed. Charles H. Nichols. New York: Dodd, Mead, 1980.

Bowman, Peter. *Beach Red*. New York: Random, 1945.

Brooks, Gwendolyn. *A Street in Bronzeville*. New York, London: Harper, 1945.

Brown, Marion. *Geechee Recollections*. Impulse, AS-9252, 1973.

Brown, Patrick James. "Jazz Poetry: Definition, Analysis, and Performance." Diss. University of Southern California, 1978.

Bruce, Lenny. "Psychopathia Sexualis." *The Sick Humor of Lenny Bruce*. Fantasy, 7003, 1958. Reissued *The Lenny Bruce Originals Volume 1*. Fantasy, FCD-60–023–2, 1991.

Byron, Don. *Tuskegee Experiments*. Words and reading by Sadiq. Elektra Nonesuch, 9 79280–2, 1992.

Carruth, Hayden. *Sitting In: Selected Writings on Jazz, Blues, and Related Topics*. Iowa City: University of Iowa, 1986.

Cherkovski, Neeli. *Ferlinghetti: A Biography*. Garden City, N.Y.: Doubleday, 1979.

Ciardi, John. "Kenneth Patchen: Poetry, and Poetry with Jazz." *Saturday Review*. 43 (May 14, 1960): 57.

Clodd, Alan, ed. *Tribute to Kenneth Patchen*. London: Enitharmon, 1977.

Coltrane, John. *Kulu Sé Mama*. Impulse 9106, 1966.

Corso, Gregory. *The Riverside Interviews: 3*. London: Binnacle, 1982.

Crane, Hart. *The Letters of Hart Crane 1916–1932*. Ed. Brom Weber. New York: Hermitage House, 1952.

Davis, Frank Marshall. *Black Man's Verse*. Chicago: Black Cat, 1935.

Ferlinghetti, Lawrence. *A Coney Island of the Mind*. New York: New Directions, 1958.

———. *The Riverside Interviews: 2*. London: Binnacle, 1980.

Ferlinghetti, Lawrence, and Kenneth Rexroth. *Poetry Reading at "The Cellar."* Fantasy, 1957.

Frazer, Vernon. *Sex Queens of the Berlin Turnpike*. Woodcrest 1001, 1988.

Gaspar, Robert Peter. "Everyone and I Stopped Breathing: Jazz in American Poetry." Diss. University of Connecticut, 1992.

Ginsberg, Allen. *Collected Poems: 1947–1980*. New York: Harper and Row, 1984.

———. *First Blues*. John Hammond Records, 1982.

Gleason, Ralph J. *Jam Session: An Anthology of Jazz*. London: Jazz Book Club, 1961. (Originally published 1958).

Haden, Charlie, and the Liberation Music Orchestra. *Dream Keeper*. Arrangements by Carla Bley. Blue Note, CDP 7 95474 2, 1991.

Harvey, Charles, ed. *Jazz Parody*. London: American Jazz Society, 1940.

"Homage to Jazz." Dec. 3–Dec. 21, 1946. New York: Samuel M. Kootz Gallery.

Hubbard, Freddie. *Sing Me a Song of Songmy*. Texts by Ilhan Mimaroğlu, Turkish poems by Fazil Hüsnü Dağlarca, ÑHA-KHÊ, Ché Guevara, and others. Atlantic, SD 1576, 1971.

Hughes, Langston. *Fields on Wonder*. New York: Knopf, 1947.

———. *One-Way Ticket*. New York: Knopf, 1949.

———. *Shakespeare in Harlem*. New York: Knopf, 1942.

———. *Weary Blues*. Verve, 841 660–2, 1990. (Originally released in 1958.)

Jacobson, Ethel. "Air de Barrelhouse." *The New York Times Magazine* (Aug. 18, 1940): 19.

Jauss, David. "Contemporary American Poetry and All That Jazz." *Crazyhorse*. 42 (Spring 1992): 125–140.

Jazz Canto: An Anthology of Jazz and Poetry, Vol. I. World Pacific 1244, 1958.

JazzSpeak. Featuring Amiri and Amina Baraka, Wanda Coleman, Mickael Lally, Michael McClure, Ishmael Reed, Archie Shepp, Quincy Troupe, et al. New Alliance, NAR CD 054, 1991.

Kerouac, Jack. *Blues and Haikus*. With Al Cohn and Zoot Sims. Rhino, R2 70939–B, 1990. (Originally released in 1959.)

———. *On the Road*. New York: Viking, 1957.

———. *Poetry for the Beat Generation*. With Steve Allen on piano. Rhino, R2 70939–A, 1990. (Originally released in 1959.)

———. *Readings by Jack Kerouac for the Beat Generation*. Rhino, R2 70939–C, 1990. (Originally released in 1959.)

Koch, Kenneth. "Biographical Notes." *The New American Poetry*. Ed. Donald M. Allen. New York: Grove, 1960.

Mariani, Paul. *William Carlos Williams: A New World Naked*. New York: McGraw Hill, 1981.

———. "Williams' Black Novel." *The Massachusetts Review* XIV, no. 1 (Winter 1973): 67–75.

Meltzer, David, ed. *The San Francisco Poets*. New York: Ballantine, 1971.

Merriam, Alan P. *A Bibliography of Jazz*. Philadelphia: American Folklore Society, 1954.

Mingus, Charles. *The Clown*. Atlantic, 7 90142–2, 1957.

———. *Let My Children Hear Music*. Columbia, CK 48910, 1972.

Murphy, Beatrice, ed. *Ebony Rhythm: An Anthology of Contemporary Negro Verse*. New York: Exposition, 1948.

Murphy, Mark. *Bop for Kerouac*. With Richie Cole. Muse, MCD 5253, 1981.

———. *Kerouac, Then and Now*, Muse, MCD 5359, 1989.

Murray, Sonny. *Sonny's Time Now!* Jihad, 1967 [Sound recording, LP only.]

Nielsen, Aldon L. "Whose Blues?" *William Carlos Williams Review*. Vol. 15, No. 2. (Fall 1989): 1–8.

New Jazz Poets. Folkways, BR 461, 1967.

Nordine, Ken. *Word Jazz Vol. 1*. Rhino, R2 70773, 1990.

Patchen, Kenneth. *Aflame and Afun of Walking Trees*. New York: New Directions, 1970. First published as *Jargon 6: Fables and Other Little Tales*. Karlsruhe/Baden, Germany: Jonathan Williams, 1953.

———. *First Will and Testament*. Norfolk, Conn.: New Directions, 1939.

———. *Kenneth Patchen Reads with the Chamber Jazz Sextet*. Cadence 3004, 1958.

———. *Kenneth Patchen Reads with Jazz in Canada*. Folkways, Fla. 9718, 1959.

———. *Memoirs of a Shy Pornographer*. New York: New Directions, 1945.

Pound, Ezra. *The Cantos of Ezra Pound.* New York: New Directions, 1970.

Rampersad, Arnold. *The Life of Langston Hughes.* 2 Volumes. New York: Oxford University Press, 1986, 1988.

Rexroth, Kenneth. *Collected Shorter Poems.* New York: New Directions, 1966.

Robson, Jeremy, ed. *Poems from Poetry and Jazz in Concert.* London: Souvenir, 1969.

Rolontz, Bob. "Whatever Became of Jazz and Poetry?" *The Jazz Word.* Eds. Dom Cerulli, Burt Korall, and Mort L. Nasatir. New York: Ballantine, 1960.

Roskolenko, Harry. "The Sounds of the Fury." *Prairie Schooner.* 33 (Summer 1959): 148–153.

Rukeyser, Muriel. *Beast in View.* New York: Doubleday, Duran, 1944.

———. *U. S. 1.* New York: Covici, Friede, 1938.

Sandburg, Carl. *Complete Poems.* New York: Harcourt, Brace, 1950.

Schmitz, Alexander. "Ideogram-Audiogram." *Paideuma: A Journal Devoted to Ezra Pound Scholarship.* Vol. 20, no. 1–2 (Spring–Fall): 43–62.

Scruggs, Anderson. "Meditation on Swing." *Hygeia,* XIX (March, 1941): 195.

Shepp, Archie. "Malcolm, Malcolm, Semper Malcolm." *Fire Music,* Impulse, MCAD-39121, 1965.

Silesky, Barry. *Ferlinghetti: The Artist of His Time.* New York: Warner, 1990.

Skau, Michael. *"Constantly Risking Absurdity": The Writings of Lawrence Ferlinghetti.* Troy, N.Y.: Whitson, 1989.

Smith, Larry R. *Kenneth Patchen.* Boston: Twayne, 1978.

———. "The Poetry-and-Jazz Movement of the United States." *Essays on California Writers.* Ed. Charles L. Crow. (*Itinerary*: Criticism, 7). Bowling Green, Ohio: Bowling Green University Press, 1978.

Truitt, James McC. "The Beats (Who Really Never Were) Are Gone." *The Washington Post* (October 23, 1960): E3.

Wagner, Linda Welshimer. *Interviews with William Carlos Williams.* New York: New Directions, 1976.

Williams, William Carlos. *The Collected Poems of William Carlos Williams.* Eds. A. Walton Litz and Christopher MacGowan. New York: New Directions, 1986–1988. 2 volumes.

———. *In the American Grain.* New York: Albert and Charles Boni, 1925.

———. "Jazz." Postcard to Fred Miller, n.d. Lockwood Memorial Library. Buffalo: State University of New York.

———. *Patterson.* New York: New Directions, 1963.

Williams, William Carlos, Lydia Carlin, and Fred Miller. "Man Orchid." *The Massachusetts Review* XIV, no. 1 (Winter 1973): 77–117.

5

Chasin' the Bird: Charlie Parker and the Enraptured Poets of the Fifties

I was always on a panic—couldn't buy clothes or a good place to live. ... The mental strain was getting worse all the time. What made it worst of all was that nobody understood our kind of music out on the [West] Coast. ... Finally, I broke down.
    —Charlie Parker

When Parker, a poet in jazz,
Gave one hundred seventy pounds to a one-ounce needle,
His music, his life,
Six hipsters from uptown
Called it a religious sacrifice
And wore turbans.
Our poet wore lonely death,
Leaving his breath in a beat.
    —Bob Kaufman

In *Bird Lives! The High Life and Hard Times of Charlie Parker* (1973), Ross Russell re-creates a meeting with the famed alto saxophonist and Dean Benedetti who, with sycophantic diligence, recorded numerous Parker performances.[1] Benedetti enters the room while Bird voraciously but methodically devours his second enormous *Comida Conquistador* dinner. "Hey, man," says Parker, "dig this crazy Mex stuff!" and Benedetti, no doubt wishing that he liked Mexican food but unable to lie to his hero, replies, "It don't kill me" (6). Russell comments:

The *don't* is deliberate. Errors in grammar and Dean's acquired, specialized, limited vocabulary are all part of the efforts he is making to become a white Negro. The highschool education received at Susanville, California, before entering the music profession, is an obstacle to his progress in the social group he esteems. In order to be in, it is necessary to master the argot of the black ghetto and jazz club. (6)

What Russell also implies, of course, is that the attraction of Parker often had just as much to do with his personality as his playing. No other figure in jazz up until then—not even Louis Armstrong—elicited such a fanatical, almost mythological attraction. Benedetti represented the consummate fan: someone who relentlessly tried to document individual genius, even at the expense of the overall performance (often he would turn off the recorder as soon as Parker stopped playing). After Parker's premature death in 1955 at the age of thirty-four, his cult following became still greater.

The jazz poets from the fifties—and here I refer to a cross section of poets from a variety of labeled groups, such as the Black Mountain writers and the Beats—were actively trying to break from tradition and find their new post-war voice. On the whole, these were anything but classically academic poets; collectively, they support Maria Damon's thesis in *The Dark End of the Street* (1993) "that the American literary avant-garde comes out of the work of the socially marginalized" (vii). (In fact, two of the eight central writers in Damon's book—Jack Spicer and Bob Kaufman—are also critical to this chapter.) In a sense, Charlie Parker proved that marginalized figures could not merely endure traditional sensibilities but could, in fact, change tradition.

As jazz musicians began copying Parker's technique and studying his solos, the poets of the time were faced with the problem of somehow integrating the vitality of his music in their poetry, an entirely different medium that was not, by nature, an improvisatory art form. The poets tried, with varying success, to bridge this difficulty, and their attempts tended to emphasize either the formal elements of music or, even more so, the biographical aspects of Parker himself. On the one hand, there was the relationship to the poetic line, and several poets, principally Robert Creeley, insisted that Bird's music directly informed their sense of method. On the other, there were the more biographical poems written by poets who were eager—perhaps desperately so—to share in Parker's magnificence. Unfortunately, too many of these poets (among them Jack Kerouac, Kenneth Ford, Howard Hart, and even Bob Kaufman) projected a God-like status on Parker, and in doing so they lost the humanness of the man: The descriptions of the music and of Parker himself became overexposed, whitened-out in adulation.

After the fashion of Dean Benedetti, this heterogeneous mix of writers viewed Parker with passionate yet distant idolatry. They did what they could "to master the argot of the black ghetto and jazz club," and with sincere efforts, but most of the time their use of lingo and hipster metaphors seemed forced, corny. Although Creeley's use of space and quirky lines may sound nothing like the longer musical lines of Parker, his Parker-inspired poems avoid cliché partly because they move away from mere portraiture. Furthermore, the poets writing about Parker in the fifties were dominantly white writers who almost never confronted any of the social issues of race, oppression, or protest—issues that were crucial to the emergence of bebop. One of the very few poets sensitive to such issues was Langston Hughes, who, in his final years, turned more to jazz than to the blues, and whose politically-charged poems provided guidance for the African-American writers in the sixties.

Although some jazz poets became drawn to Parker's suicidal life-style, all of the writers sensed that his recordings would inevitably be considered among the most dynamic artistic innovations of this century, a view even more tenaciously held by many of the musicians of the time. Gary Giddins, in his book *Celebrating Bird: The Triumph of Charlie Parker* (1987), quotes numerous players who cannot quite define their thrill and awe at hearing Parker for the first time. The trumpeter Thad Jones, for example, remembered being stationed in Guam during the forties "when all of a sudden Dizzy comes on [the radio] playing 'Shaw Nuff' with Charlie Parker. And you know," Jones continued,

I can't describe what went on in that tent. We went out of our minds! . . . It was the newness and the impact of that sound, and the technique. It was something we were probably trying to articulate ourselves and just didn't know how. And Dizzy and Bird came along and did it. They spoke our minds. (12, 15)

For musicians like Jones, the startling sounds of Parker and Gillespie jettisoned the preconceived notions of jazz and opened up a whole new perspective on modern American music. The techniques included a significantly advanced approach to harmony coupled with a velocity of fluid phrasing unparalleled by other players in jazz history. The speed alone became misleading for many who did not understand the basic foundations of jazz and who interpreted their waterfalls of sound as ungoverned, threatening statements of violent aggression. But for many musicians of the time who were yearning to break from the traditional harmonics and meter of dance band jazz but who had no established vocabulary as of yet, bebop liberated their hearing and their thinking with profound and immediate effects.

One of the fundamental innovations by Parker concerned his use of harmonic cadence: the extension of his phrases beyond the more established resolutions—a rethinking of standard chord progressions. The converse was also true, in which he concluded improvised statements prior to their harmonic resolutions. Gillespie's stratospheric trumpet lines excited listeners not merely because of his dynamic range but because of his shared conceptual approach to jazz in which the harmonic structures of the tune did not become necessary boundaries for improvisation. Many listeners with uneducated ears interpreted the startling newness of bebop as a hostile rejection of form, meter, and melody—of all musical sensibility. As Giddins points out, however, "The distancing effect of modern jazz stemmed not from any desire to estrange audiences, but from difficulties inherent in a music that, for all its emotional qualities, demanded concentration and empathy" (79).

The bebop rhythm section furthered the overall innovation by replacing the established on-the-beat background (in which the bass player often restated the drummer's beat) with more-syncopated rhythms that did not abandon the beat but rather emphasized the other rhythms inherent within the overall rhythm of the tune. Although Parker and Gillespie became the most visible figures, they were more than merely supported by their pioneering rhythm sections, featuring pianists Thelonious Monk and Bud Powell, bassists Charles Mingus and Oscar Pettiford, and drummers Max Roach and Kenny "Klook" Clarke.

What, then, made Charlie Parker stand out so prominently as a figure-head of bebop and, later, as a cult hero? Most generally, it had something to do with the sheer visibility of his presence—both his rounded, expressive physique and his position in the front line of the combo. There has also been for years a general association with the saxophone as *the* instrument of jazz. Where Gillespie and Monk became stigmatized by a clownish image, people did not interpret Bird's sense of humor with the same comedic connotations. Mainly, however, the attraction concerned Parker's two most public characteristics: first and foremost, his ability to create astonishing improvisations, but also his well-known involvement with narcotics. "If Parker's career was a frantic quest for musical fulfillment," explains Giddins,

it was continuously detoured by self-destructive impulses so gargantuan that they also became the stuff of legend. The bop king had another, by no means secret, identity as the junkie king, and many votaries unable to get close to him musically were eager to share the communion of drugs. . . . Despite his warnings, many persisted in the sometimes fatal belief that Parker drew part of his seemingly inexhaustible greatness from teaspoons of white powder. (15)

Hundreds emulated his vices without necessarily comprehending his artistic achievements. "I ran with the beboppers," explains the poet Michael McClure,

going to all their jam sessions and nightclub engagements and not really hearing their music until I had been listening to it for more than a year. I was doing it for the drugs and excitement and because you stayed up all night and slept all day. (Meltzer, 245)

Charlie Parker represented the ultimate in hipster mystique: frantic genius, coupled with romanticized overindulgence. It is no wonder that so many poets of the time—from young writers like Jack Kerouac to more-established figures such as Langston Hughes—turned to Parker and his music for inspiration. Like the graffiti "Bird Lives!" that began to mark walls only hours after Parker's death, an influx of elegies and homages for Parker appeared in numerous journals and magazines, as well as poetry collections. At times, the honest admissions of profound loss created haunting images; just as often, however, the poetry tended to rely on abstractions and clichés that rendered the poems vague and sadly ineffective. A frank discussion of the poetry about Parker from this time must acknowledge that most of the poets managed to capture only glimmers of Charlie Parker's magnitude.

It should be noted, too, that some writers, including Jake Trussell, rejected and therefore ignored the innovations by the bop musicians. Primarily a columnist and jazz disc jockey, Trussell had a passion for traditional jazz; his collection of jazz poems, *After Hours Poetry* (1958), contains very few references to modern jazz, and there are no lengthy poems that concentrate on Parker, Gillespie, or other bebop musicians.[2] His poem "Birdland," for example, tries to establish this landmark as the supreme jazz club in history, yet it makes no direct or historical references to Bird himself. Only "The Real Gone Session," an account of musicians playing posthumously in heaven, refers to Parker directly, but Trussell's ridiculous conglomerate makes no sense, musically speaking:

> There's Irving Fazola on clarinet
>   And Bix Beiderbecke blowing cornet
> Charlie Parker on alto sax
>   And Chu Berry on his tenor axe (80)[3]

Even during the zenith of bebop in the early fifties many figures supposedly "in the know" about jazz had utterly rejected Parker and his contemporaries. Probably a result of his struggle against being labeled a Bohemian Beat writer, Kenneth Rexroth tried to demythologize Parker, yet his statements now seem ridiculous. "[T]here isn't anything in Charlie Parker," he said, "that isn't in Beethoven!" (Meltzer, 27). In 1957 he dismissed the entire movement:

Even before [Charlie Parker's] death [in 1955] this influence had begun to ebb. In fact, the whole generation of the founding fathers of bop—Gillespie, Davis, Blakey, and the rest—are now at a considerable discount. The main line of development today goes back to Lester Young and by-passes them. (*Alternative Society*, 5–6)

Rexroth's bizarre criticism of bebop and Trussell's focus on traditional jazz must be evaluated, however, as utterly anachronistic, at least when compared to the importance of bop for so many other poets from the fifties, many of whom (perhaps too optimistically) equated their own literary achievements with Charlie Parker's genius.

Parker's innovations with time and rhythm, for example, inspired some writers to claim that their sense of poetics was necessarily informed by Parker's music, and of those who have made such claims, Robert Creeley may be the most outspoken. During an interview in which he discussed his influences from this decade, Creeley first turned to literary mentors and then quickly switched to music:

And I'd use Williams as a model but Williams too was—jazz was the most obvious model. It wasn't that I wanted to write like jazz but that the information of *time*, in the beat, all of that was far more accessible and immediately emphatic in jazz whereas if I went to the classic English texts for parallels there the overriding information of the statement of the emotional tone or the decor of the diction— it was far harder for me to get it. (Terrell, 39)

Of the particular jazz musicians whom Creeley admired, he often mentions Miles Davis and sometimes Thelonious Monk, but by far the most influential figure was Charlie Parker.[4] Introduced to jazz while in college, experiencing both Charlie Parker and Ezra Pound for the first time, Creeley knew that John Ashbery turned to the French surrealists for "a very active admission of the world as it's felt and confronted," but Creeley derived that same kind of inspiration from modern American music:

I was finding it in jazz, for example. And that's why Charlie Parker and Miles Davis and Thelonious Monk and those people were extraordinarily interesting to me. Simply that they seemed to have only the nature of the activity as a limit. That is, possibly they couldn't change water into stone. But then again, maybe they could. (*Contexts*, 155)

Like many of Creeley's statements about poetry and jazz, his language becomes a bit fuzzy at the crux of his argument. And yet his ambiguity sounds somewhat like Parker's own quotations. "They teach you there's a boundary line to music," Parker once said. "But, man, there's no boundary line to art" (Shapiro and Hentoff, 405).

Creeley began writing to the sounds of Charlie Parker—"just because that rhythmic insistence, I think, kept pushing me, I kept hearing it"—to the point where jazz as writing inspiration became "a physical requirement" (*Contexts*, 31–32). In an interview from 1965, when asked about his strongest literary influences on his poetry, he mentions Williams, Olson, and Pound, but concludes, "I could equally say Charlie Parker—in his

uses of silence, in his rhythmic structure" (*Contexts*, 123). "I love the syncopation of jazz," Creeley said in a different interview from 1982, "or the
way a beat could move to a set pattern of intervals, that is, units of time,
and within that structure make all these variable tempi" (Terrell, 38). "It
was a very literal hearing of that rhythm," he continued:

[My college friend] Joe Leach, characteristically, was the first friend to play me—it
must have been 1945, early 46—one of the first singles of Miles Davis and Charlie
Parker. One side was "Billie's Bounce" and the other side was "Now's the Time."
Then patterns like "Chasing the Bird," which friends who were frankly working
with the New England Conservatory of Music couldn't hear for anything. (40)

In 1953, having absorbed the sounds of Parker for seven or eight years,
Creeley wrote his poem "Chasing the Bird," which borrowed its title from
the Parker composition:

> The sun sets unevenly and the people
> go to bed.
>
> The night has a thousand eyes.
> The clouds are low, overhead.
>
> Every night it is a little bit
> more difficult, a little
>
> harder. My mind
> to me a mangle is.
>
> (*Collected*, 60)

In explicating this poem, George F. Butterick refers to the most famous
version of this tune as recorded by Parker and Davis but overinterprets
the title: "by implication the rest of the band . . . scampers to keep up with
the high-flying Parker" (Terrell, 129). Conversely, he treats the line "The
night has a thousand eyes" somewhat tentatively by ignoring the sentimental popularity of that song title (made famous in the late forties) and
briefly noting that "the 'eyes' become—if pushed that far—paranoiac, insomniac" (130); in fact, the "paranoiac" and "insomniac" qualities become
vital when addressing Parker's frenzied life-style. Yet overall, Butterick's
discussion, with its mixture of personal insight and meticulous scholarship,
dazzles. He explores "the progressive negativism of the poem," the shifts
in meter, as well as the "echo—and reversal—of Sir Edward Dyer's late
sixteenth-century [poem] 'My Mind to Me a Kingdom Is' " (130). He concludes:

"Chasing the Bird" is a confessional poem, in which revelation is withheld until the end, with its head-shaking display of self-knowledge. . . . The conscious reference of the title and the ending, together with the dignified progression of opening statements, indicate the poem is more controlled and self-critical than self-pitying. The concluding statement in which "mangle" is substituted for "kingdom" may be less an allusion to Dyer and his world of self-confidence . . . than it is a parody of such sentiment. A new tradition of wry defiance (embodied by Charlie Parker) is superimposed on the old Elizabethan optimism. (131)

Recognizing the possible connections between Olson's theory of projective verse ("projectile, percussive, prospective") and Parker's jazz, Creeley kept urging the older poet to hear the "New Sounds" of music. In Olson's essay "Projective Verse" (which first appeared in *Poetry New York*, 1950), Creeley's mentor had written, "I would argue that here, too, the LAW OF THE LINE, which projective verse creates, must be hewn to, obeyed, and that the conventions which logic has forced on syntax must be broken open as quietly as must the too set feet of the old line" (*Selected*, 21). Creeley digested the tangible relationships between poetic and musical lines, and he did his best to share this epiphany with Olson. "There is nothing being put down that can match/ that timing: Bird's," Creeley wrote Olson in a visually-active letter dated June 24, 1950:

Well, to orient yrself: wd suggest you listen to any of the following.

Miles Davis: Boplicity & reverse side.
  "   " :   Move.
The Bird   : Chasing the Bird   i got
            : Cheryl   ryhtmethe, . . .
            : Don't Blame Me
            : Donna Lee   I got R/
            : Billy's Bounce   & so on? yes. There are a
                               great many/ but each of the
                               above: sd do it.

The names to look for/ whenever getting this type:
                        musick/

Miles Davis, Chas Parker, Bud Powell, Max Roach, Milt Jackson, Al Haig, &c.

                But the above/ all yez know: on earth
                & all yez need: to know: to leave it.
                                    (Olson/Creeley, *Vol. I*, 156)

In many of his subsequent correspondences, Creeley persisted in his attempts at jazz education, but ultimately he failed to persuade Olson, who never enjoyed listening to any kind of music, jazz or otherwise.[5]

Creeley's "The Bird, the Bird, the Bird," like "Chasing the Bird," first appeared in 1953, and he dedicated the poem *"for Charles"* (presumably Olson, but possibly Parker as well):

> With the spring flowers I likewise am.
> And care for them. That they have odor.
>
> We are too garrulous (Brugm. i. §638), we
> talk not too much but too often.
>
> And yet, how otherwise to oblige the
> demon, who it is, there
>
> implacable, but content.
>
> (*Collected*, 44)[6]

The poem inverts syntax from the start (unlike "Chasing the Bird," which crescendos to its quirk in meter), and this deliberate inversion causes the voice in this poem—and in so many of Creeley's poems—to cadence unexpectedly. As Charles O. Hartman explains in *Jazz Text* (1991) about the poem "I Know a Man," "Creeley's poem does not randomly collect interesting bits of speech any more than a Parker solo randomly strings together a flurry of notes and arpeggios—though either may seem that way to an unaccustomed audience" (43).[7]

In the poem "Le Fou," Creeley himself comments on the rhythmic impulse behind the line: "who plots, then, the lines / talking, taking, always the beat from / the breath" (*Collected*, 111).[8] According to many statements, Creeley felt an integral relationship between the musical and poetic line, as seen in this passage originally printed in his preface to *All That Is Lovely in Men* (1955):

Line-wise, the most complementary sense I have found is that of musicians like Charlie Parker and Miles Davis. I am interested in how that is done, how 'time' there is held to a measure peculiarly an evidence (a hand) of the emotion which prompts (drives) the poem in the first place. If this seems hopeful, let me point to the 'line' of Miles Davis' chorus in "But Not For Me"—Bach is no different, but the time is. (*A Quick Graph*, 4)

Parker afforded new possibilities for poetic rhythms, for American idioms, and Creeley, less interested in Bird's personal life, became consumed by the ambiance of jazz and the innovations of bebop.

In 1965, reflecting on the fifties, Creeley said, "[I]t was a time when one wanted desperately an intensive and an absolutely full *experience* of whatever it was you were engaged with. So Charlie Parker—think of his place in Jack Kerouac's writing—became kind of a hero of this possibility" (*Contexts*, 47). Creeley was right: Think of Parker's importance in Kerouac's writing, and most of his major works come to mind, including *On *the Road* (1957), *Mexico City Blues* (1959), or these well-known passages from *The Subterraneans* (1958):

we went to the Red Drum to hear the jazz which that night was Charlie Parker with Honduras Jones on the drums and others interesting, probably Roger Beloit too, whom I wanted to see now, and that excitement of softnight San Francisco bop in the air but all in the cool sweet unexerting Beach . . . and up on the stand Bird Parker with solemn eyes who'd been busted fairly recently and had now returned to a kind of bop dead Frisco but had just discovered or been told about the Red Drum, the great new generation gang wailing and gathering there, so here he was on the stand, examining them with his eyes as he blew his now-settled-down-into-regulated-design "crazy" notes (17–19)

He worked diligently and earnestly to create what Ginsberg called bop prosody, and some of the jazz images from *On the Road* even read like short modernist poems, as with this one-sentence paragraph reminiscent of Pound's "In a Station of the Metro": "Holy flowers floating in the air, were all these tired faces in the dawn of Jazz America" (204). In Kerouac's prose, the twisting, minimally punctuated sentences often de-emphasize his weaker passages. But in his poetry the brevity of the lines are not as forgiving, either on the page or when read out loud. "Kerouac may well distract and irritate more than he will teach," wrote Creeley in his review of *Mexico City Blues*. "But the attempt is useful" ("Ways of Looking," 196).

Kerouac's most famous jazz poem, "Charlie Parker," which he read for the recording *Poetry for the Beat Generation* (1959), first appeared in *Mexico City Blues* (also from 1959) as three consecutive poems: "239th Chorus," "240th Chorus," and "241st Chorus." This medley exemplified his often-quoted "Note" from the collection: "I want to be considered a jazz poet blowing a long blues in an afternoon jam session on Sunday. I take 242 choruses; my ideas vary and sometimes roll from chorus to chorus or from halfway through a chorus to halfway into the next" (n.p.). The choruses are part biography (on Parker's death, on his performance with strings), part hero worship (with frequent parallels between Parker and Buddha), part gratitude for his musicianship ("This was what Charley [*sic*] Parker / Said when he played, All is Well. / You had the feeling of early-in-the-morning"), and part guilt for not saving him:

> Charley Parker, forgive me—
> Forgive me for not answering your eyes—
> For not having made an indication
> Of that which you can devise—
> Charley Parker, pray for me—
> Pray for me and everybody
> In the Nirvanas of your brain

Where you hide, indulgent and huge,
No longer Charley Parker
But the secret unsayable name
That carries with it merit
Not to be measured from here
To up, down, east, or west—
—Charley Parker, lay the bane,
off me, and every body (243)

Like the speaker in the above poem, Kerouac's protagonist in *The Subterraneans*, Leo Percepied, finds himself lost in the eyes of Parker, as
though being both judged and energized. Kerouac describes Parker as
looking

directly into my eye looking to search if really I was that great writer I thought
myself to be as if he knew my thoughts and ambitions or remembered me from
other night clubs and other coasts, other Chicagos—not a challenging look but the
king and founder of the bop generation at least the sound of it in digging his
audience digging his eyes, the secret eyes him-watching, as he just pursed his lips
and let great lungs and immortal fingers work, his eyes separate and interested
and humane, the kindest jazz musician there could be. (19)

Both Kerouac and Percepied shared an intense desire to be connected,
somehow, to this legendary figure with "immortal fingers." Parker stood
as a formidable seer of true nature, and although Percepied may suggest
that the expression is not "challenging," he also implies a curious mixture
of feeling both inspired and evaluated. Much like Dean Benedetti, Kerouac became hypnotized by Parker's artistry and presence. He elevated
Parker's creative genius to the highest levels of Buddhist enlightenment,
and yet his poetry, like the work by many of his contemporaries, became
weakest when he attempted to re-create the image of Parker as a god.

At the same time, Kerouac's description of Parker as "indulgent and
huge" in "241st Chorus" has always been, I think, one of his better lines
about Parker, for it implies the tremendous presence of Bird as a man and
as a symbol, and it also evokes the relentless desire for creative and de-
structive indulgence. Kerouac, of course, shared some of those same qualities: He was a man passionate about his art, and equally passionate in his
self-destructive behavior. In 1969, after years of excessive drinking, Kerouac died at age forty-seven. But in 1959, when he was only three years
older than Parker at his death, he probably realized that his own life was
headed towards a similar fate: burning out young like a fabulous yellow
Roman candle. In his verse, he may have begged Parker to "lay the bane,
/ off me, and every body," but in his life he wanted to be remembered
for equally huge and indulgent desires.

Like Kerouac, the poet Jack Spicer (1925–1965) lived his life with devastating neglect for his own health, and he, too, turned to Parker as a spiritual leader.[9] The biographical parallels between Spicer and Bird once inspired the poet Lew Welch to say,

The only person I have ever met that reminded me of Charles Parker was Jack Spicer. They were the same man. They were just hell-bent on self-destruction. They were both six feet plus and heavy. They were both big and strong. . . . They were very similar men and they both had the same approach to their art. (Meltzer, 216)

The two men also suffered from severe bouts of depression that caused them to doubt the validity of their work, and it is with touching honesty that Spicer begins his poem "Song for Bird and Myself" with these three admissions: "I am dissatisfied with my poetry. / I am dissatisfied with my sex life. / I am dissatisfied with the angels I believe in" (346).

Throughout this poem written in 1956, Spicer refers to Bird not as avant-garde but as "neo-classical," as someone who revived the most-respected forms of music with structure and classical elegance.[10] By referring to Parker this way, the poem recognizes the supreme order of bebop and implicitly rejects the contemptuous, belittling criticisms by many people in the United States at that time. In the poem, the poet asks Parker why artists like the two of them cannot "sell out" for the more popular forms of expression:

"Listen, Bird, why do we have to sit here dying
In a half-furnished room?
The rest of the combo
Is safe in houses
Blowing bird-brained Dixieland,
How warm and free they are. What right
Music." (346)

Parker responds:

"Man,
We
Can't stay away from the sounds.
We're *crazy*, Jack
We gotta stay here 'til
They come and get us." (346)

According to the poem, the creative act for the poet and musician is not a matter of choice but of personal urgency. Spicer, who early in the poem announced "I am dissatisfied with the angels I believe in," asks, "And are we angels, Bird?" With no pause, Parker answers, "That's what we're trying to tell 'em, Jack / There aren't any angels except when / You and me blow 'em" (348).[11]

Parker in essence instructs the poet, who listens with great intensity because he feels a spiritual kinship with the musician. Commenting on the "Terrible and pure" (347) sounds of Charlie Parker, the poet metaphorically refers to "The horse / In Cocteau," calling it "as neo-classical an idea as one can manage" as well as "the needle for which / God help us / There is no substitute" (348). The men therefore share the communion of their creative urges and passionately self-destructive desires. The poem concludes:

So Bird and I sing
Outside your window
So Bird and I die
Outside your window.
This is the wonderful world of Dixieland
Deny
The bloody motherfucking Holy Ghost.
This is the end of the poem.
You can start laughing, you bastards. This is
The end of the poem. (348)

Kenneth Rexroth may have misunderstood many things about Charlie Parker, but he was right when he compared Bird to Dylan Thomas by saying, "Both of them did communicate one central theme: Against the ruin of the world, there is only one defense—the creative act" (*Alternative Society*, 3). The same parallel, I think, could be made with Jack Spicer.

"Song for Bird and Myself" is more ambitious and successful than any individual poem in Kenneth Ford's book, *Poetry for Jazz* (1959), but, like Kerouac's *Mexico City Blues*, this collection stands out for its effort to write jazz poetry as a series. The three poems for Charlie Parker—"The Ballad of the Bird," "Bird in a World Full of People," and "Bird"—all attempt to mythologize the musician as a man larger than life, and yet, unlike the very personal dialogue in Spicer's poem, that gesture distances the speaker from the subject. When Ford labors to make Parker superhuman, the verse tends to become trite, as it does when he sustains the metaphor of a bird. "The Ballad of the Bird" suffers from too much biography; separated by the refrain "there never was a bird / like this" (15), the stanzas rarely achieve a sense of lyricism or poetic voice, nor do the biographical references stand out as being particularly interesting. "Bird in a World Full of People" emphasizes the obvious: how Parker seemed otherworldly yet was never fully embraced by the general public. Ford is best when he abandons his manipulated metaphors or his hipster catchwords and instead speaks in a more natural voice, as with the opening line to "Bird": "Let us speak plainly: Bird is dead" (40).

Howard Hart's biographical portraits of Parker are stronger, in part because he understood the music itself. A jazz drummer as well as a poet, Hart met the bebop drummer Kenny "Klook" Clarke in New York, 1952, and their introduction had a profound influence on Hart's poetry. Arun Nevader, in the introduction to Hart's *Selected Poems*, explains:

For Klook, rhythm took on a fresh lyrical dimension. It became more of an interpretation of melody than an addition to it. Hart's poetry began to develop in the same way. Rhythm often assumes certain psychological qualities in his poetry. If his work was influenced by Kenny Clarke in the early years, Hart's friendship with Elvin Jones in the early sixties helped shape his later poetry. (8)

Hart's poem "For Christianne" chronicles the whole history of jazz drumming: from Baby Dodds at the turn of the century, to drummers from the Swing era (Sid Catlett, Jo Jones, Grady Tate), edging towards bebop (Harold West, Frankie Dunlop, Kenny Clarke, Max Roach), and into the sixties (Elvin Jones). Like Etheridge Knight's poem "Jazz Drummer," which capitalizes and repeats the name "MAX ROACH" in order to punctuate the beat, Hart's poem hits the bass drum with "JONES" and "KLOOK" (three times). He capitalizes one other word in this poem—"YES"—but it is less an affirmation of hope than an urgent request for public awareness:

> Drummers and poets are used like ashtrays YES
> Purple is the color of suffering
>   because red will never suffice (71)

True to the spirit of jazz, Hart divided his *Selected Poems* into "Sets" and subtitled each set by the names of short poems. The epigraph for "Set 5" (which concludes with "For Christianne") is "Bird," a three-line poem, which breathlessly juxtaposes images and rhythms:

> antiphonal fluorescence of bamboo cane
> the burn triumphant in a soup of flowers
> absolute freedom of the imagination in a tungsten horn (59)

Hart projects the antiphonal drive in Parker, a union of personal despair with ingenious creativity—"the burn triumphant." Parker's imagination, metaphorically conceived as "a soup of flowers," thrives on his own limitless inspiration, his "tungsten horn" forging the air.

"Set 5" includes two other Parker-inspired poems, the first of which, "Moonlight on the Ganges," begins:

I am reading
    rewriting
a poem on Jazz and Snow White
In case you don't know
she was the only wife of Charlie Parker (65)

Hart cynically refers to Parker's widow, Chan Richardson, who, because she was white, received more attention than any of Parker's other wives (Rebecca Parker Davis, Geraldine Scott, and Doris Sydnor).[12] As the symbolic figure of "goodness" as well as the slang term for "white woman," "Snow White" emphasizes the mystique of lighter skins: how white women have sometimes been viewed as icons of status for African-American men. With Gillespie, Chan and Bird attend the movie *Going My Way* but "in the dubbed Scandinavian version"—a blemish to the film's purity, a watered-down version doomed for inaccuracies in translation (a metaphor, perhaps, for interracial marriages). Yet the woman becomes the focus of the poem's close:

Many's the time I heard her disagree
    with this world of pie à la mode
But she
    walking home
    enjoyed the lights of our odd town (65)

Hart implies a dual mystique: On the one hand, this white woman does not fully appreciate or endorse ethnic diversity (vanilla ice cream with pie), but, on the other, she enjoys being paraded (the lights shining on her) as an icon.

The poem "Birding with Charlie Parker," by far the longest of the three, recounts an evening at Birdland, the famed club named after Parker. The speaker arrives with friends, including his former teacher, the classical composer Charles Mills. (In this setting, "legit" music has no rank over jazz.) More commonly broke and sweetly requesting free drinks, Parker astonishes Hart by taking the tab:

You and Charles Mills equals it was beautiful
    to see feel
    and you *paid* for everything that night
Rare   Strange   BIRD
    the open heart recognized only in its closures
DIPHTHONG (67)

Parker seems all-encompassing, all-knowing: "the tryptych [*sic*] of your nonsmile a celestial smirk" (67). After the repeated question "You will tell me of your lamentations?" he finally answers,

"A little mild clapping of the hands will be sufficient!"
and in the meantime
Twenty-one little pieces of dramamine
   an egg and a good view of Deya Majorca (67)

"Birding with Charlie Parker" obsesses over "little pieces": "your hands enter the earth as fifteen / petals of the rose" (66), "The fourteen pieces of your instrument" (67), "the interstices of the floor" (67). Birdland looks "just like the Inferno," a Hell with "Bugles painted red" and "BLACK LIGHTNING" (67). Against this ruin, Parker knows his defense can only be small: bits of motion sickness pills, minimal nourishment, and dreams of the Mediterranean.

Howard Hart allows the reader to visualize Parker through evocative images set in clubs and street scenes, mixing these narratives with abstractions that might be equated with jazz. Bob Kaufman, on the other hand, moved still further away from the narrative voice and tried more directly to make the words themselves sound like jazz music. He was also, at the last, consumed by the magnificent presence of Charlie Parker. One of the most reclusive poets from this century, Kaufman lived his life much like the stereotypical jazz musician of the time: addicted to nightlife, to drugs, and to the avowedly non-academic, non-self-promoting world of the arts. "The musical form most associated with Kaufman is bebop," writes Maria Damon in her chapter about him in *The Dark End of the Street.*

Kaufman, one of whose epithets is "original bebop man," refers to Parker in a number of veiled and explicit ways...; clearly he felt an affinity for Parker's breathlessly manic music and the flamboyant, addictive, and visionary personal style of the "sweet bird of sabotage." (69)

Damon has firm ground to support her stance that "Kaufman's work reflects bebop's phrasing" (69), for despite the pitfalls often yielded by such analogies Kaufman's broken syntax, flurries of imagery, and conscious rejection of standard narrative all seem analogous to the bebop revolution of music.[13] "Jazz does not merely provide thematic material for the poet," explains Henry C. Lacey in his essay "In Memory of Bob Kaufman":

It provides also a compositional model for the seemingly spontaneous, rapid-fire lines of the Beat writer: Kaufman's poem to Charlie Parker, "Walking Parker Home" [from *Solitudes Crowded with Loneliness*], is a classic exemplification of the poet's complete appropriation of jazz theme and idiom. The poet concludes this work with a frequently invoked theme, i.e. jazz as a sustaining, transforming, vitally necessary, yes, sacred creation. (15)

Kaufman, who named his son Parker, consciously chose not to present "Walking Parker Home" as a dramatic narrative of the walk; rather, the poem re-creates a series of emotive, sensory images that combine parts of Bird's life ("Birdland nights," the influences of Coleman Hawkins and Lester Young) with the imagistic collision of beauty and horror ("visions of spikes," "beauty speared into greedy ears," and "raging fires of love").[14] "Walking Parker Home" suggests the spontaneity of jazz, with abstracted imagery and fragmented lines thrust against each other, and the speaker becomes engulfed by the music, as though jazz itself was not an invisible art form but something still more tangible—an art form that could be touched, embraced, ingested. As the poem concludes, the speaker's passion for Parker overwhelms him:

> In that Jazz corner of life
> Wrapped in a mist of sound
> His legacy, our Jazz-tinted dawn
> Wailing his triumphs of oddly begotten dreams
> Inviting the nerveless to feel once more
> That fierce dying of humans consumed
> In raging fires of Love. (5)

Throughout *Solitudes Crowded with Loneliness*, the concept of jazz as spiritual sustenance becomes an ever-present motif.[15] In "San Francisco Beat" he refers to "Eating metal jazz" (31); in "Blues Notes" Ray Charles "hurls chunks of raw soul" (20); and in the first two stanzas of "Mingus" he similarly describes jazz as something that can be physically digested:

> String-chewing bass players,
> Plucking rolled balls of sound
> From the jazz-scented night.
>
> Feeding hungry beat seekers
> Finger-shaped heartbeats,
> Driving ivory nails
> Into their greedy eyes. (27)

Some of Kaufman's generically abstract statements are often less interesting than his achievements with rhythm, but at its best the synesthesia and juxtaposition of opposites in Kaufman's poetry created refreshingly new sounds and startling imagery, much of which, to quote the opening line from "San Francisco Beat," are "Hidden in the eye of jazz" (*Solitudes*, 31). Few poets have ever equaled Kaufman's passion for the physicality of Charlie Parker as a man and a musician. One might say that Kaufman resculpted the muscular lines of bebop into verbal jazz imagery.

The vitality of Bird necessarily transformed the man into a larger figure, and, at a time when poets searched for mentors, it is particularly understandable that they would turn to Parker for inspiration. In "They Dig Booze, Jazz and Sex," an article for the *New York Daily News*, Edward Klein wrote, "Jazz is the music of the Beat Generation and the late jazz-man Charlie Parker is their god" (McDarrah, 180). Too often, however, the poets reduced their god to a cliché. If one looks at the poetry from the fifties in general—and considers the relentless, driving, forceful musical lines of Charlie Parker—it is a bit of a shock to realize how so much of the poetry written in his honor fails to capture the spirit of his music or his personality.

This had something to do, I think, with the racial discrepancy between the subject and the writers. Pioneered and propagated by African-Americans, bebop consciously rejected the commercialized white dance bands from the thirties. It revolutionized not merely the aesthetics of jazz but the social implications as well. Yet the most-popular jazz poets from the fifties were almost exclusively white writers who, with some exceptions such as Hart's "Moonlight on the Ganges," did not address issues of race. In contrast to these younger writers, Langston Hughes emerged once again as a popular voice in modern poetry, and his experiments with jazz poetry at the end of his career paved the way for the more overtly political poems by African-American writers in the sixties.

The faddish Beat movement of the fifties allowed Hughes to popularize himself through public readings, but the Beats were not entirely responsible for Hughes's popularity, for the fifties also marked a flowering of his own jazz-related work. Yes, the rhythms and sensory images of jazz appeared in Hughes's poetry as early as his first collection in 1926. "But it is in *Montage of a Dream Deferred* (1951) and *Ask Your Mama* (1961)," explains Onwuchekwa Jemie,

that Hughes attains the highest peaks of complexity in his life-long effort to integrate his poetry with music. *Montage* is written in the powerful be-bop mode of the mid-40s and the 50s, and *Ask Your Mama* is a straight jazz-poem sequence set to the accompaniment of jazz and blues. (24)[16]

Montage of a Dream Deferred, which Hughes later reprinted in its entirety in his *Selected Poems* (1959), pulses with the blues, boogie-woogie, brief riffs and longer solos, and the individual poems indeed form a montage of imagery that, more than any of his previous collections, achieves the feeling of jazz. The book opens with "Dream Boogie," where the speaker keeps coaxing the reader to listen with greater sensitivity to jazz, to hear what is beneath the beat—the dream deferred. The poem bubbles with exclamation marks, and with political observations that challenge the reader to analyze this "HAPPY BEAT."[17]

With its indented questions and exclamations, the poem zigzags like the rhythms that inspired it. But the tension of the lines is secondary to the tension of the unfinished sentences and jarring questions, which, generally speaking, represent the direct challenge presented by *Montage*: to consider the psychological conscience of the jazz musician, "something underneath," and not to dismiss the music merely as mindless entertainment. As a stand against cultural misinterpretation, the book confronts issues of race and oppression virtually ignored in the jazz poetry by the white writers of the time.[18]

One of the less obvious clues to this discrepancy lies in the hyphenated word, "RE-BOP!" which Hughes once stated was merely a watered-down version of bebop. In an often-quoted passage from "Simple on Bop Music" (*The Book of Negro Folklore*, 1958), Hughes's fictitious character responds to the claim that "Re-bop certainly sounds like scat":

"No," said Simple, "Daddy-o, you are wrong. Besides, it is not *RE*-bop. It is Be-Bop."
"What's the difference?" I asked. "Between *RE* and *BE?*"
"A lot," said Simple. "Re-Bop is an imitation like most of the white boys play. Be-Bop is the real thing like the colored boys play." (608)

Simple explains that bebop originated in racist police beatings:

"Everytime a cop hits a Negro with his billy, that old stick says, 'BOP! BOP! . . . BE-BOP! . . . MOP!! . . . BOP!' And that Negro hollers, 'Ooool-ya-koo! Ou-o-o-!'
"Old cop just beats on, 'MOP! MOP! . . . BE-BOP! MOP!' That's where Be-Bop came from, beaten right out of some Negro's head into them horns and saxophones and guitars and piano keys that plays it." (609)

Did Hughes himself regard bop as a revolutionary protest music? Was Simple's statement strictly fiction, or did the character reflect Hughes's equations of racially-motivated violence with the sounds of Charlie Parker, Dizzy Gillespie, Bud Powell, and other bebop musicians from the forties and fifties?

Simple's discussion might best be seen as part of an internal dialogue within Hughes, where, on the one hand, the music did indeed reflect an African-American rebellion and the disturbing sounds of post-World War II America; but on the other, bebop was also a nonpolitical creative act that gave him enormous pleasure. The latter is best seen in Hughes's *The First Book of Jazz* (1955), which he originally considered a work for children. The book chronicles the evolution of jazz from jug bands to bebop, and the refrain—from the title of the first chapter to the final line—is that musicians play jazz "just for fun." The section on bebop, as with most of the entries, lasts for only one page (two brief paragraphs), and some of the information seems curious at best: Among the innovators of bebop, Hughes lists Lester Young; he does not include a single bass player, such as Charles Mingus; and he cites Dizzy Gillespie as the innovator of modern jazz, with Parker (among others) listed merely as followers.[19] Nowhere in this brief discussion does Hughes suggest that bebop was in fact a form of protest music, probably because this was to be a children's book and the editors, according to Hughes, became cautious, if not anxious, about his use of language.[20] Nevertheless, the second paragraph in his discussion of bebop is remarkably contrary to Simple's explanation:

Sometimes for fun, singers sing "oo-ya-koo" syllables to boppish backgrounds today, as Cab Calloway in the 1930's sang "hi-de-hi-de-ho-de-hey," meaning nothing, or as Lionel Hampton sang "hey-baba-re-bop" in 1940, or as Louis Armstrong used to sing "scat" syllables to his music in Chicago in the 1920's, or as Jelly Roll Morton shouted meaningless words to ragtime music in the early 1900's, or as the Mother Goose rhyme said, "Hey-diddle-diddle, the cat and the fiddle," even before that—for fun. Nonsense syllables are not new in poetry or music, but they are fun. (55)

The passage so glaringly contrasts Hughes's political statements that it may seem disingenuous. But these passages are best read in the context of poems such as "Dream Boogie," where Hughes successfully unites levity of the sound and the cultural politics of the time.

Ask Your Mama: 12 Moods for Jazz became Hughes's final jazz-related project, as well as the longest poem of his career. Unlike most of his poetry, which he tended to write in one sitting, Hughes spent several months drafting numerous versions of the poem and carefully choosing the proper musical accompaniment that appeared italicized in the margins (Rampersad, Vol. II, 317).[21] "At the heart of his poem was anger," explains Rampersad,

but the crux of its form was insult. Specifically, the form invoked was the "Dozens," a ritual of insult, collectively played by both males and females, prominent in black culture. Sometimes "clean," the Dozens were also often "dirty," involving the most sordid accusations of incest and adultery. (317)

In the poem, the Dozens represented the use of words to avoid violence, and jazz became its musical counterpart, as seen, for example, in the poem "Dream Boogie" and other works. At times, Hughes referred to the music and the musicians as though invoking spirits of salvation, as in "Jazztet Muted," which cites both Bird and the alto saxophonist Ornette Coleman, a pioneer in free jazz who extended many of the principles established by Charlie Parker. Music becomes not merely sound but the ghetto itself, and the speaker cries: "HELP ME, YARDBIRD!" (77–78).

Hughes dedicated Ask Your Mama to Louis Armstrong—"the greatest horn blower of them all"—and Rampersad comments,

In this dedication to a black jazz horn blower, to a Joshua whose music, like all jazz music, threatened to blow down the walls of America in the battle of blacks for freedom, Langston further signified the spirit of rebellion and even of apocalypse at the core of the work. (319)

But *Ask Your Mama* does not end with major revolution; as Jemie later points out, the dream remains deferred (96), and though Hughes most certainly stood as a founding father for the more outspoken jazz poets of the sixties, Hughes's own literary endeavors rarely allowed for outbursts with a dramatically loud, revolutionary voice. Only after Hughes's death did his deferred dream, which he discussed more and more frequently in relation to jazz, begin to explode in African-American verse.

Langston Hughes died on March 12, 1967, twelve years to the day after Charlie Parker. Organizers of the service asked pianist Randy Weston to perform, and "Afterward, as the mourners gathered outside Benta's [Funeral Chapel]," Rampersad explains,

many were not sure what to make of the jazz and blues funeral. "O Lord, Randy, I was so confused," [the jazz singer] Lena Horne confessed. "There I was, tapping my toes and humming while y'all played, and I didn't know whether to cry for Langston or clap my hands and laugh!" (*Vol. II*, 425)

For Hughes, however, the union of grief and humor would not have seemed puzzling whatsoever. Both emotions, as simultaneous opposites, were integral to the blues and jazz, to African-American society in general. That is why he allowed his most famous comedian, Simple, to deliver the exegesis on bebop and racism, and why so many of his blues poems incorporated laughter with crying.

And Charlie Parker, who could infuse melancholy lines with a startling release of that sadness, understood this as well. He was a genius, certainly one of the most important artists of this century—so brilliant, in fact, that many listeners could not acknowledge anything beyond perfection in his playing. But, like all artists, even Parker experienced various failures. In 1946, just prior to a mental collapse, he recorded for Dial records, then run by Ross Russell. As many music critics have noted, Parker's emotional and physical decline can be clearly heard on his version of "Lover Man," and Parker never forgave Russell for issuing the cut. Yet for months after the Dial release, musicians tried meticulously to copy Bird's solo, proving that, apart from the poets of the period, there were many musicians as well as who didn't fully grasp his artistry or humanity.

Five years later, however, Parker once again recorded "Lover Man," and on this session he played with absolute authority. The difference, in fact, is somewhat overwhelming. Parker sustains his intensity while at the same time maintaining complete command of his craft. The brilliance of his phrasing actualizes what Hughes tried to express in words: how some of the most alluring and memorable jazz combines grief and joy. At the song's bridge, Parker leans into the slow melody with legato, gives a wink by quoting from "Mean to Me," returns to the smooth lyric, and then, with passionate virtuosity, releases a flurry of sixty-forth notes, fluid, precisely on the beat.

NOTES

1. Russell's book, as Gary Giddins has pointed out, "is often more roman à clef than biography" ([6]). The actual Benedetti recordings were presumed lost for many years, and their mysterious disappearance added to the mystique of Russell's book. Recently discovered and remastered, they are currently available through Mosaic records on a ten-CD collection tilted *The Complete Dean Benedetti Recordings of Charlie Parker*, which, apart from presenting the music itself, resolves some of the speculation about the recordings (for example, Benedetti did not, as most people believed, use a wire recorder.)

2. Trussell's obscure collection deserves mention mainly because of the bibliographic reference in Kennington's *The Literature of Jazz* (it is listed as one of only five jazz poetry sources), as well as his representation in *The Jazz Word* (1960), which includes very few jazz poems. For the latter, the editors wisely chose "3 A.M. Jazz Clarinet," written in 1941 and the first titled poem in *After Hours Poetry*. Despite its clichés, the poem achieves a gentle lilt, and one can indeed imagine the lonely clarinet sound emerging from the desolate morning hours. It may not be a spectacular poem, but it is spectacularly stronger than the others in the collection.

3. Trussell's undeniable enthusiasm for jazz merely sounds trite when he transposes his gushing praise into metered verse, as in his homages to Jelly Roll Morton ("Way back when jazz music / Was really startin' / No band equaled that led / By Jelly Roll Morton" [28]), Lester Young ("When Lester plays ballads / Then time stands still / The ultimate kick—/ Supreme jazz thrill" [31]), or Duke Ellington ("Of all the orchestras / In the history of jazz / I love the one most / That Duke Ellington has" [35]).

This ineffective use of rhyme and meter did not, unfortunately, terminate in the forties and fifties. In 1988 R. W. Otto published *Musical Poems*, primarily poems consisting of two quatrains, and of all the books of poetry that concentrate on jazz-related poems this is the worst. Parker dominates as the subject ("Charlie Parker," "Now Is the Time," "Charlie Parker Died," "Be-bop"), but the poems do not capture the energy of the music, the mystique of the musicians, or the spirit of the era itself.

4. These were by no means the only musicians mentioned in his many interviews and essays. In a discussion with Allen Ginsberg from 1963, for example, Creeley discussed how he wrote the different sections of *The Island* to the music of Bud Powell, John Coltrane, Nancy Wilson, and Billie Holiday (*Contexts*, 31–32).

Pancho Savery, in his reflection " 'The Character of the Speech': 56 Things for Robert Creeley," finds it curious that Creeley "doesn't mention Monk" (Terrell,

225). In fact, Creeley mentions Monk several times, once referring to him as "the kind of man who not only survived but continued right through this whole period" (*Contexts*, 48). Although this contradicts Savery's statement, it also supports many of his intriguing parallels between Monk and Creeley (see Terrell, 224–226, 228–230, 236).

5. In 1968, reflecting on his years at Black Mountain, Olson said, "Boy, there was no poetic. It was Charlie Parker. Literally, it was Charlie Parker. He was the Bob Dylan of the Fifties" (*Muthulogos* 71 Vol. 2), and Sherman Paul, responding to this statement, writes, "Charlie Parker reminds us that Olson more than any of his predecessors stresses breath" (39). There is also a brief reference to "jass" in Section IV of Olson's *The Maximus Poems* in which the poet writes, "jass is gysm" (193); Steven Tracy comments, "Olson's use of the line is in the context of his seeing the actuarial, the statistical calculator of risks and premiums, as the source of the 'Isms' of 'Vulgar Socialization.' The line puns, then, on the reference to vulgarity and on the 'ism' sound of 'gysm,' while referring to a close relationship between jazz and sexuality that Olson compares to the relationship between the actuarial and vulgar socialization" (264–265, n. 176).

What most critics fail to mention, however, is that Olson knew virtually nothing about Charlie Parker; "What he knew about Bird," explains Don Cooper, a former student of Olson's, as well as a jazz composer and bassist, "he learned from Creeley—and I'm not convinced Creeley knew a whole lot about Parker, either. Music was a bug in Olson's ear—all music, not just Charlie Parker—and I'm quoting verbatim when I say 'a bug in my ear' " (interview).

6. The obscure reference "(Brugm. I. §638)" probably refers to Karl Brugmann's *Elements of the Comparative Grammar of the Indo-Germanic Languages*; section 638 of volume 1 discusses Aryan palatalisation. Creeley may be referring to the complexity of Brugmann's definitions.

7. Hartman's book alternates the focus of the seven chapters between musicians and writers, but the general thrust of *Jazz Text* emphasizes the shared elements of improvisation and orality. The second chapter concentrates on Creeley.

8. Interestingly enough, Creeley sent the final revision of "Le Fou" in a letter to Olson dated July 7, 1950, and on the bottom of the page he added in pencil, "Thank you—Charles Parker. Et tu—Thelonius [*sic*] Bach" (*Vol. II*, 69).

9. It should be noted that Spicer was not truly a jazz enthusiast and what he knew about jazz he learned from his friend, Steve Jonas, a relatively obscure poet and musician. Jonas's poetry is filled with allusions to jazz, and his experiments with rhythm, I think, are founded in a jazz aesthetic. One of his best jazz poems, an homage to Ornette Coleman titled "One of Three Musicians," was reprinted in *The Jazz Poetry Anthology*.

10. In terms of poetics, Spicer's implied statement sounds much more mature and engaging than the rather obvious alternative as seen in the opening lines of Kerouac's "240th Chorus": "Musically as important as Beethoven, / Yet not regarded as such at all" (*Mexico City Blues*, 242).

11. Maria Damon reads this reference simply as "a characteristic sexual pun" (184), but there is a lot more at stake in this discussion than mere bathroom humor.

12. This discrepancy continues to be an issue. In Clint Eastwood's mediocre movie, *Bird* (1988), for example, Parker has no relationships besides his marriage

to Chan. Naturally, this outraged the African-American community and prompted responses such as Marilyn Marshall's article, "The *Real* Charlie Parker: What the Movie Didn't Tell You," from *Ebony* magazine (1989). Gary Giddins's *Celebrating Bird* tries to remedy this imbalance somewhat by focusing on Parker's first wife, Rebecca Parker Davis.

13. Damon is less convincing, however, when she discusses jazz itself. Her statement "The musical trademark of bebop is its fragmentary, atonal treatment of melody" (69), for example, does not seem absolutely accurate, because bebop did not treat melody atonally, nor was it strictly "fragmentary."

14. Patrick James Brown also notes the implicit irony in the poem: "For years, Parker was obscured by the more popular Hawkins and Lester [Young], whom he admired and yet resented. . . . Ironically, 'Birdland,' the New York City night club named for Parker, banished him for his abusive conduct and language; he was not allowed inside of the club which had been named for him" (133).

15. Aside from *Solitudes* (1965), Kaufman published two other major collections of poetry, *The Golden Sardine* (1967) and *The Ancient Rain: Poems 1956–1978* (1981). Although the publication dates might appear to place him primarily as a poet of the sixties, Kaufman, in fact, wrote most of his poems in the fifties. The delay in publication reflects, in part, his desire to remain anonymous and his intent to maintain the oral nature of his craft.

16. Jemie's essay "Jazz, Jive and Jam" from *Langston Hughes: An Introduction to the Poetry* (1976) remains one of the most intelligent and readable essays on Hughes and jazz music, and his discussion of *Montage* and *Ask Your Mama* persuasively compares these works to jazz music.

17. For his *Selected Poems*, Hughes replaced the capital letters with italics.

18. This is not to say, however, that these writers were unaware of such issues, nor were they unable or unwilling to interpret the sounds of modern jazz. In fact, their interpretation of bebop as a protest movement may very well have been, in some cases, the reason why it was not addressed in the verse. Kenneth Rexroth, for example, once said about modern jazz, "People get tired of being told musically, 'You motherfucker, you kept me in slavery for three hundred years' " (Meltzer, 28). Implicit in such a statement is enormous racial anxiety.

19. In 1956 Hughes modestly wrote to Arna Bontemps that "what I really know about Jazz would fill a thimble!" (Bontemps and Hughes, 349), but errors such as these—despite the editorial work done by a number of jazz scholars—show that Hughes did, in fact, have gaps in his understanding of jazz history.

20. Arnold Rampersad explains: "Not the least of his troubles with the book on jazz came from his squeamish editors. 'Have to be SO careful, no risqué titles or lyrics,' he wrote Arna Bontemps [on July 4, 1954]. 'These children's editors! Much more naive than the children!' " (Rampersad, *Vol. II*, 232).

21. Rampersad states that Hughes "fashioned musical cues integral to his poetic meaning" by "consciously taking his lead from Vachel Lindsay's *The Congo*" (*Vol. II*, 317). He also notes that "Each section, too, was freighted with allusions . . . out of the heart of lived black American culture, and that parodied and thus challenged the modernist poetry of the arcane as practiced by Melvin Tolson and others" (*Vol. II*, 317–318).

REFERENCES

Bontemps, Arna, and Langston Hughes. *Arna Bontemps-Langston Hughes Letters 1925–1967*. Ed. Charles H. Nichols. New York: Dodd, Mead, 1980.

Brown, Patrick James. "Jazz Poetry: Definition, Analysis, and Performance." Diss. University of Southern California, 1978.

Brugmann, Karl. *Elements of the Comparative Grammar of the Indo-Germanic Languages*. Trans. Joseph Wright. New York: Westermann, 1988.

Cerulli, Dom, Burt Korall, and Mort Nasatir, eds. *The Jazz Word*. New York: Ballantine, 1960.

Cooper, Don. Telephone interview. 6 Feb. 1993.

Creeley, Robert. *A Quick Graph: Collected Notes and Essays*. San Francisco: Four Seasons Foundation, 1970.

———. *The Collected Poems of Robert Creeley*. Berkeley: University of California, 1982.

———. *Contexts of Poetry: Interviews 1961–1971*. Ed. Donald Allen. Bolinas, Calif.: Four Seasons Foundation, 1973.

———. "Ways of Looking." *Poetry*. 98 (June 1961): 192–198.

Damon, Maria. *The Dark End of the Street: Margins in American Vanguard Poetry*. Minneapolis: University of Minnisota, 1993.

Ford, Kenneth. *Poetry for Jazz*. Carmel: Zocalo, 1959.

Giddins, Gary. *Celebrating Bird: The Triumph of Charlie Parker*. New York: Beech Tree, 1987.

Hart, Howard. *Selected Poems: Six Sets, 1951–1983*. Berkeley, Calif.: City Miner, 1984.

Hartman, Charles O. *Jazz Text: Voice and Improvisation in Poetry, Jazz, and Song*. Princeton: Princeton University Press, 1991.

Hughes, Langston. *Ask Your Mama: 12 Moods for Jazz*. New York: Knopf, 1961.

———. *Famous Negro Music Makers*. New York: Dodd, Mead, 1955.

———. *The First Book of Jazz*. New York: Franklin Watts, 1955.

———. *Montage of a Dream Deferred*. New York: Henry Holt, 1951.

———. *Selected Poems*. New York: Knopf, 1959.

Hughes, Langston, and Arna Bontemps, eds. *The Book of Negro Folklore*. New York: Dodd, Mead, 1958.

Jemie, Onwuchekwa. *Langston Hughes: An Introduction to the Poetry*. New York: Columbia University Press, 1965.

Kaufman, Bob. *The Ancient Rain: Poems 1956–1978*. New York: New Directions, 1981.

———. *The Golden Sardine*. San Francisco: City Lights, 1967.

———. *Solitudes Crowded with Loneliness*. New York: New Directions, 1965.

Kennington, Donald, and Danny L. Read. *The Literature of Jazz: A Critical Guide*. 2nd Ed., Rev. Chicago: American Library Association, 1980.

Kerouac, Jack. *Mexico City Blues*. New York: Grove, 1959.

———. *On the Road*. New York: Viking, 1957.

———. *Poetry for the Beat Generation*. With Steve Allen on piano. Rhino, R2 70939–A, 1990. (Originally released in 1959.)

————. *The Subterraneans*. New York: Grove, 1958.

Lacey, Henry C. "In Memory of Bob Kaufman: A Son of Rue Miro 1925–1986." *Beatitude Poetry International*. Vol. 1 (April 1992): 14–16.

Marshall, Marilyn. "The *Real* Charlie Parker: What the Movie Didn't Tell You." *Ebony* (January 1989): 128, 130, 132.

McDarrah, Fred W., ed. *Kerouac and Friends: A Beat Generation Album*. New York: William Morrow, 1985.

Meltzer, David, ed. *The San Francisco Poets*. New York: Ballantine, 1971.

Olson, Charles. *The Maximus Poems*. Ed. George F. Butterick. Berkeley: University of California, 1983.

————. *Muthulogos: The Collected Lectures and Interviews*. 2 Volumes. Ed. George F. Butterick. Bolinas, Calif.: Four Seasons Foundation, 1978.

————. *Selected Writings*. Ed. Robert Creeley. New York: New Directions, 1966.

Olson, Charles, and Robert Creeley. *Charles Olson and Robert Creeley: The Complete Correspondence*. 9 Volumes. Ed. George F. Butterick. Santa Barbara: Black Sparrow, 1980–1990.

Otto, R. W. *Musical Poems*. New York: Vantage, 1988.

Parker, Charlie. *The Complete Dean Benedetti Recordings of Charlie Parker*. Mosaic MD7–129.

Paul, Sherman. *Olson's Push*. Baton Rouge: Louisiana University Press, 1978.

Rampersad, Arnold. *The Life of Langston Hughes*. 2 Volumes. New York: Oxford University Press, 1986, 1988.

Rexroth, Kenneth. *The Alternative Society: Essays from the Other World*. New York: Herder and Herder, 1970.

Russell, Ross. *Bird Lives! The High Life and Hard Times of Charlie Parker*. New York: Charter House, 1973.

Shapiro, Nat, and Nat Hentoff, eds. *Hear Me Talkin' To Ya*. New York: Rinehard and Co., 1955.

Spicer, Jack. *The Collected Books of Jack Spicer*. Santa Barbara: Black Sparrow, 1980.

Terrell, Carroll F., ed. *Robert Creeley: The Poet's Workshop*. Orono, Maine: University of Maine, 1984.

Tracy, Steven C. *Langston Hughes and the Blues*. Urbana and Chicago: University of Illinois, 1988.

Trussell, Jake. *After Hours Poetry*. Kingsville, Tex.: Kingsville, 1958.

6

The John Coltrane Poem

Meditations
Expressions
A Love Supreme
(*I lay in solitary confinement, July 67*
Tanks rolling thru Newark
& whistled all I knew of Trane
my knowledge heartbeat
& he was dead
they
said.
　　　　　　　—Amiri Baraka

you tuck the roots in the earth,
turn back, and move
by river through the swamps
singing: a love supreme, a love supreme;
what does it all mean?
　　　　　　　—Michael S. Harper

September 15, 1963, Birmingham, Alabama. Less than three weeks prior to that Sunday, the Civil Rights Movement had been energized by the triumphant March on Washington, and, still nurtured by Martin Luther King, Jr.'s dream of equality, hundreds of African-Americans filled the Sixteenth Street Baptist Church where they had congregated before to organize protests. No one paid much attention to Robert Edward Chambliss, known as "Dynamite Bob" to his fellow Klansmen, who people later remembered had been loitering near the church. Shortly after ten in the morning, the church basement splintered into shards from detonated sticks of dynamite that wounded several of the parishioners and killed four young girls. Three of them were fourteen years old, the fourth only eleven.[1]

Everything about the murders, but particularly the innocence of the victims, induced the expected agony and appropriate outrage, not merely within the Birmingham community but across the nation. But the bombing had also temporarily crushed the momentum of the Civil Rights Movement. "It was a great moment of fulfillment, when Martin gave his 'I Have a Dream' speech," said Coretta Scott King in reflection,

and we really felt the sense of progress, that people came together, black and white, even though the South was totally segregated. . . . And then, a few weeks later, came this bombing in Birmingham, with four innocent little girls. Then you realized how intense the opposition was, and that it would take a lot more than what was being done to change the situation. (Hampton and Fayer, 174)

King himself delivered the eulogy emphasizing "the martyred heroines of a holy crusade for freedom and human dignity" while at the same time expressing his outrage: "These children—unoffending; innocent and beautiful—were the victims of one of the most vicious, heinous crimes ever perpetrated against humanity" (Washington, 221).

Shortly after this church bombing, the tenor saxophonist John Coltrane composed his tune "Alabama" in homage to the tragedy, and recorded it on November 18, 1963, just two months after the bombing.[2] According to various writers, none of whom cites primary sources, Coltrane incorporated not only his own emotional response but the rhythms in King's eulogy as well.[3] Although this song might be considered an overt political gesture, Coltrane throughout his career made no direct statements about his association with the Civil Rights Movement. Nevertheless, the outspoken African-American poets of the sixties adopted Coltrane's sound as a musical embodiment of black nationalism in the United States, and some of the most explosive poetry from that period is steeped in the music of that time.

Born in North Carolina in 1926, Coltrane spent his life in a relentless exploration of musical ideas and sounds. His career is often separated, roughly, into three periods: from the 1950s through 1960, from 1960 to 1965, and from 1965 to his death in 1967—each marking a step in Coltrane's development toward the freest forms of jazz and, on a personal level, the most spiritual forms of expression. He began as a sideman for bebop pioneers, recording with Dizzy Gillespie's orchestra as early as 1949. In the mid-fifties, Coltrane became a member of the Miles Davis quintet, and in 1957 he worked closely with Thelonious Monk, whose challenging compositions and musical sensibilities extended Coltrane's understanding of harmonics and alternative chordal progressions. Shortly thereafter Coltrane began recording as a leader on such outstanding albums as *Soultrane* (1957), *Traneing In* (1958), *Settin' the Pace* (1958), and, perhaps his greatest triumph prior to 1960, *Blue Train* (1957).

But his first major transition came in 1960, when he began to shape and control with maturity his driving, intimidatingly rapid musical phrases. At this time, he established what became known as the "classic quartet": Coltrane on tenor and soprano saxophones, McCoy Tyner on piano, Jimmy Garrison on bass, and the explosive Elvin Jones on drums. From 1960 to 1965, the quartet recorded many albums, three of which have frequently inspired poets: *My Favorite Things* (1960), *Coltrane "Live" at Birdland* featuring "Alabama" (1964), and *A Love Supreme* (1964), a virtual anthem for poets such as Michael Harper.

The new sound of the quartet featured an unmatched, percussive pulse generated in part by Jones's unfailing energy. Coltrane enhanced and countered the almost overpowering rhythm section with his elastic, dexterous use of harmonics. In 1963, Amiri Baraka (then known as LeRoi Jones) wrote,

the notes that Trane was playing in the solo became more than just one note following another, in whatever placement, to make a melody. They, the notes, came so fast and with so many overtones and undertones, that they had the effect of a piano player striking chords rapidly but somehow articulating separately each note in the chord and its vibrating sub-tones. (*Black Music* 59)

David Henderson's "Elvin Jones Gretsch Freak," subtitled "Coltrane at the Half-Note," attempts to capture that musical kinship between saxophonist and drummer. Henderson refers to the brand name of Elvin Jones's drum kit ("Gretsch") and improvises on the sound of that word until it becomes a noun, a verb, an adjective, and, most important, a sound:

```
Coltrane steps the catwalk
                elvin jones drums gretsch
                gretsch shimmy and shout
elvin drums a 1939 ford
99 pushing miles per hour   /    shoving barefoot driver
                in the heats   /
Coltrane   /    Jones
riffing              face to face
instrument charge
          stools to kneecap
many faceted rhythm structure      to      tomahawk
gretsch rocks 'n rolls          gretsch rattles (53–54)
```

From 1965 until his death in 1967, Coltrane became a pioneering figure in Free jazz in his search, as John Litweiler put it, for a still greater "release from rhythmic and harmonic constraints" (100). By 1966 both Tyner and Jones left the group and "were replaced by the light touch and ambiguous harmonic and rhythmic relationship of Alice Coltrane" and Rashied Ali (Litweiler, 101). For a brief period, Coltrane featured both Ali and Jones on drums. The tenor saxophonist Pharoah Sanders also became a permanent member of the group, and the freedom of Coltrane's sound reached its most extreme shortly before his death, as witnessed on *Interstellar Space* (1967), which he recorded with only Ali for rhythmic support.

Kimberly W. Benston's essay "Late Coltrane: A Re-membering of Orpheus" addresses the profundity of Coltrane's search for new sound, how he achieved this only "after many often tortuous dissolutions, reformations, and recrystallizations of approach as the 'heaviest spirit' (Imamu Baraka's encomium) traveled the road from apprentice to rebel to creative master" (770).[4] "Ultimately," Benston continues, "passages in Trane's music became so bright and so piercing that the sounds seemed to be words" (770), and later in the essay he notes,

The thought of giving to words and prosody values equivalent to music is an ancient one, in African and Afro-American as well as Western culture. But with modern black literature, it assumes the force of a specific idea: the notion that black language leads *toward* music. . . . This belief contains the powerful suggestions that music is the ultimate lexicon, that language, when truly apprehended, aspires to the condition of music and is brought, by the poet's articulation of black vocality, to the threshold of that condition. (772–773)

A. B. Spellman's poem "Did John's Music Kill Him?" expresses a similar idea in a more concentrated expression: "trane's horn had words in it" (Cook and Henderson, 110).

Benston points out that "The 'Coltrane poem' has, in fact, become an unmistakable genre in black poetry" (773), and this is certainly supported by Stephen Henderson's *Understanding the New Black Poetry* (1973), which includes a number of Coltrane-related poems. Some critics, such as Henry Lacey, go so far as to say that "the poem in homage to John Coltrane became [in the Sixties] an expected piece in the repertoire of the Black poet" (12), and this attitude prompted Sam Greenlee to write rather bitterly in his "Memorial for Trane" (1971): "Yeah, man, / I'll help out / with the / memorial for / Trane. / But, I wonder / how come / a people / who dig life / so much / spend / so much / time / praising the dead?" (29).[5]

Coltrane was forty when he died of liver cancer, and most of the early Coltrane poems appeared between 1967 and 1969, as posthumous reflections.[6] His premature death became immediately identifiable with the profound losses of other African-American leaders, most notably Martin

Luther King, Jr. and Malcolm X. Frank Kofsky's *Black Nationalism and the Revolution in Music* (1970) compares Coltrane to Malcolm X time and time again in their depth of influence on African-American culture, and, more important, as men who shared a desire to revolt against racial and social oppression. Kofsky's interview with Coltrane from 1966, which Kofsky includes in his book, presented questions with a direct socialist slant, as though awaiting the proper answers to supplement his general premise about the Civil Rights Movement and Coltrane's music. Kofsky spends much time discussing "Malcolm's great symbolic significance for the new generation of black musicians and his own evident identification with the black jazz artist" (67). Yet when Kofsky interviewed the musician he "worshipped as a saint or even a god" in 1966, Coltrane side-stepped many of the loaded questions in an effort to emphasize his primary concern—the creative act.[7] Here are some excerpts from that interview:

Kofsky: Some musicians have said that there's a relationship between some of Malcolm's ideas and the music, especially the new music. Do you think there's anything in that?

Coltrane: Well, I think that music, being an expression of the human heart, or of the human being itself, does express just what *is* happening. I feel it expresses the whole thing—the whole of human experience at the particular time that it is being expressed.

. . . .

Kofsky: The people who use *that* phrase ["the new black music"] argue that jazz is particularly closely related to the black community and it's an expression of what's happening there. That's why I asked you about your reaction to Malcolm X.

Coltrane: Well, I think it's up to the individual musician, call it what you may, for any reason you may. Myself, I recognize the artist. I recognize an individual when I see his contribution; and when I know a man's sound, well, to me that's him, that's this man. That's the way I look at it. Labels, I don't bother with. (225)

Whatever uncertainty may linger regarding Coltrane's political views, there is none about the common association (as seen in the poetry of that decade) between his music (particularly from the mid-sixties) and the black revolution as led by Malcolm X. Ebon's *Revolution: A Poem* (1968), for example, begins with "Legacy: In Memory of 'Trane," and Amiri Baraka's "AM/TRAK" also makes the analogy in no uncertain terms: "Trane was the spirit of the 60's / He was Malcolm X in New Super Bop Fire" (*Selected*, 336). In the liner notes for *Coltrane "Live" at Birdland* (1964), Baraka makes ironic, sweeping generalities about the United States in the early sixties: "One of the most baffling things about America is that despite its essentially vile profile, so much beauty continues to exist here" (*Black Music*, 63). Baraka interprets Coltrane's music in this light, linking the direct, aggressive sound of Coltrane's tenor with the political temperament of the time.

Baraka's association between jazz and socialist revolt is probably most clearly stated in *Dutchman*, his well-known play from 1964, in which the references to Bessie Smith and Charlie Parker could very easily be applied to John Coltrane:

Old bald-headed four-eyed ofays popping their fingers . . . and don't know yet what they're doing. They say, "I love Bessie Smith." And don't even understand that Bessie Smith is saying, "Kiss my ass, kiss my black unruly ass." . . . All the hip white boys scream for Bird. And Bird saying, "Up your ass, feeble-minded ofay! Up your ass." And they sit there talking about the tortured genius of Charlie Parker. Bird would've played not a note of music if he just walked up to East Sixty-seventh Street and killed the first ten white people he saw. (34–35)

The antagonistic, political interpretation of modern jazz can also be seen in his poem "Black Art," which he read on the drummer Sonny Murray's album, *Sonny's Time Now!* (1967):

> We want poems
> like fists beating niggers out of Jocks
> or dagger poems in the slimy bellies
> of the owner-jews. Black poems to
> smear on girdlemamma mulatto bitches
> whose brains are red jelly stuck
> between 'lizabeth taylor's toes. Stinking
> Whores! We want "poems that kill."
>
> (Baraka, 106)[8]

Infused with the political spirit of "Black Art" and *Dutchman*, Baraka's most ambitious Coltrane poem, "AM/TRAK," "is on one level a concise biography of John Coltrane," as Henry Lacey explains, "and traces the musician's apprenticeships in various bands, influences on his musical development, his battles with drugs and alcohol, the hostility of critics, and, finally, the triumphant achievement of the great John Coltrane Quartet" (14). Presented in five sections, "AM/TRAK" first introduces Coltrane's legacy with intense generalities: "scream History Love / Trane" (332). The second section sketches his early career, with an emphasis on demoralizing gigs at which he had to "walk the bars" while spouting honky-tonk licks, and his earliest musical heroes, "Rabbit, Cleanhead, Diz."[9] There is also a brief mention of alcohol abuse, all leading to his association with Davis's quintet: "Oh / scream—Miles / comes" (333). This is the link for section three, near the beginning of which we find, "Miles wd stand back and negative check / oh, he dug him—Trane" (333). The passage also includes one of many hostile reactions to Coltrane's innovative style: "Trane you blows too long" (334). Section four presents what Baraka calls "Coltrane's College"—the short-lived, astonishing collaborations with Thelonious Monk.

But it is in the fifth and final section, by far the longest, that the poem really opens up. Like Coltrane's musical explorations, which evolved with stunning rapidity after 1960, this passage in "AM/TRAK" begins with the establishment of the classic quartet ("The inimitable 4") and presents Coltrane as the sound of the times:

> black blower of the now
> The vectors from all sources—slavery, renaissance
> bop charlie parker,
> nigger absolute super-sane screams against reality
> course through him
> AS SOUND! (336)

For Baraka, as for so many of his contemporary African-American poets, Coltrane articulated the passion of a decade remembered for extreme expressions of and attacks against racism.[10] Having described these credentials, Baraka then summarizes Coltrane's career (the Philly bars, the years with Miles and Monk) and mentions important recordings (*"Meditations," "Expression," "A Love Supreme"*) before turning to his death in 1967, during the summer of the Newark riots, when Baraka was in jail: "I lay in solitary confinement."[11]

But the poem does not conclude with this tremendous sense of isolation, mistreatment, and loss. Instead, Coltrane becomes a martyr, an ever-present inspiration to whom Baraka turns while in jail, and, by implication, throughout his life:

> And yet last night I played *Meditations*
> & it told me what to do
> Live, you crazy mother
> fucker!
> Live!
>   & organize
>   yr shit
>   as rightly
>   burning! (337)

"The poet concludes," to quote Lacey again, "with the profoundly felt desire to approximate, in his life and art, the commitment, discipline, and beauty of John Coltrane's example, an example made more compelling because of the extent to which both lives—the poet's and musician's—have been characterized by change" (20).

The influence of the Black Mountain school may account for Baraka's dynamic use of form and fractured line breaks, but it is also possible to argue that the influence of jazz encouraged this sense of poetics and that Baraka's lineation is directly analogous to Coltrane's restructuring of musical sensibilities. This argument is proposed most forcefully in William Harris's *The Jazz Aesthetic: The Poetry and Poetics of Amiri Baraka* (1985). He begins by discussing Coltrane's version of "Nature Boy" from *The John Coltrane Quartet Plays* (1965):

Coltrane takes a weak Western form, a popular song, and murders it; that is, he mutilates and disembowels this shallow but bouncy tune by using discordant and aggressive sounds to attack and destroy the melody line. The angry black music devours and vomits up the fragments of the white corpse. (14)

Harris then compares Coltrane's method with the poet's:

Baraka also wants to take weak Western forms, rip them asunder, and create something new out of rubble. He transposes Coltrane's musical ideas to poetry, using them to turn white poetic forms backwards and upside down. This murderous impulse is behind all the forms of Baraka's aesthetic and art. (15)[12]

Baraka's influence, in his approach to "murdering" the Western forms of poetry and in his passion for jazz, can be seen in scores of African-American writers, including A. B. Spellman, who has also made great contributions as a jazz critic and scholar.[13] Spellman's poem, "Did John's Music Kill Him?" first appeared in Stephen Henderson's essay "Survival Motion" from *The Militant Black Writer in Africa and the United States*, a book co-written with Mercer Cook in 1969. In the first stanza, Spellman sketches the members of Coltrane's quintet—Garrison, Tyner, Jones, and Eric Dolphy on reeds—as a dramatic introduction for the poem's subject:

> then john. *little old lady*
> had a nasty mouth. *summertime*
> when the war is. *africa* ululating
> a line bunched up like itself
> into knots paints beauty black.

> (Cook and Henderson, 109)

The song titles trace back to Coltrane's first transition period—"Little Old Lady" from *Coltrane Jazz* (1960), "Summertime" from *My Favorite Things* (1960), and "Africa" from *Africa Brass* (1961)—and the poem maintains the stance that Coltrane unfailingly confronted the horrors of daily life and transformed them into haunting music.[14] Like Baraka's "AM/TRAK," the poem concludes with a gesture of spiritual rebirth:

so beat john's death words down
on me in the darker part
of evening. the black light issues
from him in the pit he made
around us. worms came clear
to me where i thought i had been
brilliant. o john death will
not contain you death
will not contain you

(Cook and Henderson, 109–110)

Askia Muhammad Touré's title poem from *JuJu* (dedicated to "John Coltrane, a Black Priest-prophet" and published in 1970), closes with a similar
expression: "and he is / NOT gone, for as I can see, can hear him still: my
Heart / my Soul my ALL vibrating—TRANE!" (16).

Using Spellman's poem as an entrée to his subject, Henderson writes,
"What Coltrane signifies for black people because of the breadth of his
vision and the incredible energy behind his spiritual quest, Malcolm X
signifies in another way—not as musician, but simply and profoundly as
black man, as Black Experience, and that experience in process of discov-
ering itself, of celebrating itself" (Cook and Henderson, 110). He then
compares Malcolm X to Martin Luther King, Jr.—"Nonviolence was not
natural. Self-defense was" (Cook and Henderson, 110)—and, with per-
suasive examples, shows how King's philosophy made him seem, at times,
out of touch with the general black populace. "The abstractions of broth-
erhood and universal love," Henderson writes, "were difficult to believe
in after a day with the Man, or after a night with the blues" (Cook and
Henderson, 110). Like Malcolm X's unflinching views on oppression, Coltrane's music represented an unsentimental look at humanity, and popular
songs of the times ("My Favorite Things," "Summertime," "Nature Boy")
became vehicles for his musical explorations. "John Coltrane like Malcolm," writes Jayne Cortez in her poem "How Long Has Trane Been
Gone?" (1969), was the "True image of Black Masculinity" (*Pissstained
Stairs*, n.p.).[15]

In his "Homage to John Coltrane" (*This Is Our Music*, 1969), the white
poet John Sinclair referred to Coltrane's "SCREAM / for the time" (n.p.),
and certainly one cannot deny that the sixties was a decade of anxiety for
all races. But in the Coltrane poetry, the "scream" is most often not for
"the time"; it is, instead, the angry expression of African-American demands for justice, for equality of opportunity. The bold verse of the sixties—unlike the understated poems by so many predecessors—
underscored the new forthrightness, the new militancy of the Civil Rights
cause.[16] The description of Coltrane's sound as a scream became, in many
cases, a way to vent outrage at the white establishment, as in Sonia San-

chez's "a/coltrane/poem" from *We a BaddDDD People* (1970). The poem
begins:

> my favorite things
> > is u/blowen
> > > yo/favorite/things.
> stretchen the mind
> > till it bursts past the con/fines of
> solo/en melodies.
> > to the many solos
> of the
> > mind/spirit. (69)

It continues in this relatively quiet voice (invoking the lullaby "are u sleepen / are u sleepen / brotha john / brotha john," which Sanchez notes in
the margin is "to be sung softly"). But in "the quiet / aftermath of assassinations" and "the massacre / of all blk / musicians," Sanchez attempts
to create a phonetic equivalent to the explosive sound of Coltrane's saxophone: "scrEEEccCHHHHH screeeeEEECHHHHHHH / sCReee-
EEECHHHHHH   SCREEEECCCCHHHH   /
SCREEEEEEEECCCHHHHHHHHHHHH / a lovesupremealovesupre-
mealovesupreme for our blk people" (69). This is followed by an expression of political fury, a direct interpretation of Coltrane's music:

> BRING IN THE WITE/MOTHA/fuckas
> ALL THE MILLIONAIRES/BANKERS/ol
> MAIN/LINE/ASS/RISTOCRATS (ALL
> THEM SO-CALLED BEAUTIFUL
> PEOPLE)
> > WHO HAVE KILLED
> WILL CONTINUE TO
> > KILL US WITH
> THEY CAPITALISM/18% OWNERSHIP
> OF THE WORLD.
> > YEH. U RIGHT
> THERE U ROCKEFELLERS. MELLONS
> > VANDERBILTS
> > > FORDS.
> > > > yeh.
> GITem.
> > PUSHem/PUNCHem/STOMPem. THEN
> LIGHT A FIRE TO
> > THEY pilgrim asses. (69–70)

More recently, Sanchez wrote of Malcolm X, "You see, what he said out
loud is what African-American people had been saying out loud forever
behind closed doors" (Hampton and Fayer, 254); in the sixties, Coltrane's

music, played "out loud," enabled poets of the time to break down the "closed doors" of African-American silence.

The dramatic tonal shift in "a/coltrane/poem" is not atypical for the Coltrane poems from the sixties, and in some ways the form mimics the sound of Coltrane who often began with a simply stated melodic line and then charged into his solos. Larry Neal's "Orishas" (*Black Boogaloo*, 1969), for example, begins almost serenely: "Is the eternal voice, Coltrane is" (26). Yet the poem goes on to express revolutionary aggression and outrage:

> The night is yours, you cloak, the armor
> of your souls, my brothers,
> battle-grooved vision locked in on the target
> shadows of the city do burning thing
> kill. kill. kill. ancestral demons
> swirl in the noise, swear in blood
> accept nothing less than the death of your enemies. (28–29)

Donald L. Graham (also known as Dante) begins his poem "soul" with condescension and anger for white musicians who, drawn to Coltrane's innovations, tried to appropriate a sound, even a culture, about which they knew nothing:

> coltrane must understand how
>   i feel when i hear
> some un-sunned-be-bop-jazz-man
>   try
>
> to find the cause of a man's hurt
>
> (Stephen Henderson, 322)

The second half of Graham's "Poem for Eric Dolphy" again broadcasts its radically anti-white stance, at the same time interpreting the "scream" of Dolphy's (and Coltrane's) horn:

> you sang for black babies in apartment
> buildings, drunks pissing in the halls
> and black chicks doing back-bends for
> pink men with slimy lips
>
> I didn't know, i didn't know you or malcolm
> or patrice or trane or me
> had i known
> i would have said
> scream eric scream
> you're a bad muthafucka
>
> (Stephen Henderson, 321)

Graham's empathy for lower-class African-Americans might be compared
to Carolyn M. Rodgers' "5 Winos" (*Songs of a Black Bird*, 1969), which
concludes:

> but the howling goes on,
> and the straining & then cursing
> and soon,
> a bottle screams on the concrete,
> scattering their mouths and juggling
> their music into the most carefully
> constructed a-melodic coltrane psalm (36)

In "Me, In Kulu Se, & Karma," Rodgers once again invokes Coltrane's
sound, this time in a first person narrative:

> moving that way going freee where pha-
> raoh and trane playing in my guts and it's me and my
> ears forgetting how to listen and just feeling oh
> yeah me i am screammmmming into the box (35)

Perhaps the best-known poem that equates Coltrane's sound with vocal
outcries is the title poem to Haki Madhubuti's *Don't Cry, Scream* (published in 1969 under the name Don L. Lee).[17] Subtitled "*(for John Coltrane / from a black poet / in a basement apt. crying dry tears of 'you ain't
gone')*," the poem begins with Coltrane's emergence, followed by expressions of pain and oppression:

> into the sixties
> a trane
> came/ out of the
> fifties with a
> golden boxcar
> riding the rails
> of novation.
>   . . . . .
> music that ached.
> murdered our minds (we reborn)
> born into a neoteric aberration.
> & suddenly
> you envy the
> BLIND man—
> you know that he will
> hear what you'll never
> see. (27)

Like Sanchez, Madhubuti takes his cue from Coltrane's music (in this case, the album *Ascension*, from the freest period of his career) and interprets the sound as a rebellious holler:

the blues exhibited illusions of manhood.
destroyed by you. Ascension into:

scream-eeeeeeeeeeeeee-ing   sing
SCREAM-EEEeeeeeeeeeee-ing   loud &
SCREAM-EEEEEEEEEEEEEE-ing   long with
                                   feeling (28)

Madhubuti's "Don't Cry, Scream" might be seen as a representative political poem from this period, for it reflects the demands made by many African-American poems from the sixties. For example, Askia Muhammad Touré's tribute to Malcolm X, "Extension," ends with free jazz—performed by Sun Ra, Pharoah Sanders, Coltrane, and Milford Graves—as the catalyst for statements for freedom:

Let the Ritual begin:
Sun Ra, Pharoah, Coltrane, Milford tune up your Afro-horns;
let the Song begin, the Wild Song of the Black Heart:
E X T E N S I O N over the crumbling ghettoes, riding
the deep, ominous night—the Crescent Moon, Evening Star;
the crumbling ghettoes exploding exploding: BAROOM, BAROOM!
(A Nation rising in Midnight Robes; let it rise, *Let the
Black Nation Rise!*) (20)

Amid violence and assassinations, the age demanded a renewed sense of pride suggested in Baraka's "AM/TRAK" and expressed still more clearly in Jayne Cortez's "How Long Has Trane Been Gone?":

Rip those dead white people off
your walls Black People
black people whose walls
should be a hall
A Black Hall Of Fame
so our children will know
will know & be proud
Proud to say I'm from Parker City—Coltrane City—Ornette City
Pharoah City living on Holiday street next to
James Brown park in the State of Malcolm (n.p.)

Baraka, Cortez, Sanchez, Madhubuti, and other outspoken African-American poets from the sixties continue to publish, but although their most recent poetry may be no less angry, it is no longer as shocking or as revolutionary.[18] In many respects, the more volatile Coltrane poems of the sixties allowed subsequent writers to be less overtly political; at the very least, they allowed the poets who followed to concentrate more on the rich legacy of jazz rather than the intensities of rage.

Michael S. Harper is the ultimate example of a poet who embraced the drive behind the earlier Coltrane poems but presented these sensibilities in a more controlled poetic voice. It's fair to say that Harper—who since the publication in 1970 of his book, *Dear John, Dear Coltrane*, has often been referred to as "the Coltrane poet"—became the dominant figure in jazz poetry of the seventies. Even now, twenty-five years later, Harper's greatest inspiration remains the music and presence of John Coltrane.[19]

Like the work of his mentor, Sterling Brown, Harper's early poetry is often political without being governed by an agenda (the way, for example, Baraka's "AM/TRAK" tries to manipulate the figure of John Coltrane into a proponent of Marxism). During an interview in 1985, I told Harper, "In your own work, jazz seems to serve as both a vehicle for traveling through history and a source of inspiration of its own. It seems important for you to bring out the musical elements while at the same time making your poems stand up as poetry," and he replied, "I'm glad you said that. It's not propaganda" (Feinstein, 7). This is a vital issue for Harper, who distinguishes between political truths and political falsehoods. Quoting from Sterling Brown's "Strong Men" ("They dragged you from homeland, / They chained you in coffles"), he commented,

And so there is a palliating influence between a strong narrative, on the one hand, and the songs, which are meant to transcend any circumstance—I mean, slavery was not a picnic for anybody, you know. Didn't really matter who the hell it was. But this was a specific reference to the American scene and we as a culture have not embraced it. I pick up anthologies all the time—that poem's not there. The poem's a *poem*. Now it's a poem of protest, and it's a poem of criticism, but it's a poem. (Feinstein, 3)

Harper insists that "jazz music is so indigenous to American culture that even if you have a predilection not to like it, you have to really be informed about it if you want to be informed about American culture" (2). Harper's use of jazz requires an intimate knowledge of the music's history, and his references to musicians or songs demand complex and well-informed associative responses. "Ode to Tenochtitlan," from *Dear John, Dear Coltrane*, typifies this collage-like structure. Harper dedicates the poem to and describes the daring actions of Tommie Smith and John Carlos, who during the medal ceremonies in the 1968 Summer Olympics, shocked the world by raising triumphant fists gloved in black. Harper pays these men his greatest compliment: "they stand before Coltrane" (85).

The title poem from that book begins with the epigraph, "*a love supreme, a love supreme*," and the poem's association with the Coltrane

composition is so integral that a brief history of the recording seems necessary. Although not recorded until 1964, *A Love Supreme* germinated
from Coltrane's spiritual and physical cleansing in 1957. It was a pivotal
year: He left the Davis quintet because, according to Harper, "Coltrane
was really bored with the music and in effect engineered his own dis-
charge" (Thomas, 81). He then performed and recorded with Thelonious
Monk. Later that same year, he quit his three vices—smoking, drinking,
and heroin—a life-threatening achievement for which, in his liner notes
for *A Love Supreme*, he praised the strength of God:

During the year 1957, I experienced, by the grace of God, a spiritual awakening
which was to lead me to a richer, fuller, more productive life. All that time, in
gratitude, I humbly asked to be given the means and privilege to make others
happy through music. I feel this has been granted through His grace. ALL
PRAISE TO GOD.

"A Love Supreme" is also a poem written by Coltrane and reproduced
on the record jacket. Repetitive and uninteresting as verse, the poem reflects Coltrane's obsession with world peace and the exaltation of God:

> I will do all I can to be worthy of Thee O Lord
> It all has to do with it.
> Thank you God.
> Peace.
> There is none other.
> God is. It is so beautiful.
> Thank you God. God is all.

It continues much the same way—a total of sixty-nine lines. But if the
poem "A Love Supreme" lacks subtlety and richness, the religious quality
of the music is undeniable; thirty years later, it continues to inspire.[20]

Coltrane divided his composition into four sections, two on either side
of the record: "Acknowledgement," "Resolution," "Pursuance," and
"Psalm." "Acknowledgement" begins with Jones's gongs and shimmering
cymbals, the tenor saxophone briefly rising above the gentle trills of Tyner's piano, which then fade into Garrison's emerging rhythmic bass pattern: The initial free rhythms meld into a structured pulse like sets of
iambs (x' x', x' x'). The drums modulate from the open rhythms established at the beginning of the movement to that same beat—(x' x', x' x')—
and as soon as Jones and Garrison lock into their rhythm, Tyner re-enters
on piano. And then Coltrane joins the trio with commanding gestures.
Each musician now driving with the rhythm, the bass line becomes less
insistent, though the underlying pulse is always present. Towards the end
of his solo, Coltrane incorporates the bass rhythm (x' x') and, substituting
various pitches within the rhythm, concludes his improvisation using only

four beats as his foundation. The tenor fades out, leaving the rhythm section alone for a brief moment. And then, in deep bass vocals, the musicians begin to sing the refrain: a love supreme, a love supreme.

Like the ostinato bass line in the composition, the phrase *"a love supreme"* recurs throughout "Dear John, Dear Coltrane," first as an epigraph and finally as a coda. The poem begins with the fractured images of "Sex fingers toes" and then introduces Coltrane's childhood: his home in North Carolina, his father's church. Yet the fragments in the first line might suggest a larger, more universal African-American history that Coltrane shares and, for Harper, represents. "The appendages in the marketplace," explains Robert Stepto, "in all their suggestiveness of barter and sale as well as of unrealized craftsmanship and art-making, may be Coltrane's, but most certainly they are, in the historical continuum, the fingers, toes, and sex of slaves in the pen and on the block" (5). As Harper states in his liner notes to a reissued collection of Coltrane's music, "The poem begins with a catalogue of sexual trophies, for whites, a lesson to blacks not to assert their manhood, and that black men are suspect because they are potent."[21] For Coltrane, repressed sexuality has its outlet in jazz. "There is no substitute for pain," Harper says, and from that pain, "by river through swamps," emerges a chant, a song of hope if not salvation, a pulse: *"a love supreme, a love supreme."*

If the first stanza of "Dear John, Dear Coltrane" acknowledges pain, the second describes relief through art. Yet the poem presents an engaging oxymoron: If the jazz musician expends sexuality in performance, then the player becomes spent, impotent; but it is this new, odd variant on sublimation that revitalizes the performer. The reference to Coltrane's "genitals gone or going, / seed burned out" suggests that the self-purification "that makes you clean" results from a devouring of one's fertility. Coltrane energizes his sound from the raw resources of his soul; "genitals and sweat" nourish "the tenor sex cannibal / heart." If, as Harper implies, Coltrane cannot assert his manhood because he is so potent, then the artist must use his "impotence" to "fuel" his music.

The third stanza, all in italics, acts as a song within the poem. It is vocal. "The antiphonal, call-response / retort stanza," Harper explains, "simulates the black church, and gives the answer to renewal to any questions— 'cause I am' " (liner notes). In part, Harper refers to Coltrane's father's church, yet the phrase "cause I am" is more than a rhythmic pattern; it is an expansive answer, with the "I" encompassing "all":

> *Why you so black?*
> *cause I am*
> *why you so funky?*
> *cause I am*
> *why you so black?*

cause I am
why you so sweet?
cause I am
why you so black?
cause I am
a love supreme, a love supreme (75)

If only momentarily, the stanza releases the tension in the poem.

In the final stanza, Harper shifts from the abstract to the specific—to the end of Coltrane's life, when his cancerous liver became increasingly painful and debilitating. Yet Coltrane continued to perform; he was used to pain, having spent a lifetime with severe tooth decay. The opening lines of this stanza—"So sick / you couldn't play Naima" (75)—are particularly poignant, for "Naima" remained a favorite composition, one Coltrane wrote to express his love for his first wife, a song he continued to use as a source of development.[22]

The poem repeatedly asserts that "there is no substitute for pain," for out of pain arises purity. The "tenor sax cannibal / heart" from the second stanza transforms in the fourth into "the inflated heart," "the tenor kiss." The poem concludes in "tenor love," "*a love supreme.*"[23] The four stanzas of "Dear John, Dear Coltrane" create, then, a significant progression: a recognition of disease and pain; the hope that one can become "clean" through impotence; a vocal repetition that strives to answer all questions; and, finally, praise for the purity that results from pain, a prayerful affirmation of spirituality. Indeed, the poem is structured like *A Love Supreme*—in four parts which, as a whole, strive for a supreme love: Acknowledgement, Resolution, Pursuance, Psalm.

Dear John, Dear Coltrane also includes important poems in honor of Coltrane's dynamic rhythm section. "Effendi," named after the composition by McCoy Tyner, begins: "The piano hums / again the clear / story of our coming, / enchained, severed, / our tongues gone" (46). Like the opening to "Dear John, Dear Coltrane," the allusions to slavery enhance both the sense of history and pathos. In fact, many of the themes expressed in "Dear John, Dear Coltrane" reappear in this poem for Tyner—"experience and pain" (46), for example, create a spirit "pure, new, even lovely" (47)—as well as several other related poems from the collection. In "Elvin's Blues," an homage to Elvin Jones and one of the strongest poems in the book, Harper focuses on the use of drugs and sexuality: "Sniffed, dilating my nostrils, / the cocaine creeps up my / leg, smacks into my groin" (12). In "Dirge for Trane," he concentrates on the devastating news of Coltrane's death, and, like the italicized refrain "*a love supreme,*" the repetition of "*gone, gone, gone, gone, gone*" rings in our ears like a chant.

In "Here Where Coltrane Is," from Harper's second book of poetry

(*History Is Your Own Heartbeat*, 1971), the poet again juxtaposes dissimilar and evocative imagery while maintaining a strong narrative. Like so many of Harper's works, this poem presents pain—a speaker who, suffering from the cold of winter and, worse, from witnessing the death of a family member, turns to Coltrane's music for solace:

> I play "Alabama"
> on a warped record player
> skipping the scratches
> on your faces over the fibrous
> conical hairs of plastic
> under the wooden floors. (32)

Like the gesture in the final line of the poem "Reuben Reuben," in which the speaker turns to jazz after the death of his son, here the musical elegy for the girls killed in the Birmingham church bombing enables the speaker to face his own tragedy, and the poem concludes with a reference to Coltrane in the process of composing:[24]

> Dreaming on a train from New York
> to Philly, you hand out six
> notes which become an anthem
> to our memories of you:
> oak, birch, maple,
> apple, cocoa, rubber.
> For this reason Martin is dead;
> for this reason Malcolm is dead;
> for this reason Coltrane is dead;
> in the eyes of my first son are the browns
> of these men and their music. (33)

The ending suggests that these men have died because of their race. But it is also a testimony to those who expend themselves for issues broader and more significant than any individual life. For this reason if for no other they need to be recognized, to be welcomed.

Indeed, Harper's poem "Welcome," from *Dear John, Dear Coltrane*, invokes Coltrane indirectly—"Now tenor kiss / 'Welcome' / tenor love" (30)—and reads like a plea for jazz to be embraced:

> When the moon's
> scientists excavate
> these puritan
> paranoid scars
> black feathered
> jazz
> will again speak

its loving entreaty:
"Welcome", finally. (30)

Fortunately, in the last fifteen years there has been a radical shift in acceptance; even the tiny subgenre of "the Coltrane poem" has an international audience. Like African-American poets rebelling against racism, other minority cultures have turned to Coltrane as a musical, if not spiritual, leader. In "Glass" from *Black + Blues* (1976), for example, the West Indian poet Edward Kamau Brathwaite offers a political observation that makes the sixties sound like a dream deferred:[25]

i hear them screaming
REVOLUTION
as the world revolves round
marcus malcolm mississippi memphis

but there aint no vein of revolution
only the blues
and coltrane's gospel pain (25)

In 1969, John Taggart edited *Maps #3: Poems for John Coltrane*, which includes poems by eighteen writers.[26] Three of the works appear in Spanish as well as in translation: Fernando Arbelaez's "Aire de Blue Para Coltrane," which uses images kaleidoscopically to suggest the associative nature of improvised phrases; J. G. Cobo-Borda's "Coltrane," which sketches a slightly more biographical encounter with the musician ("irreparable pain / at the edge of real surprise. / in the guillotine of his lips / a note vibrates" [36]); and Jaime Ferrán's "Coltrane Blues," which describes Coltrane's sound, as well as his death, as a reminder of what the poet sees as mankind's dark essence:

ten years
            from nineteen hundred
fifty-seven
            the soprano saxophone
of John Coltrane
            shows us
a forgotten path,
            In the mist
a few words are repeated
like a broken thanksgiving
suddenly
            the record has cracked
                        We have
to begin again:

In the beginning
there was only rhythm and sadness . . . (63–64)[27]

In Japan, Kazuko Shiraishi remains the best known poet writing about
jazz, and *Seasons of Sacred Lust* (1978) includes her lengthy tribute, "Dedicated to the Late John Coltrane" (1978). Here the musician's magnificence makes him seem one with nature:

> Coltrane almost became a sky
> He became a cascade of will
> Carrying the sounds
> He made them fall
> Pouring them out
> We know the monsoon
> In John's long lasting solo
> The blazing rain continues (44–45)

Asian-Americans have also turned to Coltrane for inspiration, as seen in
Garrett Hongo's "Roots" (*Yellow Light*, 1982), in which the speaker, who
at one point says, "So now I study spells in Sanskrit / and memorize a
tenor sax lick" (49), later unites the seemingly disparate impulses:

> And so, my sutra comes around midnight,
> and I chant it to the tune of "A Love Supreme":
>
> MAKA HANYA HARAMITA SHIN GYO
> A LOVE SUPREME
> A LOVE SUPREME
> SUPREME, SUPREME
> A LOVE SUPREME
> GYA TE GYA TE
> HA RA GYA TE
> HARA SO GYA TE
> SOWA KA
> HAN NYA SHIN GYO (49–50)

Joy Harjo, one of the strongest contemporary Native American poets,
continues to incorporate jazz into poems such as "Healing Animal" from
In Mad Love and War (1990), where the music of Coltrane becomes "the
collected heartbeat of" a Papago Indian tribe:

> And I ask you
> *what bitter words are ruining your soft-skinned village,*
> because I want to make a poem that will cup
>   the inside of your throat
> like the fire in the palm of a healing animal. Like
> the way Coltrane knew love in the fluid shape

of a saxophone
          that could change into the wings of a blue angel.
He tasted the bittersweet roots of this crazy world,
and spit them out into the center of our musical
                    jazzed globe. (38)

The tone of the John Coltrane poem has become noticeably less anti-white, and not so visually aggressive on the page, but the politics of the sixties have not been abandoned by more-recent poets, nor has the church bombing from 1963 been forgotten. Tom Dent's "Coltrane's Alabama" (*Blue Lights and River Songs*, 1982) begins somewhat obviously ("yes, Coltrane / it is a woeful song / you sing") but departs from the biographical elements and sustains a metaphor of mud and flood:

red mud sticks
to my brain
shards of broken
glass
punctured my heart
it is raintime
woetime
& the flood cannot
wash
the blood
away (41)

In Jan Selving's "Dancing to Ellington," the speaker describes her father, a doctor "who years later / would tell me he couldn't bear / to have supper with us / after seeing a 17-year-old / patient with his skull caved in" (Feinstein and Komunyakaa, *The Jazz Poetry Anthology*, 191). Ellington's "Fleurette Africaine" inspires the father's release of tension, but it is Coltrane's "Alabama" that allows the speaker to "remember those nights / I followed the sound of jazz / to the place I could watch / my father dance" (191).

What most of these varied Coltrane poems share is the desire to give this musical genius a still greater audience. In 1965 John Sinclair published his "Homage to John Coltrane," one of the few tributes to appear during the musician's lifetime.[28] The poet implores John Coltrane to

teach us to stand
like men
in the face of the most devastating insensi-
tivity. can touch us
where the hand or mouth or

eye
   can't go. can see. can be
a man. make a love
from centuries of unplumbed music
& a common metal tool
anyone can misuse. (33–34)

For a quarter of a century, more poets have responded to Coltrane's music
than to that of any other jazz figure. Beyond politics, beyond race or
gender, there exists a profound admiration for this musician, which is why
so many of these poems plead with their readers to acknowledge the spirituality he sought to attain in works such as *A Love Supreme*. This plea
takes many forms in the history of the Coltrane poem, from the conclusion
of Sanchez's "a/coltrane/poem"—"a love supreme. / for each / other / if
we just / lissssssSSSTEN" (72)—to the persistent rhythms in Michael Stillman's "In Memoriam John Coltrane":

   Listen to the coal
rolling, rolling through the cold
   steady rain, wheel on

   wheel, listen to the
turning of the wheels this night
   black as coal dust, steel

   on steel, listen to
these cars carry coal, listen
   to the coal train roll.

                       (Feinstein and Komunyakaa, 207)

NOTES

1. Some of these details were obtained from *Voices of Freedom: An Oral History of the Civil Rights Movement from the 1950s through the 1980s* (1990), edited
by Henry Hampton and Steve Fayer. Chapter 11, titled "The Sixteenth Street
Church Bombing," also includes reflections by James Bevel, Diane Nash, Fred
Shuttlesworth, Coretta Scott King, David Vann, and Burke Marshall; all are worth
reading, and the book in general is a tremendous addition to Civil Rights literature.

2. Although recorded in the studio, the tune "Alabama" appears on the album
Coltrane "Live" at Birdland (released in 1964).

3. In his liner notes to the LP collection *John Coltrane*, the poet Michael Harper explained that "the song ['Alabama'] was composed while John Coltrane was
reading a speech by Martin Luther King, Jr. eulogizing five [*sic*] black girls blown
up in an Alabama church—Birmingham, 1963—from the rhythms of King's eulogy
Coltrane composed 'Alabama,' while on a train traveling from New York to Philadelphia." In Bill Cole's biography, *John Coltrane* (1976), he concurs that "the

melodic line of the piece was developed from the rhythmic inflections of a speech given by Dr. Martin Luther King" (150). In *Chasin' the Trane* (1975), J. C. Thomas claims that "John Coltrane heard the news [of the bombing] that afternoon on a radio broadcast" (167); C. O. Simpkins, in *Coltrane: A Biography* (1975), writes, "While riding a plane on the way to a performance in the United States, John read this speech [by King]. From its rhythm, he wrote the composition, *Alabama*" [*sic*] (171). Quite obviously, the necessity for a thorough and reliable biographical study of Coltrane's life remains.

4. The reference to Baraka refers to the dedication in *Black Music* (published in 1968 under LeRoi Jones) which reads, "For John Coltrane / the heaviest spirit." Benston's own hagiographic descriptions of Coltrane often diminish the effectiveness of his adulation, and many readers might be put off by phrases such as, "Trane himself became the sun and the node, the zero point of the universe, and all things (incarnated by a variety of rhythmic/percussional accompaniments) swirled in dynamic flux around him" (770). On the other hand, Jim Stevens's introduction to *Bright Moments*, a small collection of jazz poems, states that his "thoughts on the possibilities of a Jazz-poetry come from a range of sources" ([7]), at which point he mentions Benston's essay as one of only two sources.

5. Greenlee, interestingly enough, wrote on the back of his book: "My chief literary influences are Charlie Parker, Lester Young, Miles Davis and Billie Holiday. As a writer, I consider myself a jazz musician whose instrument is a typewriter."

6. An important study of the Coltrane poem is Günter H. Lenz's "Black Poetry and Black Music: History and Tradition: Michael Harper and John Coltrane" from *History and Tradition in Afro-American Culture*, which Lenz edited in 1984. Although Lenz fills his massive paragraphs with underlining for emphasis (making both the intellectual content and the visual presentation difficult to follow), he has nevertheless compiled a wealth of material concerning John Coltrane and poetics, with a special emphasis on Harper's writing.

7. This interview was reprinted in C. O. Simpkins's *Coltrane: A Biography* (1975), and Simpkins has a similar reaction: "In doing this interview, Kofsky had a particular stereotype of a progressive Black musician in mind, and posed questions that aimed at fitting John into his mold. John's answers, however, gave testimony to his broadness" (212).

8. Baraka also wrote the liner notes for this recording, and his concluding paragraph, in which he addresses the "deep music," displays his writing at its worst in which vapid generalities strive for ultimate, spiritual expressions: "It goes all through you, makes the circle of excitement and adventure, from earth to heaven, man in between going both ways, elliptical and perfect as anything" (Jones, *Black Music*, 179).

9. For those unfamiliar with the allusions, Lacey explains that the names "are, respectively, alto saxophonist of Ellington fame, Johnny Hodges, saxophonist-singer Eddie Vinson and, founding father of bebop, John Burks [*sic*] Gillespie, all of whom employed Coltrane in his developing years" (15). Still more insightful is Lacey's interpretation of "Trees in the shining night forest," which he sees as "a pointed allusion to Langston Hughes' poem 'Jazzonia' " (15).

10. There is another by no means understated agenda in the poem, and it concerns Baraka's Marxist stance at that time, which he then imposed on the jazz

figures. Monk's drummer Shadow Wilson becomes "Comrade Shadow," and even Lacey, who proposes "AM/TRAK" to be the greatest Coltrane poem (and one of the finest poems from the sixties), concludes, "Reference to Coltrane's music as 'red records of the history of ourselves' borders on the superfluous. Moreover, by placing him in the camp of the dialectical materialists, the poet, at least momentarily, undermines the overt spirituality of Coltrane's music, especially the later recordings, including those catalogued near the end of the poem. Even the light-hearted, Marxist-inspired aside to Don Lee and all other 'reactionaries,' is out of harmony with the general tenor of the poem" (18).

11. Baraka's association among the riots, Coltrane's death, and his own incarceration became a national issue and one not limited to his personal narrative. For example, Robert Kelly's poem, "Newark," collected in John Taggart's anthology of John Coltrane poems, begins: "John Coltrane died this morning. LeRoi's in jail" (13).

12. Harris also quotes an interesting passage from Henry Louis Gates's essay, "The 'Blackness of Blackness': A Critique of the Sign and the Signifying Monkey," in which Gates discusses the form of structural disassembling and uses a musical analogy: "Repeating a form and then inverting it through a process of variation is central to jazz—a stellar example is John Coltrane's rendition of 'My Favorite Things,' compared to Julie Andrews' vapid version" (Harris, 15).

13. Of particular importance is his book *Four Lives in the Bebop Business* (1966), a study of Ornette Coleman, Herbie Nichols, Jackie McLean, and Cecil Taylor.

14. In 1965 Spellman wrote in his poem "John Coltrane": "listen to *summertime*, think of spring, negroes / cats in the closet, anything that makes a rock / of your eye. imagine you steal. you are frightened / you want to help. you are sorry you are born with ears" (*The Beautiful Days*, n.p.).

15. Henderson, as an aside, includes a paragraph about Julius Lester in which he concludes: "He writes sparse evocative poetry, but his most beautiful poem he saved for his son. He baptized him in blackness. He named him Malcolm Coltrane!" (Cook and Henderson, 114).

16. Not all writers, of course, embraced the dynamically loud voice or tone. Nikki Giovanni's "Revolutionary Music," for example, makes references to the popular African-American singers of the time. The poem's conclusion seems directly in line with the emotional responses to Coltrane's music, though the tone seems far more understated than many of the poems by her contemporaries: "we be digging all / our revolutionary / music consciously or un / cause sam cooke said 'a change is gonna come' " (Henderson, 281–282).

17. Henry Lacey refers to this poem as "the first and[,] perhaps, most well known of the poems in homage to Coltrane" (13), but it is neither. Significantly less well known than Harper's "Dear John, Dear Coltrane," Madhubuti's work first appeared in 1969 and therefore postdates poems such as John Sinclair's "Homage to John Coltrane" (*This is Our Music*, 1965), A. B. Spellman's "John Coltrane" (*The Beautiful Days*, 1965), Ebon's "Revolution" (*Revolution: A Poem*, 1968), or Eugene Perkins's "Eulogy for Coltrane" (*Black Is Beautiful*, 1968), to name just a few.

18. Representative of the changing sensibilities, the recent reprintings of Mad-

hubuti's "Don't Cry, Scream" have, by the poet's request, omitted the passage attacking homosexuals.

19. Harper's only collections of poetry since *Images of Kin* have been *Healing Song for the Inner Ear* (1985), which includes quite a number of Coltrane-related poems, and *Honorable Amendments* (1995), but the jazz poems in these books seem far less engaging than those in his earlier collections. Like a musician quoting old familiar phrases, these poems repeat various book titles ("Nightmare begins responsibility," "History Is Your Own Heartbeat") and Coltrane songs ("A Love Supreme"), but they become predictable. Unlike Coltrane, who constantly tried to explore new avenues with his craft, Harper seems to have fallen back on his own clichés.

The *New York Times* reviewed *Healing Song* and proclaimed that this anxiously-awaited volume proves that Harper remains one of the most vital poets of our time. The reviewer also stated: "I don't find it farfetched at all to compare the sound Mr. Harper gets in his poems to the jazz solos of Harry Carney. In fact, Carney's singular landmark recording, 'Picasso,' may be one of the analogues Mr. Harper employs to organize his verse" (Chappell, 15). However, the solo version of "Picasso" was performed and composed by the tenor saxophonist Coleman Hawkins. (Carney played baritone and never recorded the tune.) It seems to me that the reviewer's desire to like this long-awaited collection obscured the book's inherent weaknesses.

20. The jazz critic Whitney Balliett had surprisingly little sympathy for Coltrane's attempts at attaining a spirituality in his music; referring to *A Love Supreme* and other recordings, Balliett stated in 1968 that "attempts to write program music succeed only in the mind of the composer or performer. One man's requiem is another man's polka" (107). Coltrane, he continues, "had a blank, aggressive tone, and in his moments of frenzy, which were frequent, he repeated series of manic shrieks, wails, and screams that hurt the ear and stopped the mind. (His apologists were fond of pointing out that none of us really know what *music* should or should not sound like, but instinct, which can instantly isolate ugliness or beauty, knows better)" (107). Balliett nominates *Crescent* as Coltrane's greatest triumph, placing it with the company of works by Armstrong, Bechet, and Parker. But his highly critical reflection on Coltrane concludes, "People said they heard the dark night of the Negro in Coltrane's wildest music, but what they really heard was a heroic and unique lyrical voice at the mercy of its own power" (108).

21. These liner notes appeared on the two-record set, *John Coltrane* (Prestige 24003), which collected *Soultrane* and *Traneing In*. Although those individual recordings have been reissued on compact disc, the Prestige twofer has not (but most likely will). Harper repeated this statement, verbatim, in an interview with John O'Brien, in which Harper added, "Black men are suspect because they are potent, and potency is obviously a great part of Coltrane's playing and of the music of contemporary black musicians" (97).

22. Harper claims to have written "Dear John, Dear Coltrane" prior to Coltrane's death. In an interview from 1985, he stated that he "knew that Coltrane was ill," adding, "I certainly had a vision about this, and it was just a disturbing vision, so much so that I did not publish the poem. I felt that this was almost sacrilege" (Feinstein, 5).

23. Al Young's "The John Coltrane Dance" from *Dancing* (1969) also expresses

an awareness both of the cost of Coltrane's music and of the spiritual act itself. Young writes parenthetically "(I know sound cures)" (20) and concludes, "In this long day of spirit / let song be night / & the showering of notes / stars in that beloved firmament" (21).

24. Discussing the actual history of Coltrane's composition, Harper wrote that "Alabama" was "a tune he'd composed after reading a eulogy of four Birmingham children blown up in church—the eulogy by Martin Luther King, Jr.—while riding from New York to Philadelphia to visit his mother. The melody was a blues-dirge celebration ending in the simulation of a human cry" ("Introducing the Blues," 19).

25. In that same collection, Brathwaite includes a poem titled "Trane" that refers to the musician still more directly, but the images sound rather trite and obvious: Coltrane "leans against the bar / and pours his old unhappy longing in the saxophone" (26).

26. Many of the poems seem to have no relationship to Coltrane except, perhaps, for a profoundly personal connection between the poet and the music. Taggart's introductory statement admits, "There's the risk that a collection of poems which begin variously from the music of John Coltrane . . . may turn out to be a collection of aesthetic and sterile games. But I think it's a risk worth taking; you could even say it's *demanded* from this liberty to hear, to make what we can from it, as evidence that John Coltrane's music is still very much with us" (*i*).

27. Cobo-Borda's poem was translated by Evelyn Pagán and John Taggart, and Ferrán's poem was translated by Joan Howard and Walter R. Keller.

28. In 1967 Sinclair published a collection of his Coltrane poems titled *Meditations: A Suite for John Coltrane.*

REFERENCES

Balliett, Whitney. *Ecstacy at the Onion: Thirty-one Pieces on Jazz.* Indianapolis: Bobbs-Merril, 1971.

Baraka, Amiri. *Selected Poetry of Amiri Baraka/LeRoi Jones.* New York: Morrow, 1979.

Benston, Kimberly W. "Late Coltrane: A Re-membering of Orpheus." *The Massachusetts Review* (Winter 1977): 770–781.

Brathwaite, Edward Kamau. *Black & Blues.* Cuba: Premio Casa de las Americas, 1976.

Chappell, Fred. "Sepia Photographs and Jazz Solos." *New York Times* Section 7 (Oct. 13, 1985): 15.

Cole, Bill. *John Coltrane.* New York: Schirmer, 1976.

Coltrane, John. "A Love Supreme." *A Love Supreme* (Impulse 77): 1964.

Cook, Mercer, and Stephen E. Henderson. *The Militant Black Writer in Africa and the United States.* Madison: University of Wisconsin, 1969.

Cortez, Jayne. *Pisstained Stairs and the Monkey Man's Wares.* New York: Phrase Text, 1969.

Dent, Tom. *Blue Light and River Songs.* Detroit: Lotus, 1982.

Ebon. *Revolution: A Poem.* Chicago: Third World, 1968.

Feinstein, Sascha. "John Coltrane and Poetics: An Interview with Michael S. Harper." *Indiana Review.* 12 (Spring 1989): 1–12.

Feinstein, Sascha and Yusef Komunyakaa, eds. *The Jazz Poetry Anthology*. Bloomington: Indiana University Press, 1991.

Greenlee, Sam. *Blues for an African Princess*. Chicago: Third World, 1971.

Hampton, Henry, and Steve Fayer, eds. *Voices of Freedom: An Oral History of the Civil Rights Movement from the 1950s through the 1980s*. New York: Bantam, 1990.

Harjo, Joy. *In Mad Love and War*. Middletown, Conn.: Wesleyan University Press, 1990.

Harper, Michael S. *Dear John, Dear Coltrane*. Pittsburgh: University of Pittsburgh, 1970.

———. *Healing Song for the Inner Ear*. Chicago: University of Illinois, 1985.

———. *History Is Your Own Heartbeat*. Chicago: University of Illinois, 1971.

———. *Honorable Amendments*. Chicago: University of Illinois, 1995.

———. "Introducing the Blues." *American Poetry Review* 6 (January/February 1977): 19.

———. Liner notes. *John Coltrane* (Prestige 24003).

Harris, William J. *The Jazz Aesthetic: The Poetry and Poetics of Amiri Baraka*. Columbia: University of Missouri Press, 1985.

Henderson, David. *De Mayor of Harlem*. New York: Dutton, 1970.

Henderson, Stephen, ed. *Understanding the New Black Poetry*. New York: Morrow, 1973.

Hongo, Garrett Kaoru. *Yellow Light*. Middletown, Conn.: Wesleyan University Press, 1982.

Jones, LeRoi. *Black Music*. New York: Morrow, 1968.

———. *Dutchman and The Slave*. New York: Morrow, 1964.

Kofsky, Frank. *Black Nationalism and the Revolution in Music*. New York: Pathfinder, 1970.

Lacey, Henry C. "Baraka's 'AM/TRAK': Everybody's Coltrane Poem." *Obsidian II*. Vol. 1, nos. 1 and 2 (Spring/Summer 1986): 12–21.

Lenz, Günter H., ed. *History and Tradition in Afro-American Culture*. Frankfurt and New York: Campus Verlag, 1984.

Litweiler, John. *The Freedom Principle: Jazz after 1958*. New York: Morrow, 1984.

Madhubuti, Haki (Don L. Lee). *Don't Cry, Scream*. Detroit: Broadside, 1969.

Neal, Larry. *Black Boogaloo*. San Francisco: Journal of Black Poetry, 1969.

O'Brien, John, ed. *Interviews with Black Writers*. New York: Liveright, 1973.

Perkins, Eugene. *Black Is Beautiful*. Chicago: Free Black, 1968.

Rodgers, Carolyn M. *Songs of a Black Bird*. Chicago: Third World, 1969.

Sanchez, Sonia. *We a BaddDDD People*. Detroit: Broadside, 1970.

Shiraishi, Kazuko. *Seasons of Sacred Lust*. New York: New Directions, 1978.

Simpkins, Cuthbert Ormond. *Coltrane: A Biography*. Philadelphia: Herndon, 1975.

Sinclair, John. *Meditations: A Suite for John Coltrane*. Detroit: Artist's Workshop, 1967.

———. *This is Our Music*. Detroit: Artist's Workshop, 1965.

Spellman, A. B. *The Beautiful Days*. New York: Poets, 1965.

———. *Four Lives in the Bebop Business*. New York: Schocken, 1966.

Stephens, Jim, ed. *Bright Moments*. Madison: Abraxas, 1980.

Stepto, Robert B. "Michael Harper's Extended Tree: John Coltrane and Sterling Brown," *The Hollins Critic*, 8, 3 (June, 1976): 2–16.

Taggart, John, ed. *Maps #3: Poems for John Coltrane.* Syracuse: Syracuse University Press, [1969].

Thomas, J. C. *Chasin' the Trane.* New York: Doubleday, 1975.

Touré, Askia Muhammad. *JuJu.* Chicago: Third World, 1970.

Washington, James Melvin, ed. *A Testament of Hope: The Essential Writings of Martin Luther King, Jr.* San Francisco: Harper and Row, 1986.

Young, Al. *Dancing.* New York: Corinth, 1969.

Goodbye Porkpie Hat: Farewells and Remembrances

The line "You so beautiful but you got to die someday" is the story of humankind in nine words.
——Whitney Balliett

Cold chestnuts flowering April
& you're falling from heaven in a shower of eighth notes
to the cobbled street below & foaming dappled horses
plunge beneath the still green waters of the Grand Canal.
——Lynda Hull

"It is 12:20 in New York a Friday / three days after Bastille Day, yes / it is 1959 and I go get a shoeshine" (O'Hara, 325). Yes, it is July 17, 1959, and the speaker in Frank O'Hara's "The Day Lady Died" begins his walk through the Manhattan streets, doing what he can to repress the fact that Billie Holiday, the seemingly immortal Lady Day, is gone. He describes the afternoon in slow motion as though recounting an anxiety dream (he finds himself "practically going to sleep with quandriness") and each detail, no matter how mundane, takes on monumental importance, much like the stories that answer the common question, "Where were you when J. F. K. was shot?" When he buys some foreign smokes at a corner tobacconist, his eyes flash to the cover of the *New York Post*, at that time a respectable paper, and the photograph of Holiday makes his haze dissipate to memory:

and I am sweating a lot by now and thinking of
leaning on the john door in the FIVE SPOT
while she whispered a song along the keyboard
to Mal Waldron and everyone and I stopped breathing (325)

Since its publication in O'Hara's *Lunch Poems* (1964), "The Day Lady Died" has probably become the most famous of all jazz poems, mainly because of its regular reprintings in a variety of anthologies.[1] O'Hara's created persona consciously avoids mentioning Holiday, and this kind of elegy, in which the subject is barely addressed, distinguishes his poem from most jazz elegies (and most elegies in general, for that matter). But even though "The Day Lady Died" may not be a representative jazz poem in terms of its approach, the gesture is similar to a great many tributes that followed: urgent expressions of loss for the passing of major jazz figures and, in many cases, entire eras.

Looking for a moment at all of the jazz homages in poetry, it is clear that five artists dominate as a subject: Billie Holiday, Bessie Smith, Thelonious Monk, Charlie Parker, and John Coltrane. Their brilliant and influential musicianship not withstanding, the biographical histories of these artists also account for their popularity among poets who have been drawn to their tragic and brief lives. Monk, who lived to be sixty-four, may be the exception here, though his eccentricities have fascinated poets almost as much as his music. As explained in earlier chapters, Parker and Coltrane became cultural icons in part because of the pathos of their premature deaths. Bessie Smith's fatal car accident continues to be reported as a death resulting from white doctors who refused to treat her. Billie Holiday, who died at age forty-two, lived long enough to publish an autobiography that chronicled her disastrous childhood and relentless abuse; like Parker, her well-known drug addictions characterized her almost as much as her celebrated artistry.[2]

In emphasizing their early deaths and personal idiosyncrasies, I do not mean to belittle or dismiss the significance of their creative accomplishments. But it is telling that poets have turned more to Bessie Smith than, say, Louis Armstrong; that Parker became the source for scores of poems, yet Gillespie has been mentioned primarily in passing; that Holiday completely overshadows other singers, including Sarah Vaughan and Ella Fitzgerald; and that Coltrane should become the figure for Civil Rights, despite the fact that Sonny Rollins, to whom Coltrane was initially compared unfavorably, made a far more directed political statement with his record, *Freedom Suite* (1958). The reason for such aggrandizement is obvious: There is something grossly ironic—perhaps in an exploitive way—about true geniuses who never, at least during their lifetimes, received their deserved acclaim, and there is also the insidious but persistent cliché that unites creativity with personal suffering.

By the mid-seventies, an astonishing number of jazz musicians were dead, and their deaths, in conjunction with the emergence of rock and roll, almost annihilated the popularity of jazz in the United States. The legendary Louis Armstrong, born circa 1900, passed away in 1971. One of his greatest successors, the swing trumpeter Charlie Shavers (1917–1971), had his mouthpiece buried with Armstrong, but Shavers himself died of throat cancer just two days later. The primary tenor sax soloists from the Swing Era all died poor, virtually uncelebrated, and feeling like gutted human beings: Lester Young (1928–1964), Coleman Hawkins (1901–1969), and Ben Webster (1909–1973). Among the few innovators on the baritone saxophone, Serge Chaloff (1923–1957) and Lars Gullin (1928–1976) died prematurely from complications related to narcotics, and Harry Carney (1910–1974) passed away just four months after the death of his band leader and hero, Duke Ellington (1899–1974). Johnny Hodges (1907–1970), probably the most featured altoist from the Ellington band, refused to acknowledge medical warnings that would have prohibited him from Ellington's demanding schedule and ended up dying in a dentist's office.

The loss of modern jazz innovators was, if anything, still more devastating. Many of the young trumpet players suddenly, unbelievably, were gone: Fats Navarro (1923–1950), age twenty-seven, tuberculosis; Clifford Brown (1930–1956), age twenty-six, car crash; Booker Little (1938–1961), age twenty-three, uremia; Lee Morgan (1938–1972), age thirty-three, shot to death; Kenny Dorham (1924–1972), age forty-eight, kidney failure. The brilliant multi-instrumentalist Eric Dolphy died from diabetes in 1964 at age thirty-six. The saxophonists Cannonball Adderley (1928–1975), Gene Ammons (1925–1974), Paul Desmond (1924–1977), Booker Ervin (1930–1970), and Rahsaan Roland Kirk (1936–1977) all died between the ages of forty and fifty-two, as did Sonny Criss (1927–1977), who shot himself. The seminal electric guitar player, Charlie Christian (1916–1942), was thirty-five when he died, and Wes Montgomery (1925–1968), the carrier of his flame, only lived to be forty-three; Grant Green (1931–1979), a superb yet underrated guitarist, died at forty-seven. Pianists Art Tatum (1909–1956), Tad Dameron (1917–1965), Herbie Nichols (1919–1963), Bud Powell (1924–1966), and Bill Evans (1929–1980) reached the ages of forty-seven, forty-eight, forty-four, forty-one, and fifty-one, respectively. Powell's piano-playing younger brother, Richie (1931–1956), died at age twenty-four in the same car accident as Clifford Brown. Jimmy Blanton (1918–1942), the most important bassist from the first half of this century, died of tuberculosis, and Scott LaFaro (1936–1961), one of Blanton's most significant successors, was killed in a car crash; both died in their twenties. The bassist, composer, and band leader Charles Mingus (1922–1979) lived to be fifty-seven, only slightly older than many of his contemporaries. Saxophonists Wardell Gray (1921–1955) and Albert Ayler (1936–1970) both died mysteriously at age thirty-four, Gray's body recovered in the Las Vegas desert, Ayler's in New York City's East River.

These lists go on. "What a sense of loss to be a witness to the tail end," wrote Gerald Early in his evocative essay, "The Passing of Jazz's Old Guard,"

the burning out forever of that magnificent light of great music with its tough
carnality and its depth of telling resonance that made not only storytellers but also
heroes of its practitioners. They were the last heroes of jazz; never again will there
be the likes of Dexter Gordon and Wardell Gray—hair slicked hard, big pants
blowing in the wind, hats cocked to the side, pointed-toe shoes walking in rhyme
and rhythm with the corner boys—battling on their tenor saxes in an endless
version of "The Steeplechase." (308–309)

Early's essay concentrates on Monk, Mingus, and Sonny Stitt, but in the
above passage he suggests a still more profound loss—that of an entire
era. Not only were the giants of jazz dying in a shockingly concentrated
time period, but the whole romance of the music, as well as the dynamic
innovations of jazz, had apparently ceased. The seventies promoted a fusion with rock that replaced the suaveness of modern jazz described by
Early. Worse, many major record labels simply stopped pressing jazz recordings because they were not selling to the American public.

And yet, the number of jazz poems written during the seventies exploded exponentially. Part of this had to do with the intense desire to
capture the spirit of an ignored history. Poets confronted their own anguish, damned society for consistently praising genius with posthumous
honors, attempted to re-create the vitality of jazz, and, through detailed
descriptions and dramatic narratives, tried to immortalize both the music
and the individual musicians. Generally speaking, these elegies took two
major forms: first, grave expressions of sorrow that look at tragedy simply
as tragedy; and second, poems that offer a more instructive gesture—that
people must learn from and not perpetuate the reprehensible treatment
of great jazz artists.

Eugene Perkins, a poet who has written extensively about jazz and who
is now known as Useni Eugene Perkins, exemplified the sweeping feelings
of despair in his poem "Death of Jazz" (Silhouette, 1970), which describes
the demise of early jazz and then questions if the music has any future. It
begins, "they buried / jelly roll morton / without remembering / his name"
and continues with a series of head-shaking details: Charlie Parker's alto
gets auctioned "to a music / critic who / thought / paul whiteman / invented
jazz"; Lester Young's porkpie hat, a trademark, gets sat upon and flat-
tened by an opera-loving old woman; Leadbelly's "obituary column / listed
him as a vaudeville / performer"; someone mistakes Fats Navarro for an
American Indian and performs a mock dance; no one, the poem claims,
knows if Bud Powell or Tadd Dameron are alive or dead (they were both
deceased), and "who cares"; "even record collectors," Perkins concludes,
"have faint memories" (66).[3]

Apart from this feeling of doom at watching an entire culture dissipate,
Perkins's poem also suggests enormous sadness and regret at witnessing
such lack of respect and admiration for these triumphant musicians. And

so many jazz elegies, particularly those from the seventies, plaintively bear witness to that sadness. For example, poems in tribute to the innovators of modern jazz guitar—Charlie Christian and Wes Montgomery—inevitably focus on their premature deaths: Christian in 1942 from tuberculosis and pneumonia (age thirty-five) and Montgomery in 1968 from heart failure (age forty-three). Perkins's "Boss Guitar (for Wes Montgomery)" begins "Charlie (Christian) died / even younger" (34) and concludes,

> Charlie would've dug your style
> you had so much in common.
> fluent moves/drive/soul/and of
> course these beautiful chords
> you played so well. (35)

Quincy Troupe's "Elegy for Wes" (1972) also mentions Christian ("Charlie left his 'Solo Flight' / & went off" to "pay / his last dues") and concludes with the simple chant, "We will miss you Wes, / We will miss you Wes" (5).

These elegies dwell on the sadness of death, but many others are fueled by anger, particularly when addressing racial discrimination. The poems written about Bessie Smith's death, for example, perpetuate the story that she had been denied access to a white hospital and, because of that refusal, died from blood loss. The most famous literary account of this tragedy is still probably Edward Albee's drama from 1960, *The Death of Bessie Smith*, but many poets have referred to and condemned the tragedy. Jayne Cortez, for example, opens her first book of poems *Pisstained Stairs and the Monkey Man's Wares* (1969) with "The Road," an allusion to "the same road that downed Bessie" and amputated her arm (n.p.).

Chris Albertson's biography *Bessie* (1972) explains that Smith, in fact, was not driven to a white hospital and, furthermore, died of hemorrhaging that could not have been stopped under any circumstances (215–226). Albertson in no way belittles the overt racism of the thirties, but he does make an effort to describe the exact details of that night. Nevertheless, the power of myth and, more important, the need to react against racial injustices beyond this particular incident have caused the legendary account of Smith's accident to overshadow Albertson's proposition. Political poems governed by rage over Smith's apparent denial continue to be written, including Houston A. Baker, Jr.'s "Of Walker White's Father in the Rain" (*Blues Journeys Home*, 1985), which begins, "Denied, / like Bessie, / Bleeding in southern rain, / You felt your body jolted / Above gurney wheels" and continues, "Now, like Bessie on back roads dying, / You are discovered a son of Ham, / A son-in-law's dark inquiry set the staff humming: / 'God-dammed *Nigger* . . . My God!' " (23).

The accounts of Smith's death may be controversial, but certain post-

humous details about the Empress of the Blues are uncontested: Denied
a headstone for thirty-three years, Smith also had a chintzy funeral service,
one described in Alvin Aubert's "Bessie Smith's Funeral" from *Against
the Blues* (1972):

> Naked bulbs retreat
> From slaking so much darkness, turn
> To dalliance with lilies and a casket
> Textured to the dime-store toy that reins
> The impish hands of a child close by. (8)

In "Bessie," the previous poem from that collection, Aubert writes: "Forgive my late arrival. / Forgive this late late rose. / Forgive the lazar place
/ That would not let you in. / Bessie, forgive my sin" (7). Like Kerouac
begging Parker—"Forgive me—/ Forgive me for not answering your
eyes—/ ... lay the bane, / off me, and every body" (243)—the poet, as a
final gesture, requests, "And serve me, / Bessie, in this time / Of our most
common need" (7).[4]

Implicit in such elegies is the hope that people learn from these horrors,
that the poems, in fact, instruct. There is, for example, the abstract acknowledgment on the part of the speaker in Philip Levine's "I Remember
Clifford" (*One for the Rose*, 1981) in which he hears

> for the first time the high clear trumpet
> of Clifford Brown calling us all
> such a short time. My heart quickened
> and in my long coat, breathless
> and stumbling, I ran
> through the swirling snow
> to the familiar sequined door
> knowing it would open on something new. (79)

But politically- or racially-charged poems offer more-direct instruction,
such as those that invoke "Strange Fruit," a song of lynching (originally
a poem) made famous by Billie Holiday. In Cyrus Cassells's "Strange
Fruit," the speaker tentatively admits, "As a boy, / I was frightened by
Billie's song," but learns the horrible importance of it when Emmett Till
"was lynched / For 'eyeball rape' ": "And then the strange fruit was given
/ A face, a body like my own—" (Feinstein and Komunyakaa, 30–31).[5]
The speaker concludes in prayer: "And I'm dreaming the death of fear, /
That one word, if we could grasp it, / Which might stop a child from
becoming strange fruit" (31). Joy Harjo's poem, also titled "Strange Fruit"
(1990), begins with images of white-hooded Klansmen and burning
crosses, but to make us aware that she is invoking Holiday's song for the

present—not just the past—Harjo dedicates the poem at the bottom of the page as such:

(For Jacqueline Peters, a vital writer, activist in her early thirties, who was lynched in Lafayette, California, in June 1986. She had been working to start a local NAACP chapter, in response to the lynching of a twenty-three-year-old black man, Timothy Lee, in November 1985, when she was hanged in an olive tree by the Ku Klux Klan.) (12)

In addition to loss and anger, most of the jazz elegies emphasize how America has neglected its cultural heritage, and many of the poems for jazz expatriates, such as the tenor saxophonist Ben Webster, remind us how jazz has consistently been received more warmly overseas than in our own country. Both Ron Welburn and Howard Hart invoke Webster's final studio session, *Did You Call?*, which he recorded in 1972, one year before he died. Welburn's poem "Ben Webster: 'Did You Call Her Today?' " (1981) begins, "we do not care if you were / gruff and robust in / your ways" (11), but adds that an unnamed woman, who "might / not care about the careless / love pumping through your powerful tenor" (11), has waited for hours to hear from him. The poem suggests that Webster never found the time, or perhaps did not have the energy, to keep in touch. Hart's "Ben Webster and a Lady" (1984) is a dramatic monologue spoken by Webster himself. Webster reports that someone heard his phone ringing, wonders if it was a particular woman (whose identity is also left anonymous), and then explains how he has been gigging at "this little place" and that "Holland is strange" (16). The poem ends, "You know the number of the pool parlor / the best yes in Amsterdam / Call there" (16). Although in some ways opposite to each other, both poems share a tone of homelessness, of unsettled wandering and emotional detachment from the world.

Bud Powell (1924–1966) lived in Paris from 1959 to 1964, preferring Europe to the United States, where he had suffered racial beatings, mental breakdowns, and a good deal of shock therapy. Several poets have paid homage to Powell, though Clayton Eshleman has written more than most, and four of his poems concentrate exclusively on this innovator of bebop piano playing. "Bud Powell's story is never complete" writes Eshleman in *The Name Encanyoned River* (139), and all of his poems for Powell, though not necessarily written as a series, read like a relentless effort to recognize the injustices Powell endured. The poems bear witness to a writer coming to terms with the death of a monumental figure, and, when studied together, they play off of (and sometimes even explicate) repeated images of Powell's desperate life-style, a union of pity with genius, fragility with great endurance.

Powell died on August 4, 1966, and four days later Eshleman composed a prose poem titled "Bud Powell 1925 [*sic*]–1966" (*Indiana*, 1969), an homage that includes this statement about Powell and creativity: "He paid, probably since he was born, and without respite, in a way that no matter what happens to me I never will. A man does not swing who has not suffered, but to suffer is not to swing" (83). As a testimony to that suffering, Eshleman's poem "Bud Powell" from *The Gull Wall* (1975) describes the pianist as someone approximating a ravaged animal scavenging for food:

> locked in his Paris bathroom so he wouldn't wander.
> Sipping his lunch from the cat
> saucer on the floor.
> I see him curled there, nursing his litter,
> his great swollen dugs,
> his sleepy Buddha face
> looks down through the lotus pond
> sees the damned, astral miles below,
> amongst them a little unmoving Clayton Jr.
> placed by his mother on a bed of keys,
> Powell compassionately extended his tongue,
> licked my laid out senses (24)

In "Un Poco Loco," a poem published four years later in 1979, Eshleman describes Powell in a similar way: "The image of a man playing blues / who earlier that day / sipped lunch on all fours" where "the sipped milk becomes a dug root" (*The Name Encanyoned River*, 139).[6] In the poem "The Bison Keyboard" (*Hotel Cro-Magnon*, 1989), Powell "bites into the horizon / wearing keyboard braces" (139) with what Eshleman calls "Tiresias intensity":

> At the keyboard, Powell clawed for blood, as if stabbing at a bison sacrifice.
> Thus he proposes a grand dilemma: the living, no matter how grand their C
>   chords,
> lack the Tiresian recipe: to be all soul and bison vivid, a cunnilinctrice of
>   the goddess trench. (100)

The portrait presents Powell with much greater heroism than those images from earlier works, pathetic glances at a gutted spirit, but even "The Bison Keyboard" concludes with the master of bebop failing to find security or direction:

> On his cell wall in Creedmore asylum, Powell is said to have sketched, in
>   chalk, a keyboard.

Powell, now the ghost of a grand, stared at this keyboard.
"O how get home, Tiresias? How drink bison music in this hellish trench?"
   (100)

Jazz elegies have concentrated on African-American musicians not only because of the explosive themes of racism and cultural neglect but also because the primary innovators in jazz have been African-Americans. Indeed, some argue that all of the innovators have been African-Americans, but in a list of notable exceptions one might include the pianist Bill Evans and the bassist Scott LaFaro. In addition to other exceptional performances, Evans and LaFaro recorded in 1961 what is generally considered essential material: *Live at the Village Vanguard* and *Waltz for Debby*. With Evans as leader, the trio featured the drummer Paul Motion as well as LaFaro, then twenty-five, whose remarkable technique and musical sensibilities gave notice to other bassists that new standards would have to be met. These two recordings offer some of the most sublime moments in jazz. But they have also become legendary because they occurred just days before LaFaro died in an automobile accident.

The poet Bill Zavatsky knew Evans well and helped him begin work on an autobiography (left unfinished because Evans didn't think it was important enough). Zavatsky's poem "To the Pianist Bill Evans" from *Theories of Rain* (published in 1975, five years before Evans' death) elegizes Scott LaFaro and offers sympathy for the pianist. It begins with a brief acknowledgment that we can forget tragedy when listening to music, but soon, reflecting on the jazz and the players no longer alive, the loss sets in:

> When I hear you
> play "My Foolish Heart"
> I am clouded
>
> remembering more than
> Scott LaFaro's charred bass
> as it rested
>
> against a Yonkers wall
> in its transit
> from accidental fire
>
> like a shadowy
> grace note
> exploding (48)

Like the internalized thoughts of someone reacting to tragedy, Zavatsky blends one image into another; soon it becomes unclear—and this is not a critical statement—whether the speaker is Evans himself or the poem's narrator: "I imagined being / trapped inside, still / see it in my heart" (49). The poem allows us to approximate Evans's anguish, how he turned to music for solace, how jazz could comfort in ways beyond his known drug habit:

> the gentle rise
> and circle of
> cinders in
>
> February air
> in their transit
> from fire
>
> into music,
> into memory, a space
> where heroin
>
> does not slowly wave
> its blazing arm (49–50)

Like jazz lines, and like bewildering thoughts of sadness, the lines in this poem drift into each other with no full stops. Repeated images—fire, the human heart, fingers and hands, wood, wires, smoke—appear and reappear in flurries, so that the actual bass, with its strings and vulnerable neck, become the hair and neck of LaFaro, and, later the "in- / transigent wire, / inanimate wood" of Evans's piano. In a sense, LaFaro's death becomes the epicenter of resonating concern: Evans's obsession over the death, the speaker's sympathetic interpretation of Evans's grief, and our own responses to this tragedy and others like it.

In contrast to those poems that mourn individual losses, however, some jazz poems, even those from the sixties, respond to the deaths but take an anti-elegiac stance, particularly Larry Neal's "Don't Say Goodbye to the Pork-Pie Hat" from *Black Boogaloo* (1969). The poem refers to Charles Mingus's musical elegy, "Goodbye Porkpie Hat," written after he learned that Lester Young, who was famous for wearing those flat-topped hats, had died. Dedicated to *"Mingus, Bird, Prez, Langston, and them,"* the poem reads like a passionate appeal not to forget the myriad of jazz musicians from Jelly Roll Morton, Fats Waller, and Willie "the Lion" Smith to Charlie Parker, Ornette Coleman, and Sun Ra. (Neal often makes these references in shorthand—for example "Eric," "Tad," "Dinah" for Dolphy, Dameron, and Washington; like Michael Harper, he assumes an intimate knowledge of the music.) In short, Neal stresses that the "spirit lives" and that we must celebrate that sound, "dig it," as he repeats so often toward the conclusion, and not bury the spirit of jazz with the bodies of these musicians.

Similarly, Lawson Fusao Inada's poem "Filling the Gap" from *Before the War* (1971) tries hard to convince the reader that the speaker does not "like to mourn the dead" because "what didn't, never will" (87). "When Bird died," the speaker tells us, "I didn't mind: / I had things to do" (86). Clifford Brown's death evokes an equally casual reaction. The depressing descriptions of Billie Holiday and Lester Young at the end of their careers should be seen, apparently, as mere facts of life. In essence, the poem celebrates the present and concludes with the "moaning" and "alterable cry" of love making. Ironically, however, the litany of tragic deaths suggests the opposite: These losses become, in retrospect, real wounds whose gaps need filling. The speaker insists that death should be dismissed without obsessive meditation, but the image of Lester Young, the strongest image in the poem, pulls us back to a disturbing past—"a sick reunion" with Count Basie where Young is "tottering," his "saxophone / dragging him like a stage-hook" (86–87).

Although the jazz world has lost many legendary figures in the last decade—including Miles Davis, Art Blakey, Dizzy Gillespie, Stan Getz, Dexter Gordon, and Sarah Vaughan—few of the deaths have been grossly premature, and, at the risk of sounding dispassionate or cynical, I suspect that this corresponds with the declining number of jazz elegies being written.[7] The death of the trumpeter Chet Baker in 1988, however, has inspired numerous tributes. Mysteriously, Baker fell from a window ledge in an Amsterdam hotel, and shortly thereafter people began to speculate about the possible connections with his well-known drug associations: Was this a deal gone bad? Was he so smacked out that he finally "got lost" forever?

Like the alto saxophonist Art Pepper, Baker cheated death for years, somehow avoiding what seemed to be an inevitable, tragic end. His face, which once looked like the epitome of fifties cool, had been eaten away by heroin, the deep creases making him appear one-third again his age. Still, the bizarre fall that killed him left most people feeling confused, not expecting him to die *that way*, and most of the recent tributes to Baker have focused on his death, including Yusef Komunyakaa's "Speed Ball":

> Didn't Chet Baker know
> They made each great white hope
> Jump hoops of fire on the edge
> Of midnight gigs that never happened?
>
> Miles hipped him at The Lighthouse
> About horse, said not to feel guilty
> About *Down Beat* in '53. Chet stole
> Gasoline to sniff, doctored with Beiderbecke's
>
> Chicago style. But it wasn't long
> Before he was a toothless lion
> Gazing up at his face like a stranger's
> Caught by tinted lens & brass. Steel-

Blue stare from Oklahoma whispering for
"A kind of high that scares everyone
To death." Maybe a bop angel, Slim
Greer, pulled him from that hotel window. (151–152)

Komunyakaa's poem begins with a question of urgency, but Miller Williams's elegy "The Death of Chet Baker" does not really gain momentum until it too asks a pressing question: "What do we feel, now that he's gone?" (9). Williams's poem continues to press the reader with questions about pity and pain, and then, as though resigned to the fact that the questions cannot be adequately answered, presents the realities of loss:

He had his dreams and methadone,
we have tapes and CDs,
Time after Time, When Your Lover Has Gone.

CDs do what was done before
over and over and over and over,
never adding a note more
if we should listen to them forever. (9–10)

The poem concludes with a strange stanza, italicized and titled "*Epitaph*"; its final couplet reads, "*The body here beneath this stone/was Chet Baker, who has flown*" (10), and it is unclear how ironic Williams intends to be, or how appropriate that irony is to the poem. The glib rhythms and rhymes seem to undermine the emotion in the penultimate stanza:

Wherever we are he isn't there.
Love him. Love him in the loss
for all the things he did with air.
The Thrill Is Gone. Poor Chet. Poor us. (10)

Ai's poem for Chet Baker, "Archangel" (*Greed*, 1993), includes some lines that, in much the same way as Williams's "*Epitaph*," seem a little trite or too easy, such as "you earned the wings / that were too late to save you, / but not too late to raise you / up to junkie heaven" (68). But in general, Ai's poem re-creates the essence of Chet Baker, not through memory but, quite literally, in spirit. Baker visits the speaker in her dreams, and suddenly she's transported to Paris. In one of the strongest parts of the poem, Ai describes with her characteristically honest tone the sexual flirtations of that moment:

I had high breasts
and my dress was cut low.
You leaned close to me, so close;
yet, did not touch.

"I don't need to," you said, "it's the dope,
it's the rush
so much better than lust.
Hush, take a deep breath
and you'll just go to sleep like I did."
I knew you were hustling me,
that underneath the hipster philosophy
lay the same old Chet out to score. (67)

Baker leaves the table, gets his fix in the public bathroom, then leaves
with a prostitute. He returns long enough to blow a kiss and wish the
speaker, in French, good luck. When he rises from out of the dream, an
image that concludes the poem ("into flight, / as the cool, jazzy, starry
night / opened its arms to retrieve you"), Ai does not disappoint the reader
with the cliché "Then I woke up." Instead, Baker ascends the way we
imagine a body's spirit rises. Our mind's eye moves skyward, but the unsentimental physical description of his death balances the celestial images
with the grimmer realities of mortality:

You said when you slammed into the pavement,
Amsterdam shook, then settled back into apathy,
the way we all do, when we are through
with the foolishness of living. (67)

Mark Doty's poem for Chet Baker, "Almost Blue" from *My Alexandria*
(1993), meditates on Baker's trumpet tone, first with anachronistic analogies ("If Hart Crane played trumpet/he'd sound like you" [14]) and then
with more biographical sketches that quickly meld into wondrous abstractions and landscapes:

two weeks before the end, Chet,
and you're playing like anything,

singing *stay little valentine*
stay

and taking so long there are worlds sinking
between the notes, this exhalation

no longer a voice but a rush of air,
brutal, from the tunnels under the river,

the barges' late whistles you only hear
when the traffic's stilled

by snow (14–15)

Like his description of Baker's music as "a rush of air," the poem itself exhales the images and rhythms. Even the jagged syntax and sweeping statements of emotion seem perfectly in place:

> Too many rooms unrented
>
> in this residential hotel,
> and you don't want to know
>
> why they're making that noise in the hall;
> you're going to wake up in any one of the
>
> how many ten thousand
> locations of trouble and longing
>
> *going out of business forever everything must go*
> wake up and start wanting. (15–16)

In fact, it's quite difficult to discuss this poem in sections or stanzas, for it does not read like a formal narrative—this happened, and then this, and then this—but like a jazz solo that you don't want to dissect so much as enjoy. "Almost Blue" maintains a soft, quiet tone, yet it builds its emotion from the continuous flow of rhythm and the deft repetition of imagery. The first two-thirds of the poem introduce us to Baker's life: the "dark city," "sleep's hellgate," his voice singing standards, "a little pearl of junk," the "residential hotel," need and desire. The last third improvises on those images, inverts them, and presents his death:

> It's so much better when you don't want:
> nothing falls then, nothing lost
>
> but sleep and who wanted that
> in the pearl this suspended world is,
>
> in the warm suspension and glaze
> of this song everything stays up
>
> almost forever in the long
> glide sung into the vein,
>
> one note held almost impossibly
> almost blue and the lyric takes so long
>
> to open, a little blood
> blooming: *there's no love song   finer*
>
> *but how strange the change*
> *from major to minor*
>
> *everytime*
> *we say goodbye*

and you leaning into that warm
haze from the window, Amsterdam,

late afternoon glimmer
a blur of buds

breathing in the lindens
and you let go and why not (16–17)

In the notes for *My Alexandria*, Doty dedicates his poem to Lynda Hull, whose own poetry constantly returns to "locations of trouble and longing" (Doty, 16), as witnessed in her poem "Hollywood Jazz" from *Ghost Money* (1986), which begins with a description that unites the dark throatiness of jazz with the dangerous, evocative urban landscape:

Who says it's cool says wrong.
    For it rises from the city's
        sweltering geometry of rooms,

fire escapes, and flares from the heels
    of corner boys on Occidental
        posing with small-time criminal

intent—all pneumatic grace. This
    is the music that plays at the moment
        in every late-night *noir* flick (43)

But if comparisons must be made, Hull's tribute to Baker, "Lost Fugue for Chet" from *Star Ledger* (1991), is her most astonishing jazz-inspired work. The poem asks probing questions about the nature of Baker's psyche and artistry; it presents vivid, painterly images of the Amsterdam panorama as a necessary backdrop for his music; and it unflinchingly delves into the dark world of jazz and narcotics.

The opening to "Lost Fugue for Chet" is reminiscent, perhaps, of O'Hara's reference to the newspaper photo of Holiday, but not slavishly so, and unlike O'Hara's poem the details recounted in this walk through the Amsterdam streets recall a more detailed history of the poem's subject, a musician who led a life reminiscent of "furled petals turning in & in upon themselves" (79):

A single spot slides the trumpet's flare then stops
    at that face, the extraordinary ruins thumb-marked
with the hollows of heroin, the rest chiaroscuroed.
    Amsterdam, the final gig, canals & countless

stone bridges arc, glimmering in lamps. Later this week
  his Badlands face, handsome in a print from thirty
years ago, will follow me from the obituary page
  insistent as windblown papers by the black cathedral

of St. Nicholas standing closed today: pigeon shit
  & feathers, posters swathing tarnished doors, a litter
of syringes. (78)

Filled with relentless introspection and variations on Baker's "Let's Get Lost," the speaker admits to passionate, personal associations with addiction ("I've never forgotten, never— / *this is the tied-off vein, this is 3 A.M. terror / thrumming, this is the carnation of blood clouding / the syringe*" [80]), establishing a remarkable intimacy between speaker and subject.

Like too many artists in this chapter, Lynda Hull (1954–1994) died prematurely and unexpectedly from a car crash. "Our response to horror," writes Mark Doty in the "After Word" to Hull's posthumously published *The Only World* (1995), "is silence," but he adds: "Another is to make what one can, to create with all the more ardor and fury" (79). Perhaps, as Doty suggests, the creative act is the most we can ask for when facing tragedy, and perhaps the conclusion to her elegy might be read as a more universal gesture, where the release into the winds and waters of Amsterdam allows the human spirit to become as vibrant, invisible, and everlasting as jazz:

From the trumpet, pawned, redeemed, pawned again
you formed one wrenching blue arrangement, a phrase endlessly
  complicated as that twilit dive through smoke, applause,

the pale haunted rooms. Cold chestnuts flowering April
  & you're falling from heaven in a shower of eighth notes
to the cobbled street below & foaming dappled horses
  plunge beneath the still green waters of the Grand Canal. (80)

NOTES

1. Possible exceptions include Langston Hughes's "The Weary Blues" and Michael Harper's "Dear John, Dear Coltrane."

2. Both Billie Holiday and Thelonious Monk deserve separate chapters. Apart from those poems discussed in this chapter, the many homages to Billie Holiday include Langston Hughes's "Song for Billie Holiday" (*One-Way Ticket*, 1949), possibly the first poem in her honor; Walter DeLegall's "Elegy for a Lady," anthologized by Pool in 1962 and possibly the first elegy; and Alexis De Veaux's book *Don't Explain: A Song for Billie Holiday* (1980), a biography of Holiday written entirely in verse. Whereas almost all of the poems for Holiday were written posthumously, Monk had numerous poems written in his honor during his lifetime—more than any musician, in fact—and they include entire books of poems,

such as Dave Etter's *Well You Needn't: The Thelonious Monk Poems* (1975) and Art Lange's *The Monk Poems* (1977). John Sinclair's *Thelonious: A Book of Monk* has yet to be published, but one selection appeared in *We Just Change the Beat: Selected Poems* (1988).

3. Unfortunately, Perkins misspells "Navarro" as "narvaro"; when the poem reappeared in *Midnight Blues in the Afternoon* (1992, second edition), it was misspelled as "navaro." Although this may seem petty, one of the sad commentaries about jazz poetry in general has to do with the sloppy scholarship—errors in names and dates that undermine the tributes. Just glancing at the elegies for this chapter, I have noticed numerous misspellings of names (particularly "Thelonious"). Lillian Morrison's tribute "For Billie Holiday" refers to her birth and death dates (1915–1959) but incorrectly lists her death date as 1958; the dates for Clayton Eshleman's "Bud Powell (1925–1966)" should more accurately be 1924–1966; and so on.

4. Not all poems about Bessie Smith concentrate on the tragedy of her death, including two poems from 1962: John Berryman's "Dream Song 68" (*The Dream Songs*) and Robert Hayden's "Homage to the Empress of the Blues" (*A Ballad of Remembrance*). Berryman invokes Smith's voice for setting the buoyant atmosphere of the poem; Hayden presents Smith in her elaborate costumes, her flamboyant presentation a welcomed relief from the tensions of the unadorned world.

5. "Emmett Till's body," explain the editors to *Voices of Freedom*, "was discovered in the Tallahatchie River. A cotton gin fan was tied to his neck with barbed wire" (Hampton and Fayer, 5). The first chapter to that book offers a detailed account of the murder as told by witnesses and relatives.

6. This poem originally appeared in *Hades in Manganese* (1981) as "The American Sublime." Eshleman changed the title to "Un Poco Loco," a composition by Powell, when the poem was reprinted in *The Name Encanyoned River* (1986).

7. There have been some major exceptions to this statement, including the deaths of bassist Jaco Pastorius (1951–1987), guitarist Emily Remler (1957–1991), and trumpeter Woody Shaw (1944–1989), among others. Art Pepper (1925–1982) survived extraordinary substance abuse (his accounts in *Straight Life* make it one of the most haunting jazz autobiographies ever written), but there have been surprisingly few jazz poems in his honor or about his life—with some significant exceptions, including David Meltzer's "18:VI:82" from *The Name: Selected Poetry 1973–1983* (1984) and Edward Hirsch's "Art Pepper" from *Earthly Measures* (1994).

REFERENCES

Ai. *Greed*. New York: Norton, 1993.

Albee, Edward. *The Zoo Story; The Death of Bessie Smith; The Sandbox: Three Plays*. New York: Coward-McCann, 1960.

Albertson, Chris. *Bessie*. New York: Scarborough, 1972.

Aubert, Alvin. *Against the Blues*. Detroit: Broadside, 1972.

Baker, Houston A., Jr. *Blues Journeys Home*. Detroit: Lotus, 1985.

Balliett, Whitney. Letter to the author. 13 February 1988.

Berryman, John. *The Dream Songs*. New York: Farrar, Straus, Giroux, 1969.

Cortez, Jayne. *Pissstained Stairs and the Monkey Man's Wares*. New York: Phase Text, 1969.

De Veaux, Alexis. *Don't Explain: A Song of Billie Holiday.* New York: Harper and Row, 1980.

Doty, Mark. *My Alexandria.* Urbana: University of Illinois Press, 1993.

Early, Gerald. *Tuxedo Junction.* New York: Ecco, 1989.

Eshleman, Clayton. *Hades in Manganese.* Santa Barbara: Black Sparrow, 1981.

———. *Hotel Cro-Magnon.* Santa Rosa: Black Sparrow, 1989.

———. *Indiana.* Los Angeles: Black Sparrow, 1969.

———. *The Gull Wall.* Los Angeles: Black Sparrow, 1975.

———. *The Name Encanyoned River.* Santa Barbara: Black Sparrow, 1986.

Etter, Dave. *Well You Needn't: The Thelonious Monk Poems.* Independence, Mo.: Raindust, 1975.

Feinstein, Sascha, and Yusef Komunyakaa, eds. *The Jazz Poetry Anthology.* Bloomington: Indiana University Press, 1991.

Hampton, Henry, and Stever Fayer, eds. *Voices of Freedom: An Oral History of the Civil Rights Movement from the 1950s through the 1980s.* New York: Bantam, 1990.

Harjo, Joy. *In Mad Love and War.* Middletown, Conn.: Wesleyan University Press, 1990.

Hart, Howard. *Selected Poems: Six Sets, 1951–1983.* Berkeley: City Miner, 1984.

Hayden, Robert. *A Ballad of Remembrance.* London: Paul Breman, 1962.

Hirsch, Edward. *Earthly Measures.* New York: Knopf, 1994.

Hughes, Langston. *One-Way Ticket.* New York: Knopf, 1949.

Hull, Lynda. *Ghost Money.* Amherst: University of Massachusetts, 1986.

———. *The Only World.* New York: HarperPerennial, 1995.

———. *Star Ledger.* Iowa City: University of Iowa, 1991.

Inada, Lawson Fusao. *Before the War.* New York: Morrow, 1971.

Kerouac, Jack. *Mexico City Blues.* New York: Grove, 1959.

Komunyakaa, Yusef. "Speed Ball." *New England Review* 16, 1 (Winter 1994): 151–152.

Lange, Art. *The Monk Poems.* New York: Frontward Books, 1977.

Levine, Philip. *One for the Rose.* New York: Atheneum, 1981.

Meltzer, David. *The Name: Selected Poetry 1973–1983.* California: Black Sparrow, 1984.

Morrison, Lillian. *The Ghosts of Jersey City & Other Poems.* New York: Thomas Y. Crowell, 1967.

Neal, Larry. *Black Boogaloo.* San Francisco: Journal of Black Poetry, 1969.

O'Hara, Frank. *The Collected Poems of Frank O'Hara.* Ed. Donald Allen. New York: Knopf, 1971.

Perkins, Useni Eugene. *Midnight Blue in the Afternoon.* Second Edition. Detroit: INESU, 1992.

———. *Silhouette.* Chicago: Free Black, 1970.

Pool, Rosey E., ed. *Beyond the Blues: New Poems by American Negroes.* Kent, England: Hand and Flower, 1962.

Sinclair, John. *We Just Change the Beat: Selected Poems.* Roseville, Mich.: Ridgeway, 1988.

Troupe, Quincy. *Embryo.* New York: Barlenmir, 1972.

Welburn, Ron. *Heartland*. Detroit: Lotus, 1981.

Williams, Miller. *Adjusting to the Light*. Columbia: University of Missouri Press, 1992.

Zavatsky, Bill. *Theories of Rain*. New York: Sun, 1975.

An Enormous Yes: Contemporary Jazz Poetry

For me, jazz works primarily as a kind of discovery, as a way for me to discover that emotional mystery behind things. It helps me get to a place I thought I had forgotten.
　　　　—Yusef Komunyakaa

My father, who used to bicycle thirty miles one way to court my mother, had this record [Coleman Hawkins' Body and Soul] *among his dust-needled 78s. He'd already worn out several copies before I learned to love it from memory, never knowing until much later what a cause it had stirred.*
　　　　—Al Young

To say that recent American poetry has not been as revolutionary as poetry from previous decades is not, in itself, a revolutionary statement, nor is it a condemnation. "The mainstream of American poetry," writes Jonathan Holden about contemporary verse, "has continued to be, whether narrative or meditative, in a Realistic mode that is essentially egalitarian, university-based, middle-class, and written in free verse that has, by and large, vastly improved since the sixties" (Myers and Wojahn, 273). Holden supports James Breslin's stand in *From Modern to Contemporary: American Poetry, 1945–1965*, and Breslin's well-known metaphors regarding poetry in the eighties bear repeating because they also pertain to contemporary jazz and jazz poetry:

If American poetry in the middle fifties resembled a peaceful public park on a pleasant summer Sunday afternoon, and if by the early sixties it had been transformed into a war zone, the air heavy with manifestos, then by the early 1980s the atmosphere has lightened and the scene more resembles a small affluent town in Northern California. (250)

We appear to be living at a time when the creative arts seem much less tumultuous, less life-on-the-line, and it is for that reason, I think, that contemporary poets engaged in jazz have tended to leapfrog the present and celebrate the musicians of the past, when jazz and poetry kept progressing with sharklike urgency.

The rapid development of jazz from the turn of the century through the sixties has caused many critics to evaluate contemporary jazz artists in relation to their innovative predecessors. Whitney Balliett, for example, recently stated that the prodigies who now dominate jazz are "conservatives bent on refurbishing" hard bop, which is why he refers to them as "the neos" (98). On the one hand, jazz enthusiasts have witnessed in the last ten years a remarkable resurgence, featuring musicians whose technical abilities have staggered audiences, and many of these players have embraced their musical history—bypassing what in the seventies seemed like a required fusion with rock and celebrating in their sound and ideology the music of Duke Ellington, Thelonious Monk, John Coltrane, and many others. In contrast to the image of the jazz musician as a junkie, these younger players, generally speaking, now live cleaner lives, and the music that used to be performed exclusively in small, often dingy clubs now fills expensive concert halls. On the other hand, Gerald Early seems justified to lament being "witness to the tail end," "the burning out forever of that magnificent light of great music" (308). Because jazz seems at present to be stalled in its once furious evolutionary development, some question whether it has, in fact, run its course.

Writing about contemporary jazz poems, at least in terms of the social and cultural implications, does not yield neat analogies, such as those established between early American poetry and early American music; Beat poetry and Bebop; or John Coltrane and Black Nationalism. But there are some significant parallels concerning a change in tone, and Breslin's overview of contemporary poetry parallels the more specific movement in jazz poetry. In the last twenty-five years or so, jazz poems have become noticeably less dynamic visually than the poetry from the fifties and sixties, which tried more deliberately to emulate the rhythms of jazz in the verse. In the fifties, jazz culture infused poetry with hip, Daddy-O vernacular, jagging the syntax and, often, the appearance on the page. By the end of the next decade, the "scream" of Coltrane's horn ballooned the lettering into capitalized statements and sent the poetic lines cascading. In contrast, jazz poems since 1970 have been, generally speaking, rather quiet and strongly narrative.

But within that period—from 1970 to the present—a subtle but significant transition in jazz poetry has occurred, and this change concerns tone:

In contrast to the overwhelming number of elegies written in the seventies, the more-recent jazz poems, reflecting the human grieving process, tend to celebrate jazz musicians and their music. In fact, an inventory of the careers of several ranking poets whose work has been centrally concerned with jazz—William Matthews, Yusef Komunyakaa, Hayden Carruth, and Al Young, for instance—reveals an emergent pattern: The grief that occupied their poetic center in the seventies has largely given way to hagiography, as they have in their more recent work reinvoked the memories of famous players, celebrating their artistic triumphs and inspirational musicianship in the process.

In terms of this changing emphasis from elegy to celebration, William Matthews' career as a poet perfectly reflects a more global transition. Like many jazz poems from the seventies, those from Matthews' first book, *Ruining the New Road* (1970), focus on emotional upheaval, on devastation. "Coleman Hawkins (d. 1969), RIP" describes this powerful tenor saxophonist ("a river of muscles") whose life concluded with brief moments of satisfaction ("eggs scrambled just right in a diner"), a manic work schedule ("eight gigs in nine nights"), and estranged values ("a new Leica / for the fun of having one")—all summed up by the simple line, "Gasps and twitches." Matthews' persona responds with personal anguish: "It's like having the breath / knocked out of me / and wearing the lost air for a leash" (10). Where Hawkins uses the "dank music / of his breath" to create arresting sounds, the speaker simply has his breath taken out of him, as though the very source of inspiration has gone.

"Blues for John Coltrane, Dead at 41" concerns itself even less with the genius of the performer and still more directly with despair. The speaker imagines "death's salmon breath / leaping back up the saxophone / with its wet kiss" (9) and meditates on the premature death of Coltrane who, in fact, did not live to reach his forty-first birthday. Like the wind knocked out of the speaker in the Hawkins poem, this loss overwhelms the speaker: "I feel it in my feet / as if the house were rocked / by waves from a soundless speedboat / planing by, full throttle" (9). Thus, in his poems for Coltrane and Hawkins, Matthews seems unable to present portraits that transcend his grief.

By Matthews' third book, *Rising and Falling* (1979), the jazz poems still concentrate on elegy, but the poet hints of an identification between speaker and subject, particularly in "Bud Powell, Paris, 1959" and "Listening to Lester Young." The portrait of Powell begins with grim observation, a statement of the young poet's disturbed awareness of Powell's decline: "I'd never seen pain so bland" (24). Powell's extreme substance abuse—he was an alcoholic, not a junkie as the poem implies—"had eaten his technique" until it was almost unbearable to watch.[1] Matthews sets the scene: "Two bucks for a Scotch in this dump, / I thought, and I bought me / another," adding, "I was young and pain / rose to my ceiling like warmth, / like a story that makes us come true / in the present" (24). We can sense the speaker's urgent need to share in, if not save, this man's life. But while his hero remains a myth—"Nobody played as well / as Powell, and neither did he"—the man behind the myth degenerates to shocking decay. Despite the trenchant difference between Powell's life-threatening decline and the discomfort of adolescent confusion, the speaker salvages at least one empathetic shard of wisdom: "Pain loves pain / and calls it company, and it is" (24).

In "Listening to Lester Young," pain is once again the dominant motif. The poem begins one year prior to Young's death (he left for Paris in 1959, returning to New York on March 14 and dying on the Ides) and several years after his ordeal with the United States Army in 1944, when he experienced the extremes of prejudice that left him emotionally and artistically scarred:

> It's 1958. Lester Young minces
> out, spraddle-legged as if pain
> were something he could step over
> by raising his groin, and begins
> to play. (28)

The poem offers no hint of Young's dynamic performances from the late thirties or of his youthful lyricism, which Matthews once described in an essay titled "Billie Holiday and Lester Young on 'Me, Myself, and I' ":

Young's tone was pale and wispy and languidly understated. He had none of the burly vibrato or rushing, masculine lyricism of Coleman Hawkins, who ruled the tenor when Lester came on the scene. Young never seemed urgent and could run longer and farther behind the beat than any musician who could also swing, which he never failed to do. . . . He played with an unmatched tenderness, as if suffering and pleasure were impossible without each other. (*Curiosities*, 116)

In its omission of any such reference to tenderness, however, the first stanza heightens the pathos and resignation of Young's decline.

In the second stanza, a stranger attempts to enter Young's mythic world, and the fact that this person is a "jazz writer" certainly evokes an emotional connection with Matthews. The writer lets his ice skates fall from his hands, and his eager tone—"It's Lester Young! *Hey Prez*" (28)—suggests desperation to touch fame. But he fails to realize, or perhaps momentarily forgets, that Young is beyond adulation at this point in his career. The saxophonist cuts all of the youthful speaker's enthusiasm with one short, apathetic comment: "*You dropped your shit*" (28).

Then the poem charges forward in time, and the speaker begins to interact not with the musician himself but with the music:

> It's 1976 and I'm listening
> to Lester Young through stereo equipment
> so good I can hear his breath rasp,
> water from a dry pond—(28)

As with the elegy for Coleman Hawkins, sound becomes breath, and with uninterrupted rhythm, "Listening to Lester Young" moves quickly to a close through a series of associative rising and falling images inspired by "water from a dry pond":

> its bottom etched, like a palm,
> with strange marks, a language
> that was never born
> and in which palmists therefore
> can easily read the future. (29)

Taken one way, the last lines suggest our inability to understand completely the sounds of a man whose life has ended in disarray and despair. Taken another, they imply that we can all respond to jazz in absolute terms—despite the abstraction of the art form—because no associative reflection is any less valid than another; in other words, because people have no absolute language for sound, they "can easily read the future," and if there is an intimacy in listening to recordings, then it must have to do with this appreciation. Although "Listening to Lester Young" provides a nearly hopeless portrait, it nevertheless allows the speaker to participate in and learn from the lives of his heroes.

Two of the jazz poems from Matthews' *Flood* (1983) move still further from elegy, suggesting that *Flood* might be a pivotal work for him in its dramatic distancing from elegiac despair.[2] "Bmp Bmp," for example, improvises on the playfulness of Sidney Bechet, the New Orleans clarinetist and first master of the soprano saxophone. "The poem," Matthews explains in a note, "describes a cadenza Bechet takes on 'Tin Roof Blues' on his *Back to Memphis* album with Sammy Price, recorded in 1956" (*Flood*, 71).[3] But the poem does more than describe a moment; it captures the whole spirit of Bechet's ability, how this reedman, born in 1897, was consistently able to transform the mundane into the supernal in his explosively brilliant performances:

> And then he's up, loop
> and slur and spiral, and a long, drifting note
> at the top, from which, like a child decided
> to come home before he's called, he begins to drift

back down, insouciant and exact, and ambles
in the door of the joyous and tacky chorus
just on time for the band to leave together,
headed for the *Tin Roof Blues*. (61)

Bechet's solo surges as he lips his inflections with the perfect balance between tension and release, which Matthews adroitly associates with World
War II planes rising from aircraft carriers, how they "would dip off the
lip, and catch the right / resistance from wet air and strain up" (61). Still,
the tension here has nothing to do with anxiety or pressure; instead, the
poem concentrates on what Philip Larkin called the "enormous yes" of
Bechet's playing (*Whitsun Weddings*, 16).[4]

Similarly, Matthews' poem "Unrelenting Flood" captures the sheer
pleasure of the music by Art Tatum, a pianist who was blind in one eye
and virtually blind in the other. The poem begins with a stop/start rhythm,
an effort by the speaker to understand the process of improvisation
("White key. Black key. No,/that's wrong. It's all tactile" [*Flood*, 37]) and
then swiftly moves with a push of rhythm, emphasizing the "sunlight" and
"joy" of Tatum's abilities:

Think how blind and near-
blind pianists range along
their keyboards by clambering
over notes a sighted man
would notice to leave out,
by stringing it all on one
longing, the way bee-fingered,
blind, mountainous Art
Tatum did, the way we like
joy to arrive: in such
unrelenting flood the only
way we can describe it
is by music or another
beautiful abstraction,
like a ray of sunlight
in a child's drawing
running straight to a pig's ear,
tethering us all to our star. (37)

In effect, the poem simultaneously celebrates Tatum's artistry and instructs other poets how to use visual imagery to describe an invisible art.

In recent years, Matthews has moved still further from his original elegiac tone. *A Happy Childhood* (1984) includes the marvelous "Alice
Zeno Talking, and Her Son George Lewis the Jazz Clarinettist in Atten-
dance," where Alice Zeno is in command, her famous son virtually silent,

yet the musicality of her voice evokes the lyricism of Lewis's New Orleans style clarinet. *Blues If You Want* (1989) includes several poems titled after famous jazz standards ("Smoke Gets in Your Eyes," "Moonlight in Vermont," "It Don't Mean a Thing If It Ain't Got That Swing") as well as a few direct references to jazz. Mainly, however, the book sustains a jazz feel, with variations on related themes, including the blues, that read a bit like jazz improvisations but not in the acutely self-conscious style of, say, Kerouac's *Mexico City Blues*.

In "The Buddy Bolden Cylinder," a recent but uncollected piece, the speaker inevitably accepts the truth—that Bolden's insanity destroyed any chance to record his music, that there is no cylinder to be found—but not before meditating on the fantasy of finding such a scroll, the kind of fantasies we need.[5] Matthews' most recent book, *Time and Money* (1995), includes three poems for the bassist and composer Charles Mingus. In "Mingus at The Showplace" Matthews reflects on autobiographical experiences where the speaker, like the youngster in his Powell poem, awkwardly interacts with this legendary jazz figure.[6] Here again the speaker seems too young to grasp the full magnificence of these players yet is old enough to realize how much can be learned from listening. He shows the great bassist one of his "miserable" poems, and Mingus chooses dismissal rather than condescension. Unlike the emerging poet, however, the weak pianist in the band does not receive Mingus's patience, and the poem closes with a gesture and statement that seem both shocking and comical: Mingus fires the pianist, watches him leave, and comments, "We've suffered a diminuendo in personnel" (5). To a degree, the poem thanks Mingus for not attacking the bad verse, for withholding what could have been a savage assault. And it thanks him, too, for one of many remarkable evenings in downtown New York. Matthews realizes how these jazz musicians have nurtured his craft, and his poems swell with gratitude.

Analogies between poets and musicians can seem arbitrary and often uninstructive, but if the poems by Matthews sound like the suave and lyrical jazz solos by Lester Young, then the work by Yusef Komunyakaa sounds much more like Thelonious Monk, who knew how to balance clustered chords with elevator shafts of silence. In a sense, much of Komunyakaa's poetry seems governed by the Monk title "Ugly Beauty." His poetry boldly juxtaposes conflicting images, setting up predominantly unresolved tensions, and yet his speakers often discover how jazz can excavate buried resilience.

This bittersweet combination of dissonance and resolution propels the movement of both jazz poems in Komunyakaa's first book, *Copacetic* (1984). "Elegy for Thelonious" begins, "Damn the snow. / Its senseless beauty / pours a hard light / through the hemlock. / Thelonious is dead" (40). The speaker moves in and out of reflection, thinking of Monk tunes and Monk's fingers on the keyboards—"The ghost of bebop / from 52nd

Street, / footprints in the snow" (40)—and after he curses the month itself
("Damn February"), he conjures a vivid image of the pianist, with his hat
doubling as trademark and death mask. "Let's go to Minton's," the
speaker says to himself, urging on memories that challenge death: "Lord,
/ there's Thelonious / wearing that old funky hat / pulled over his eyes"
(40).

The second jazz poem, "Copacetic Mingus," presents a different kind
of challenge, one that has less to do with death and more to do with love.
Here Komunyakaa describes the bassist "Running big hands down / the
upright's wide hips, / rocking his moon-eyed mistress" (41). Midway
through the poem, the speaker suggests unspoken depression (it is clear
that Mingus has died), yet he turns to Mingus on record, *Pithecanthropus
Erectus*, and "the raw strings / unwaxed with rosin" speak to him again,
recapture the romance of 1973 when he heard the bassist live. The "Hyperbolic bass line" comforts and instructs: "Hard love, it's hard love" (41).

In the poems for Monk and Mingus, Komunyakaa offers music as a
form of immortality. The poems acknowledge a sense of anguish, but the
overwhelming emotion—the one sustained by each poem and related to
the reader—concerns the prevailing and positive quality of the creative
act. We witness musicians who have lived intensely, and their recorded
music, as well as the memories of musicians, overshadows loss. There is
an urgency in the poet's tone, as though the speaker fully identifies with
the need to create in spite or even because of personal hardships. "You
taught me a heavy love / for jazz, how words can hurt / more than a quick
jab," says the speaker in "More Girl Than Boy," adding, "You always
could make that piano / talk like somebody's mama" (*Copacetic*, 10). The
poems for Monk and Mingus celebrate the individual musicians, and they
also, by implication, address the "hard love" of writing poetry or playing
jazz.

For Komunyakaa, jazz also functions as a vehicle for personal discovery.
"I wanted to write a poem that dealt with childhood," he recently said,
"so I put on Louis Armstrong" (Kelly, 647). The poem he then wrote,
"Venus's Fly-traps" (*Magic City*, 1993), does not overtly address jazz but
tries to emulate "jazz and syncopated rhythms" (Kelly, 647). Indeed, the
influence of jazz on Komunyakaa's poetry might be felt as much in the
rhythms of the verse as in the actual subject matter, and this aural connection is most apparent in his poems from his chapbook *February in
Sydney*, later collected in *Neon Vernacular*. In "The Plea," for example,
the jazz-influenced refrain "bop, bop, bebop, rebop" sets the pace and
motion of the poem even more than the alternating indentation.[7] Like
Monk's use of dissonance and silence, Komunyakaa offers imagery that
seems too large to visualize while giving the reader the space to think,
respond. In "The Plea," Thelonious himself appears "bright as that /
golden plea of gospel / under everything / Monk wrung from the keys"

(163), and this golden light beneath the midnight pitch swells in a "slow dance of waves" that illuminates the speaker's consciousness. "Each undying note," he tells us,

> resounds in my head;
> there's a cry in every pocket
> & low swell of unhappy
> lust I've suffered,
> & round about midnight the odor of sex
> & salvation quivers in each song
> the wooden hammers
> strike from wire strings
> like anger stolen back
> from the soil. (164)

Like "The Plea" and its repeated line "bop, bop, bebop, rebop," the unpunctuated poem "Blue Light Lounge Sutra for the Performance Poets at Harold Park Hotel" uses the refrain "the need gotta be / so deep" (*Neon Vernacular*, 176) as a way of pushing the lines forward, and the dynamics of its rhythm have made it one of Komunyakaa's most successful in terms of performance, whether reading it solo or with musical accompaniment. The center of the poem cadences with "blow that saxophone," and as the speaker repeats "you gotta get into it," the poem offers precise descriptions of wild abstractions: "so deep you can vomit up ghosts"; "so deep the bomb locked / in rust opens like a fist"; "if you wanna dance / this boogie be ready / to let the devil use your head / for a drum" (176–177). "Blue Light Lounge Sutra" glorifies a "basic / animal need" to create, to perform on the deepest spiritual level.

The title poem to *February in Sydney*, like so many poems in *Neon Vernacular*, explores bewilderment and despair in response to violence and racism, but it also dramatizes the creative act as a way of coping, even triumphing:

> Dexter Gordon's tenor sax
> plays "April in Paris"
> inside my head all the way back
> on the bus from Double Bay.
> *Round Midnight*, the '50s,
> cool cobblestone streets
> resound footsteps of Bebop
> musicians with whiskey-laced voices
> from a boundless dream in French.
> Bud, Prez, Webster, & The Hawk,
> their names run together
> like mellifluous riffs.
> Painful gods jive talk through

bloodstained reeds & shiny brass
where music is an anesthetic.
Unreadable faces from the human void
float like torn pages across the bus
windows. An old anger drips into my throat,
& I try thinking something good,
letting the precious bad
settle to the salty bottom.
Another scene keeps repeating itself:
I emerge from the dark theatre,
passing a woman who grabs her red purse
& hugs it to her like a heart attack.
Tremolo. Dexter comes back to rest
behind my eyelids. A loneliness
lingers like a silver needle
under my black skin,
as I try to feel how it is
to scream for help through a horn. (178)

Framed by references to Dexter Gordon, the poem pays homage to four other innovators—Bud Powell, Lester Young, Ben Webster, and Coleman Hawkins—and the ease with which the speaker releases their nicknames evokes, by association, the huge history of jazz. But this poem is less about that history than it is about self-discovery. Although the speaker in "February in Sydney" initially assumes that the "music is an anesthetic," jazz becomes an instructional aesthetic—not something that numbs his emotion but an art that allows him to respond, to face the "old anger." Like most of Komunyakaa's jazz poems, this piece invokes jazz as a vehicle for introspective explorations of the past that necessarily inform the present.

Komunyakaa's jazz poems are full of discovery and wonder but they do not seem nostalgic, and this is one of the crucial differences between his work and Hayden Carruth's poetry. Carruth's nostalgia has much to do with his favorite styles of jazz: Whereas Komunyakaa clearly prefers players from the fifties and sixties, Carruth is one of the few contemporary writers who focuses more on musicians from the Swing era, and in general Carruth's tributes threaten to boil over with enthusiasm for the music.

This buoyancy does not infuse all of Carruth's jazz poems. For example, in *Nothing for Tigers* (1965), one of his earliest books, his elegy "Billie Holiday" reads like an epitaph—one of his least optimistic jazz poems and possibly his first:

Here lies a lady. Day was her double pain,
Pride and compassion equally gone wrong.
At night she sang, "Do you conceive my song?"
And answered in her torn voice, "Don't explain." (50)

But this same book includes a more representative jazz poem, "Freedom and Discipline," and here Carruth discusses how music acts as an education, how jazz must be seen as an art form superior, in a sense, to poetry. "Why I went to verse-making," the speaker says, "is unknowable, this / grubbing art" (78–79). Poetry for him seems "locked / in discipline" yet "sworn to / freedom" (79), and this philosophy is elaborated in considerable detail in his essay "Influences: The Formal Idea of Jazz" from *Sitting In* (1986). "For myself," Carruth explains, "I know my sensibility was better attuned to jazz than to any other artistic mode; but the rest of my personality was unfit for it. . . . The truth is, whether for good or ill and to the extent—is it any at all?—that we enjoy freedom of choice in this world, poetry for me was, and is, second-best to jazz" (29). In this spirit, his poem "Freedom and Discipline" concludes:

> Freedom and discipline concur
> only in ecstacy, all else
>
> is shoveling out the muck.
> Give me my old hot horn. (79)

Carruth's long poem "Paragraphs" from *Brothers, I Loved You All* (1978) closely expresses his envy of jazz musicians while approaching the "ecstacy" of jazz he sought to achieve in his art. Paragraph "11" at first seems almost like a found poem—just a list of names. (In a later poem, "Letter to Maxine Sullivan," Carruth's speaker says, "oh / the names, names, lovely old names calling to me always through echoing dark" [*Collected*, 364].) But this section builds momentum, creating a rhythmic drive through the sounds of these players' names: Cozy Cole, Zutty Singleton, Specs Powell, J. C. Higginbotham, Nappy Lamar, Pops Foster. By the end of the passage, we realize that it is anything but a eulogy, either in tone or content. In fact, several of these musicians were alive when Carruth wrote the piece, and some are still living. Instead, we become aware of his pleasure in paying tribute to these players, with such intensity that this section's closing line—"Brothers I loved you all"—titles the book.

"Paragraphs" winds through varied landscapes and histories and concludes with three paragraphs—"26," "27," and "28"—that epitomize the poem's vitality.[8] This trio of paragraphs features a jam session with the pianist Albert Ammons, Vic Dickenson on trombone, and Big Sid Catlett on drums, all mythic figures for Carruth:[9]

26

A day   very solid   February 12th, 1944
cheerless in New York City
                    (while I kneedeep

elsewhere in historical war
was wrecking Beauty's sleep
and her long dream)
                    a day (blank, gray) at four
in the afternoon, overheated in the W.O.R.
Recording Studios. Gum wrappers *and* dust
and a stale smell. A day. The cast
was Albert Ammons, Lips Page, Vic Dickenson,
Don Byas, Israel
Crosby, and Big Sid Catlett. (*And* it was Abe Linkhorn's
birthday.) And Milt Gabler
presided over the glass with a nod, a sign. Ammons
counted off
                    a-waaaaan,,, *tu!*

          and went feeling
his way on the keys gently,
                    while Catlett summoned

27

the exact beat from—
          say from the sounding depths, the universe . . .
When Dickenson came on it was all established,
no guessing, and he started with a blur
as usual, smears, brays—Christ
the dirtiest noise imaginable
                    belches, farts
                              curses
but it was music
                    music now
                    with Ammons trilling in counterpoise.
Byas next, meditative, soft/
                    then Page
with that tone like the torn edge
of reality:
          and so the climax, long dying riffs—
groans, wild with pain—
and Crosby throbbing *and* Catlett riding stiff
yet it was music   music.
                    (Man, doan
fall in that bag,
          you caint describe it.)
                    Piano & drum,
Ammons & Catlett drove the others. *And* it was done
and they listened *and* heard themselves
          better than they were, for they had come

28

high above themselves. Above everything, flux, ooze,
loss, need, shame, improbability/   the awfulness
of guy-wrong,   sex-wrack,   horse & booze,
the whole goddam mess,
And Gabler said, "We'll press it"   *and* it was
     "Bottom Blues"
BOTTOM BLUES   five men knowing it well   blacks
     & jews
yet music, music   high
in the celebration of fear, strange joy
of pain: blown out, beaten out
                         a moment ecstatic
in the history
     of creative mind and heart/ not singular, not the rarity
we think, but real and a glory
our human shining, shekinah . . .   Ah,
                    holy spirit, ninefold
I druther've bin a-settin there, supernumerary
cockroach i' th' corner, a-listenin, a-listenin,,,,,,
          than be the Prazedint ov the Wuurld. (97–99)

"Paragraphs" overflows with pleasure yet maintains its form, much like the music described; despite the formal restraints, the feel or sound of the poem is improvisatory. In a sense, the poem approximates the thrill and tension of Dickenson's trombone improvising lyrical solos over Catlett's steady beat.

A more recent but equally rambunctious poem, "What a Wonder among the Instruments Is the Walloping Tramboone!" (*Collected Shorter Poems*, 378–380), opens with an exuberant description of the trombone's sound, followed by a plea—so common in Carruth's writing—that we embrace the great players from the past:

That elephantine bray in the upper register, that sagacious rumbling down
     below, that glissing whoop,
A human glory, a nobility—but arch, the good words for goodness have
     been bollixed in our degradation.
Recall then from the darkness of your adolescence, my still empowering
     spirit, the names of gladness,
J. C. Higgenbotham, Jim Harrison, Wilbur de Paris, Kid Ory, George Lugg,
     Dickie Wells, Trummy Young, Honore Dutry, Jimmy Archey,
And although in retrospection Teagarden was overrated, the white names
     too, Miff Mole, Floyd O'Brien, Brad Gowans, Lou McGarity, Vernon
     Brown,
May all their persons be never forgotten and their music continue in the
     ears of the chosen forever!

                                   (*Collected Shorter*, 378)

The twenty-seven long lines of this poem, which wrap around like trombone slides, first preach the gospel of many players and then focus on Carruth's hero: "Spirit, let me revere and celebrate in poetry the life of Vic Dickenson, and let me mourn his death" (379). Although this is indeed an elegy, it is one that repeatedly celebrates Dickenson's most dynamic moments on the bandstand:

> Dickenson, no other could sing as you, your blasts, burbles, and bellowings,
>   those upward leaps, those staccato descensions,
> Your smears, blurs, coughs, your tone veering from muted to stentorian,
>   your confidences, your insults,
> All made in music, musically. Never was such range of feeling so integrated
>   in one man or instrument. (379)

He refers to Dickenson as "King of the Zulus," a phrase he used thirty years earlier in the poem "New Orleans," which begins, "I am a trombone" and features the refrain "O King of the Zulus, consecrate me!" (*Collected Shorter*, 44). The mythos of Dickenson and the beauty of his playing become indistinguishable, and as they appear in Carruth's poetry, they form a hosanna to this exceptional artist who is still unknown to most Americans. In fact, Carruth's poems read like treasure maps pointing to Dickenson's LPs.

Other poets, employing different techniques, have also invoked musicians from the past in an effort to immortalize them. David Hilton's "Blind Saxophonist Dies," for example, commemorates Rahsaan Roland Kirk, and this poem incorporates the musician's thoughts and spoken voice to create an active presence. The poem opens with an obituary notice, a "small photo & caption [that] make / him a circus act" by emphasizing Kirk's ability to play numerous horns simultaneously rather than by focusing on his artistry or musicianship. Hilton sketches the history of Kirk's debilitating life, from the blinding of his eyes in youth to his crippling strokes. But the tone changes dramatically by the second half of the poem. Beneath a "blue midnight ceiling / of the jammed club," the crowd starts chanting Rahsaan's italicized name, again and again in variations, and Kirk leaves the poem in triumph, quoting from his famous song title, and preaching with hip *carpe diem* insistency:

> when asked about his
> massive stroke he said
>
> "that happened
> that's over with
> that's done

now bright moments
bright moments
everyone"

(Feinstein and Komunyakaa, 84)

This call for "bright moments" could be a mantra for Al Young, whose whole life, it seems, has been governed by jazz musicians and their music. In his reflection "The Years with Miles" from *Kinds of Blue* (1984), Young talks about jazz, not merely as an attraction but as a spiritual guide:[10]

Positioned at the D's in the alphabetized jazz section, I flipped through dozens of Miles Davis LPs, finding it tough to believe I knew most of them by heart. Even more surprising was my instant realization that the music compressed in those vinyl grooves had played a strange and indefinable role in shaping me and the years I'd grown up in; years that saw me wobble down from the hills of adolescence toward the slippery banks of maturity. (45)

Like Bob Kaufman's descriptions of jazz, Young's metaphors often suggest that the music can be physically ingested—chewed, squeezed, swallowed. In "Jungle Strut," from *The Blues Don't Change* (1982), he applauds the saxophonist Gene "Jug" Ammons and his father, the pianist Albert Ammons, for leaving "this dry world / a treasure tray of cocktails for the ear" (129). The poem concludes with a wink to those who know the saxophonist by his nickname and personal history: "The wine poured from your jug (when you weren't / locked up in one) was aging and tasty." (129). In "Billie," from that same collection, sound once again becomes an intoxicant ("I suck on my lemon, I squeeze my lime / into bright but heady drink"), which then fills his body ("She who is singing enters my mouth, / a portion at a time: an arm, a leg, a nipple, an eye, strands of hair" [121]). As the poem concludes with the speaker's request, "Warm me again now with / the red of your Cleopatra breath" (122), Holiday becomes not merely lifelike but life affirming.[11]

To be sure, Young does not attempt to revise the past or ignore tragedy; occasionally he shows us the debilitations of physical decay, as in the conclusion of "Lester Leaps In" from *The Blues Don't Change*:

Here lived a man so hard and softspoken
he had to be cool enough to hold his horn
at angles as sharp as he was heartbroken
in order to blow what it's like being born. (130)

But even in his earliest work, such as those poems from *Dancing* (1969), we can see his emphasis on the creative act rather than emotional or physical decline. "Dance of the Infidels," one of his best poems from *Dancing*, was written in memory of Bud Powell (who wrote a tune by the same title), and begins with an acknowledgment of Powell's personal displacement as an American jazz musician and as an expatriate: "The smooth smell of Manhattan taxis, / Parisian taxis, it doesn't matter" (9). The opening could easily have been an appropriate introduction for a portrait of Powell's decline, but instead the speaker turns to the music, a Paris concert with Art Blakey and Lee Morgan, and in a moving gesture addresses Powell posthumously with a casual aside—"The world, in case / youre losing touch again, keeps wanting the same / old thing" (9). He concludes, "I know / this world is terrible & that one must, above all, / hold onto the heart & the hearts of others. / I love *you*" (10).

Young's love for Powell and his music is just one example among many where the poet embraces these figures with such fine portraiture that they become accessible on the page, and this is certainly true of "A Dance for Ma Rainey," also from *The Blues Don't Change*. "I'm going to be just like you," says the speaker at the start of the poem, later adding,

> I'm going to cry so sweet
> & so low
> & so dangerous,
> Ma,
> that the message is going to reach you
> back in 1922
> where you shimmer
> snaggle-toothed
> perfumed &
> powdered
> in your bauble beads (7)

Now suddenly alive, Ma Rainey becomes a figure who can instruct, whose voice transformed "redblooded american agony" into a form of salvation, so that "beautiful brave black people" will no longer require drugs and violence for identity (7). Like the jazz portraits by Carruth, Komunyakaa, and Matthews, those by Young present the humanity in these legendary figures and in doing so revitalize their legacies.

In addition, Young has for years written about contemporary musicians. *The Blues Don't Change*, for example, includes "The Art of Benny Carter" and "A Little Poem about Jazz," the latter of which is dedicated to Miles Davis (who died a decade after publication). *Heaven: Collected Poems 1956–1990* includes three poems written when the musicians were in top form: "Thelonious: An Intro" from 1964, "Dexter Gordon at Keystone Korner" from 1977, and "Jackie McLean: Alto Saxophone," written over three years in the late sixties. If the work by Useni Eugene Perkins represents the jazz elegy as a statement of despair, Young has shown the other extreme by de-emphasizing tragedy and reinvigorating the legacy of those musicians.

Young's willingness to address living musicians distinguishes him from most other poets currently writing as well as those from the past. The great majority of jazz poetry concentrates on modern jazz musicians from the fifties and sixties—particularly Charlie Parker, Thelonious Monk, and John Coltrane—and even Young also focuses on that period. An understandable romance hovers over those formative years in jazz, when those extraordinary musicians changed the sound of the music more dramatically than any other group of artists before or since. It is surely revealing to note that although John Coltrane died a generation ago, the Coltrane poem lives and in fact multiplies. One waits in eager anticipation to discover the range and extent of this preeminent musician's influence on the jazz poetry of the future.

It will indeed be interesting to see how far-reaching the influence of jazz will extend. This chapter, for example, has focused primarily on four American men, but an equally valid and engaging conclusion could have been written solely on women writers—such as Jayne Cortez, Wanda Coleman, Joy Harjo, and Ntozake Shange—or international writers. From Ireland, for example, the poet Michael Longley recently wrote, "Jazz is arguably the twentieth century's most significant contribution to the culture of the world." Anselm Hollo, originally from Helsinki, agrees: "I cannot imagine a world without jazz, be it hot or cool; it is one of the relatively few good reasons one has for enduring this century." Charles Simic, in a less emphatic but deeply personal statement, once described his years in New York City listening to Thelonious Monk as "the happiest times of my life."

Contemporary jazz poems time and again offer urgent notice of and gratitude for the music and its innovators. Like the blues and jazz, the history of jazz poetry offers the extremes of emotions, from Sterling Brown's blues poetry to those, like William Matthews' "Unrelenting Flood," celebrating jazz as an art that fills our soul "the way we like / joy to arrive" (*Flood*, 37). Whatever the tone of these poems, jazz has yielded discovery and inspiration, a process explained by Yusef Komunyakaa: "As I listen to [Eric] Dolphy or Dexter [Gordon], I think their music works like a refrain underneath my life keeping it all together and in focus. If I'm having a writer's block, a couple of days of Coltrane or Miles does the trick" (Kelly, 661). These "names of gladness," to quote Hayden Carruth, bring us again and again to the music; "May these words," says Carruth in the conclusion to his Vic Dickenson tribute, "point to you and your recorded masterwork forever, / Which means as long as our kind can endure" (*Collected*, 380). Similarly, Al Young writes:

I lived long enough to get this down onto paper, knowing well that—like notations on musical score paper—it'll go on being strictly dead stuff, an artifact, until another human being runs it through that most marvelous of instruments, imagination, and transforms the look of it into sound by breathing sense and meaning and feeling back into these blues. (*Drowning in the Sea of Love*, 136)

In the work by hundreds of writers around the world, we witness the extraordinary influence of jazz music and its mythic anecdotal history. For those who use "that most marvelous of instruments" to combine jazz with poetry, the music actively instructs poetic sensibilities. The varied works by these writers directs others to the limitless synesthetic unions of these two art forms. And it was in that spirit of discovery and joy that Etheridge Knight wrote this inscription shortly before he died: "Be / making / sounds / Words / be / beautiful."

NOTES

1. In his notes from *Rising and Falling*, Matthews explains, "In the poems for Bud Powell and [the New Orleans bassist] Alcide Pavageau I've given Powell a heroin habit and Pavageau (by implication) a limp, for reasons the poems developed. They are not necessarily good biography" (viii). The discrepancy between actual biography and poetic license evokes a number of creative and ethical issues that are worth pursuing—but not here.

2. A third poem, "Averted Eyes," concentrates on the pathos of Wardell Gray's premature death, but even here Matthews does not dwell on the sadness in the same way that he does in his tributes to Hawkins and Coltrane.

3. In a letter from 1988, Matthews wrote: "I'm not aware of any different rhythmic attention in poems about music and poems about other things, except possibly in the Bechet poem, where the shape of his solo influenced the shape of my sentences somehow. I think whatever I know about rhythm in poetry I learned as much from music as from literary study or reading, but there's no way to demonstrate that; I just know it."

4. Like Matthews' poem, Larkin's "For Sidney Bechet" is not an elegy. (Larkin wrote his poem prior to Bechet's death.) But Larkin's radically anti-modernist aesthetic, particularly evident in his collection of essays, *All What Jazz*, made all his years as a jazz critic seem like an extended elegy for Dixieland and early jazz.

5. Bolden seems to be the perfectly mythic figure for jazz poems, and one of the best poems written in his memory is Robert Sargent's "Touching the Past" from *Aspects of a Southern Story* (1983) and reprinted in *The Jazz Poetry Anthology*.

6. The three Mingus poems, plus a fourth one, have been reprinted as a series in the first issue of *Brilliant Corners: A Journal of Jazz & Literature*, which features an interview with Matthews discussing these poems.

Two other poems about Mingus worth noting are Elaine Cohen's "In Memoriam Mingus (1922–79)" and Ira Sadoff's "Mingus: Last Speech." Cohen's poem is one of the strongest pieces in Chris Parker's uneven anthology *B Flat, Bebop, Scat*

(1986) and, like Harper's "Dear John, Dear Coltrane," it attempts to cover the range of the musician's life, from his childhood to his cremation. Sadoff's wonderful narrative (from *Emotional Traffic*, 1989) is actually an elegy for Eric Dolphy from the perspective of Charles Mingus. "When Eric left," the poem begins, "we played / lost" (68). A splendid writer, Sadoff has often turned to jazz for inspiration.

7. "Many times," Komunyakaa explains, "in the jazz-related poem there's a refrain. Sometimes I will use a refrain during composition—something that I return to—but I'll go back later and remove it. Essentially, the refrain keeps me going—moving on with the same tone pretty much throughout the poem" (Kelly, 657). In "The Plea" and a few others, he obviously decided that the refrain was necessary.

8. In *Sitting In*, Carruth reprinted this series as one long poem titled "Three Paragraphs."

9. This session appeared as a 78 (Commodore 1516) titled "Albert Ammons Rhythm Kings." One side featured "Bottom Blues," discussed in the poem, and the other "Jamin' the Boogie." In a later poem, "An Expatiation on the Combining of Weathers at Thirty-Seventh and Indiana Where the Southern More or Less Crosses the Dog," Carruth imagines himself playing with Ammons and Catlett, among others (*Tell Me Again*, 1989).

10. *Kinds of Blue* is one of three books, all of which bear the subtitle "Musical Memoirs." The other two are *Bodies & Soul* (1981) and *Things Ain't What They Used to Be* (1987). Selections from these books, as well as an essay on Robert Johnson, appear in *Drowning in the Sea of Love* (1995).

11. This gesture is similar to the final couplet in Bill Zavatsky's "Elegy," dedicated to Bill Evans: "The sunlight and the shade you carried us / We drank, tasting our bitter lives more sweetly / From the spring of song that never stops its kiss" (Feinstein and Komunyakaa, 245). It is interesting to compare this poem to his elegy from the seventies, "To the Pianist Bill Evans" (discussed in the previous chapter); whereas that poem concluded with a hand-holding gesture, a need for comfort, the speaker in "Elegy" seems more serene and less stricken by death.

REFERENCES

Balliett, Whitney. "Young Guns." *The New Yorker* (June 5, 1995): 97–99.
Breslin, James E. B. *From Modern to Contemporary: American Poetry, 1945–1965*. Chicago: University of Chicago, 1983.
Carruth, Hayden. *Brothers, I Loved You All*. New York: Sheep Meadow Press, 1978.
———. *Collected Shorter Poems 1946–1991*. Port Townsend: Copper Canyon, 1992.
———. *Nothing for Tigers: Poems 1959–1964*. New York: Macmillan, 1965.
———. *Sitting In: Selected Writings on Jazz, Blues, and Related Topics*. Iowa City: University of Iowa, 1986.
———. *Tell Me Again How the White Heron Rises and Flies across the Nacreous River toward the Distant Islands*. New York: New Directions, 1989.
Early, Gerald. *Tuxedo Junction*. New York: Ecco, 1989.

Feinstein, Sascha, and Yusef Komunyakaa, eds. *The Jazz Poetry Anthology*. Bloomington: Indiana University Press, 1991.

Hollo, Anselm. Letter to author. 4 June 1994.

Kelly, Robert, moderator. "Jazz Poetry: A Conversation." Interview with Yusef Komunyakaa and William Matthews. *The Georgia Review*. Vol. XLVI, no. 4 (Winter 1992): 645–661.

Komunyakaa, Yusef. *Copacetic*. Middletown, Conn.: Wesleyan University Press, 1984.

———. *February in Sydney*. Unionville: Matchbooks, 1989.

———. *Magic City*. Middletown, Conn.: Wesleyan University Press, 1993.

———. *Neon Vernacular: New and Selected Poems*. Middletown, Conn.: Wesleyan University Press, 1993.

Larkin, Philip. *All What Jazz*. New York: Farrar, Straus, Giroux, 1985.

———. *The Whitsun Weddings*. London: Faber and Faber, 1964.

Longley, Michael. Letter to author. 28 June 1994.

Matthews, William. *Blues If You Want*. Boston: Houghton Mifflin, 1989.

———. "The Buddy Bolden Cylinder." *Poetry*. Vol. CLIX, no. 1 (October 1991): 26–27.

———. *Curiosities*. Ann Arbor: University of Michigan, 1989.

———. *Flood*. Boston: Little, Brown and Company, 1983.

———. *A Happy Childhood*. Boston: Little, Brown and Company, 1984.

———. Letter to the author. 4 November 1988.

———. *Rising and Falling*. Boston: Little, Brown and Company, 1979.

———. *Ruining the New Road*. New York: Random, 1970.

———. *Time & Money*. Boston: Houghton Mifflin, 1995.

Myers, Jack, and David Wojahn, eds. *A Profile of Twentieth-Century American Poetry*. Carbondale and Edwardsville: Southern Illinois University Press, 1991.

Parker, Chris, ed. *B Flat, Bebop, Scat: Jazz Short Stories & Poems*. London: Quartet, 1986.

Sadoff, Ira. *Emotional Traffic*. Boston: Godine, 1989.

Sargent, Robert. *Aspects of a Southern Story*. Washington, D.C.: Word Works, 1983.

Simic, Charles. Letter to author. 5 Sept. 1994.

Young, Al. *The Blues Don't Change: New and Selected Poems*. Baton Rouge: Louisiana University Press, 1982.

———. *Bodies & Soul*. Berkeley: Creative Arts, 1981.

———. *Dancing*. New York: Corrinth, 1969.

———. *Drowning in the Sea of Love*. New Jersey: Ecco, 1995.

———. *Heaven: Collected Poems 1956–1990*. Berkeley: Creative Arts, 1992.

———. *Kinds of Blue*. San Francisco: Creative Arts, 1984.

———. *Things Ain't What They Used to Be*. Berkeley: Creative Arts, 1987.

Index

About the Author

SASCHA FEINSTEIN is Assistant Professor of English at Lycoming College and is the editor of *Brilliant Corners: A Journal of Jazz & Literature*. He is the coeditor (with Yusef Komunyakaa) of *The Jazz Poetry Anthology* (1991) and *The Second Set* (1996). His jazz-related poetry and prose have appeared in journals such as *The Southern Review, The North American Review,* and *Paideuma.*

ISBN 0-313-29515-8

90000>

EAN

9 780313 295157

HARDCOVER BAR CODE